TEXTBOOK OF SYRIAN SEMITIC INSCRIPTIONS

VOLUME III
PHOENICIAN INSCRIPTIONS

TEXTBOOK OF SYRIAN SEMITIC INSCRIPTIONS

VOLUME III

PHOENICIAN INSCRIPTIONS
including inscriptions in the
mixed dialect of Arslan Tash

BY

JOHN C. L. GIBSON

READER IN HEBREW AND SEMITIC LANGUAGES
UNIVERSITY OF EDINBURGH

CLARENDON PRESS · OXFORD
1982

Oxford University Press, Walton Street, Oxford OX2 6DP

OXFORD LONDON GLASGOW
NEW YORK TORONTO MELBOURNE AUCKLAND
KUALA LUMPUR SINGAPORE HONG KONG TOKYO
DELHI BOMBAY CALCUTTA MADRAS KARACHI
NAIROBI DAR ES SALAAM CAPE TOWN
AND ASSOCIATE COMPANIES IN
BEIRUT BERLIN IBADAN MEXICO CITY

© J. C. L. Gibson 1982

Published in the United States by Oxford University Press, New York

British Library Cataloguing in Publication Data

Gibson, John Clark Love
Textbook of Syrian Semitic Inscriptions.
Vol. 3: Phoenician Inscriptions
1. Inscriptions, Semitic
1. Title
492   PJ3085   80-40403

ISBN 0-19-813199-2

Produced by Typeset International, Jerusalem

Printed in Great Britain
at the University Press, Oxford
by Eric Buckley
Printer to the University

PREFACE

THE present volume is devoted to inscriptions in the Phoenician language which, unlike Hebrew and Aramaic (see vols. I and II), is known to us almost entirely from unvocalized epigraphic sources. It is divided into two parts at about the 6th century BC, inscriptions prior to that being called Old Phoenician, those after it Phoenician *simpliciter.* The first part includes all but the most fragmentary of the extant Old Phoenician texts. It also contains a chapter on the two incantations from Arslan Tash, which are commonly classified as Old Phoenician but are in the view taken here more accurately regarded as artificial compositions which mix Aramaic forms with Phoenician. The second part is more selective in its contents, restricting itself to the longer and more important inscriptions and the more interesting of the shorter texts. A distinction is made in both parts between inscriptions in the dialect of Byblos and those (the majority) that are written (with some local variations, especially in Cyprus) in the dialect spoken in the region of Sidon and Tyre. The last named was the leading Phoenician city in the period of colonial and commercial expansion in the early 1st millennium BC, and it was in most cases its dialect that was transported overseas, though one or two inscriptions (notably those from Lapethos and Pyrgi) provide evidence that the people of Byblos, and at one remove, as it were, the Phoenicians of Cyprus, also had a share in that movement.

Regrettably it has not been possible within the limits of size and cost laid down by the Delegates of the Press to make room for inscriptions in Punic, the name given to the Phoenician dialect or group of dialects which developed in Carthage and the western Mediterranean from the 6th or 5th centuries BC onwards. Most of these take us beyond the early period on which the *Textbook* as a whole has concentrated; but I had hoped to include a small selection in order to introduce students to some of the unique epigraphic problems which they present, particularly in the spheres of orthography and phonology. This ambition has had for the time being to be postponed.

For the sake of consistency the title *Syrian Semitic* has been retained for the present volume; but I would like to announce that it will not be used in any future editions of the *Textbook*. It is, as several reviewers have pointed out and as I now accept, based on a Greek and Latin usage of the name Syria which had no counterpart in the Semitic world from which the inscriptions come, and it ought clearly to be abandoned.

My grateful thanks are due to the authors, editors, and publishers whose illustrations have been reproduced in the figures and plates or have been used as the basis of my own sketches; details of the publications where the originals may be found are given in the List of Illustrations which follows this Preface.

J. C. L. GIBSON

New College, Edinburgh
Spring 1979

CONTENTS

Phoenician Inscriptions

LIST OF ILLUSTRATIONS

Figures 9–14 and all the Plates are reproduced, and Figures 1–8 and 15–17 sketched by myself from the sources indicated below. The Figures should not be relied upon by themselves where exact work is required; the same warning applies in the case of the Tables of scripts. Inscriptions not illustrated are, for chapters I–IV, included in Driver's *Semitic Writing* (3rd edit.) and, for chapters V–VII (with one or two exceptions), in Lidzbarski's *Handbuch der nordsemitischen Epigraphik,* books which should be available in most University and College libraries.

FIGURES (pp. 182–187)

PLATES (at end)

ABBREVIATIONS OF JOURNALS AND WORKS CITED

AIUON	*Annali dell'Istituto Universitario Orientale di Napoli.*
Albright, 'Inscriptions'	W. F. Albright, 'The Phoenician inscriptions of the tenth century B.C. from Byblus', *JAOS* 67 (1947), 153–60.
ANEP	J. B. Pritchard (ed.), *The Ancient Near East in Pictures* (Princeton, 1954). Supplementary vol.; see *ANET*.
ANET	J. B. Pritchard (ed.), *Ancient Near Eastern Texts relating to the Old Testament*, 2nd edit. (Princeton, 1955), and with continuing pagination, Supplementary volume of Texts and Pictures (1969).
Arch. Or.	*Archiv Orientální.*
Avishur, 'Stylistic features'	Y. Avishur, 'Studies of stylistic features common to the Phoenician inscriptions and the Bible', *Ug.-Forsch.* 8 (1976), 1–22.
Bange, *Vowel-Letters*	L. A. Bange, *A Study of the Use of Vowel-Letters in Alphabetic Consonantal Writing* (München, 1971).
BASOR	*Bulletin of the American Schools of Oriental Research.*
Benz, *Names*	F. L. Benz, *Personal Names in the Phoenician and Punic Inscriptions* (Rome, 1972).
Bibl. Or.	*Bibliotheca Orientalis.*
Birnbaum, *Scripts*	S. A. Birnbaum, *The Hebrew Scripts*, 2 vols. (London, 1954–7; 1971).
BMB	*Bulletin du Musée de Beyrouth.*
CBQ	*Catholic Biblical Quarterly.*
CIS i (with number of text)	*Corpus Inscriptionum Semiticarum, Pars Prima Inscriptiones Phoenicias Continens* (Paris, 1881 ff.).

*CML*² (with number
of text)
    J. C. L. Gibson, *Canaanite Myths and Legends,*
2nd edit. (originally edited by G. R. Driver)
(Edinburgh, 1978).

CRAIBL
    *Comptes rendus des séances de l'Académie des
inscriptions et belles-lettres.*

Diringer, *Alphabet*
    D. Diringer, *The Alphabet: A Key to the
History of Mankind* (London, 1948).

DISO
    C.-F. Jean, J. Hoftijzer, *Dictionnaire des
inscriptions sémitiques de l'ouest* (Leiden,
1965).

Dotan, 'Stress
position'
    A. Dotan, 'Stress position and vowel shift in
Phoenician and Punic', *Israel Oriental Studies*
6 (1976), 71–121.

Driver, *Writing*
    G. R. Driver, *Semitic Writing: From
Pictograph to Alphabet,* 3rd edit. (London,
1976).

Dunand, *Byblia
Grammata*
    M. Dunand, *Byblia Grammata: Documents et
recherches sur le développement de l'écriture en
Phénicie* (Beyrouth, 1945).

EA (with number
of text)
    J. A. Knudtzon, *Die El-Amarna Tafeln*
(Leipzig, 1915).

EHO
    F. M. Cross, D. N. Freedman, *Early Hebrew
Orthography: A study of the Epigraphic
Evidence* (New Haven, 1952).

Ephemeris
    M. Lidzbarski, *Ephemeris für semitische
Epigaphik,* 3 vols. (Giessen, 1902–15).

Friedrich, *Grammatik*
    J. Friedrich, W. Röllig, *Phönizisch-punische
Grammatik,* 2nd edit. (Rome, 1970).

Ginsberg, 'Ugaritico-
Phoenicia'
    H. L. Ginsberg, 'Ugaritico-Phoenicia',
JANES 5 (1973), 131–47.

Greenfield, 'Scripture'
    J. C. Greenfield, 'Scripture and inscription:
The literary and rhetorical element in some
early Phoenician inscriptions' in H.
Goedicke (ed.), *Near Eastern Studies in Honor
of W. F. Albright* (Baltimore, 1971), 253–68.

Guzzo Amadasi, *Iscrizioni*
(with page number)
    Maria Giulia Guzzo Amadasi, *Le iscrizioni
fenicie e puniche delle colonie in occidente*
(Rome, 1967).

Harden, *Phoenicians*	D. Harden, *The Phoenicians (Ancient Peoples and Places,* no. 26) (London, 1962).
Harris, *Grammar*	Z. S. Harris, *A Grammar of the Phoenician Language* (New Haven, 1936).
HTR	*Harvard Theological Review.*
IEJ	*Israel Exploration Journal.*
JA	*Journal asiatique.*
JANES	*The Journal of the Ancient Near Eastern Society of Columbia University.*
JAOS	*Journal of the American Oriental Society.*
JNES	*Journal of Near Eastern Studies.*
JRAS	*Journal of the Royal Asiatic Society.*
JSS	*Journal of Semitic Studies.*
KAI (with number of text)	H. Donner, W. Röllig, *Kanaanäische und aramäische Inschriften,* 3 vols. (Wiesbaden, 1962–4). 2nd edit., 1966–69.
KI (with number of text)	M. Lidzbarski, *Kanaanäische Inschriften* (Giessen, 1907).
Lipiński, 'Miscellanea'	E. Lipiński, 'From Karatepe to Pyrgi: Middle Phoenician miscellanea', *RSF* 2 (1974), 45–61.
Lipiński, 'North Semitic texts'	E. Lipiński, 'North Semitic texts from the first millennium B.C.' in W. Beyerlin (ed.), *Near Eastern Religious Texts relating to the Old Testament,* Engl. transl. (London, 1978), 227–68.
McCarter, *Antiquity*	P. K. McCarter, *The Antiquity of the Greek Alphabet and the Early Phoenician Scripts* (Missoula, 1975).
Magnanini, *Iscrizioni* (with page number)	P. Magnanini, *Le iscrizioni fenicie dell' oriente* (Rome, 1973).
Masson and Sznycer, *Recherches*	O. Masson, M. Sznycer, *Recherches sur les Phéniciens à Chypre* (Genève-Paris, 1972).
Moscati, *Phoenicians*	S. Moscati, *The World of the Phoenicians,* Engl. transl. (London, 1968).
MUSJ	*Mélanges de l'Université Saint Joseph* (Beirut).
NEB	*New English Bible.*
NESE	*Neue Ephemeris für semitische Epigraphik.*

NSE (with page number)	M. Lidzbarski, *Handbuch der nordsemitischen Epigraphik* (Weimar, 1898).
NSI (with number of text)	G. A. Cooke, *A Text-book of North-Semitic Inscriptions* (Oxford, 1903).
Or. Ant.	*Oriens Antiquus.*
Peckham, *Scripts*	J. B. Peckham, *The Development of the Late Phoenician Scripts* (Cambridge, Massachusetts, 1968).
Poenulus	Citations from the Punic passages in the 'Poenulus' of Plautus; see Segert, *Grammar*, pp. 266–7, and in more detail M. Sznycer, *Les passages puniques en transcription latine dans le 'Poenulus' de Plaute* (Paris, 1967).
RA	*Revue d'assyriologie et d'archéologie orientale.*
RB	*Revue biblique internationale.*
RÉS (with number of text)	*Répertoire d'épigraphie sémitique* (Paris, 1900 ff.).
RHR	*Revue de l'histoire des religions.*
Röllig, 'Beiträge'	W. Röllig, 'Beiträge zur nordsemitischen Epigraphik (1–4)' *WO* 5 (1969–70), 108–25.
RSF	*Rivista di studi fenici.*
RSO	*Rivista degli studi orientali.*
Segert, *Grammar*	S. Segert, *A Grammar of Phoenician and Punic* (Munich, 1976).
Teixidor, 'Bulletin' (with year)	J. Teixidor, 'Bulletin d'épigraphie sémitique', printed at the end of successive volumes of the periodical *Syria*, beginning 1967.
Ug.-Forsch.	*Ugarit-Forschungen. Internationales Jahrbuch für die Altertumskunde Syrien-Palästinas.*
VT	*Vetus Testamentum.*
WO	*Die Welt des Orients.*
ZA	*Zeitschrift für Assyriologie und verwandte Gebiete.*
ZAW	*Zeitschrift für die alttestamentliche ·Wissenschaft.*
ZDMG	*Zeitschrift der Deutschen Morgenländischen Gesellschaft.*
ZDPV	*Zeitschrift des Deutschen Palästina-Vereins.*

SIGLA USED IN TRANSCRIBING AND TRANSLITERATING

°	over a letter indicates that it is doubtful.
–	indicates the presence of an undecipherable letter.
1,5,10,	etc., indicate numerical signs.
. or '	indicates a separating dot or stroke.
[　]	in Semitic text enclose restorations of missing or faded portions; thus גבל [.מלך].
....	in Semitic text indicate missing or faded portions of uncertain length.
<　>	in Semitic text enclose letters omitted in error by the mason or scribe; thus סכן.בס<כ>נם.
{　}	in Semitic text enclose letters added in error by the mason or scribe; thus אל{ו}ל. ...
[　]	in English text enclose translations of restored portions.
(　)	in English text enclose additions to improve the sense.
[　]	in the commentary enclose phonological reconstructions; thus נחת = [nōḥat].

Personal and place-names are, if of frequent occurrence or of known structure, given in a conventional English form; thus Ahiram (properly ['ḥīrōm]), Eshmunazar, Milkyatan, Astarte, Kilamuwa, Ptolemy, etc. Otherwise straight transliteration is used; thus BMH, MKL, PDRŠŠ', etc.

NOTE ON PHOENICIAN PHONOLOGY AND GRAMMAR

Apart from transliterations of names and words in vocalized sources in Akkadian, Greek, or Latin, we possess no direct evidence for the pronunciation or indeed for the morphology of ancient Phoenician. We have, therefore, while being aware of the pitfalls, to rely for many of our phonological and grammatical reconstructions on the analogy of Hebrew and other better-known Semitic languages. In this short Note, apart from the paragraph on consonants, I restrict myself to commenting on three problematic areas where recent important studies have clarified or modified the treatment given in the standard Grammars.

1. CONSONANTS

The consonantal phonemes of Phoenician seem to have been as in classical Hebrew except that the Phoenicians did not possess the lateralized [ś] ([sl]) of the latter, otherwise as inventors of the writing system they would have devised a symbol for it. In Phoen. this [ś] appears as [š] with the exception of the word עסר 'ten' (Hebr. עשר). Though it is not attested prior to the 5 cent. BC (**28** Eshmunazar 1), it is better to assume that an anomalous change [sl] > [s] took place with this word in the proto-Phoen. stage than that [š] gave way to [s] in the mid-1 millenn. under Aram. influence. Most other irregularities in the usage of consonants, e.g. שׁ for ס in some inscrs. from Cyprus, do, however, seem to be due to influence from a local language, though some, e.g. the weakening of the laryngals and phrayngals evidenced in late, mainly Punic texts, can be paralleled from the history of Hebrew.

2. VOWELS AND STRESS

The characteristic Canaanite shift of stressed [ā] to [ō], which is attested as early as the El-Amarna glosses (14 cent. BC), is reflected in both Phoen. and Hebr., but not in equal measure. Whereas there is in Hebr. a significant number of forms in which it is expected but does not appear, the shift is carried through into Phoen. with, as far as we can judge, complete consistency. It even operates in a number of cases where the stressed [ā] arises at a much later stage through phonological change. Thus Canaanite [maqāmu] 'place' becomes [maqōm] in both Phoen. (cp. Poenulus *macom*) and Hebr.

Canaanite [dagānu] 'the god Dagon; corn' becomes [dagōn] (cp. Greek translit. Δαγων) in Phoen. but both [dagōn] 'the god Dagon' and [dagān] 'corn' in Hebr.

Canaanite [qāma] (< proto-Sem. [qáwama]) 'he stood' becomes [qōm] in Phoen. (cp. Poenulus *chon* 'he was') but [qām] in Hebr.

Canaanite ['álaya] 'he went up' becomes first ['alay] (Ahiram עלי) and then ['alò] (cp. Poenulus *avo* 'may he live!'; precative perf.) in Phoen. but ['alā] in Hebr.

Canaanite [našá'tī] 'I carried' becomes [našōtī] in Phoen. (cp. Poenulus *nasot*) but [naśātī] in Hebr.

Canaanite [šáma'a] 'he heard' becomes [šama'] in Phoen. as in Hebr. but (after the lapse of the pharyngal) [šamō] in Punic (cp. Greek translit. σαμω).

Contrary to the claim of the Grammars (Harris, p. 26; Friedrich, pp. 29 ff.), the shift does not operate where a stressed [ā] results not from Canaanite [ā] (or its equivalent like [ay] or [a']) but follows upon the well-known changes in the position and role of the stress that took place in all the Syrian or Northwest Semitic languages around 1200–1100 BC. The examples of transliterations which are regarded as showing a shift of this stress-induced [ā] (< Canaanite [a]) to [ō] are remarkably few and cannot bear the weight put on them. Thus e.g. the Phoen. form [labōn] 'white' reflected in the Greek translit. λαβον prob. goes back to Canaanite [labānu] rather than [lábanu], and it is the Hebr. [labān] which is irregular in the same way as the form [dagān] mentioned earlier. The Grammars also cite in this connection forms like Latin *Baliaton* (= בעליתן), where in Hebr. the vowel is stressed short [a] not [ā], apparently assuming a development [yátana] 'he gave' > [yatan] > [yatān] > [yatōn]. Just as common, however, are forms like Greek Βαλεαζαρος (= בעלעזר) and Akkad. *Ilu-ia-ta-a-nu* (= אליתן) which presuppose short [a] as in Hebrew. It seems wiser to explain the forms with [ō] occurring in proper names as nominal forms on the pattern of Hebr. [qatā/ōl] or [qattā/ōl] than to regard them as regular and ignore the examples which adhere to the practice of Hebrew. There is, therefore, no reason to doubt that normal Phoen. nouns like דבר and verbs like עזר are to be vocalized [dabār] and ['azar] the same as in Hebrew. Similarly the fem. ending in nouns should be vocalized [at] not [ōt] (the fem. ending in verbs was not stressed and therefore remained [ā] (< [at]); thus [qatālā]).

See further on these matters Dotan, 'Stress position', and my article 'Stress and vocalic change in Hebrew: A diachronic study', *Journal of Linguistics* 2 (1966), 35 ff.

[*Note*: as in previous volumes, the stress is not marked unless it falls on a penultimate syllable; nor is the *Shewa* vowel, which need not normally be distinguished from absence of vowel or zero.]

3. THE DEFINITE ARTICLE

In *Near Eastern Studies in Honor of W. F. Albright* (1971), 326 ff., T. O. Lambdin proposes a solution to the problem why in Phoen. the article does not seem to be used in many places where on the analogy of Hebr. we are led to expect it. The Grammars are non-committal on this subject. According to Lambdin the answer lies in extending syncope of [h] to those places. Thus there is clearly on the Hebr. model syncope in e.g. בספר ז (**13** Kilamuwa i 14), but it may also be assumed after some longer prepositions (e.g. על גבלם; **15** Karatepe A i 14); after the copula (e.g. ואלם; ibid. A i 8); after the object marker (e.g. אית אדם; ibid. A iii 19); and within many construct relations. Lambdin argues further that Phoen. developed a special construction with demonstratives in which, when 'this' is added to a construct relation, the article is put with the member which it modifies. Thus in **25** Yehaumilk 4 המזבח נחשת ז means 'this altar of bronze', whereas עם ארץ ז in *ll.* 10–11, in which syncope of [h] is to be assumed, means 'the people of this land'. This particular argument is unacceptable because of העפת חרץ in *l.* 5, where a demonstrative is lacking (see the Note to *l.* 4). But in general his thesis is an attractive one, going far towards removing the impression that Phoen. is inconsistent (Harris, *Grammar,* p. 56) in its use of the article. However, the more one examines it the more exceptions one finds; see e.g. the Note to **28** Eshmunazar 22, and the strong rebuttal of his case by G. Coacci Polselli in *RSF* 5 (1977), 117 ff. The matter clearly requires further investigation, and it would in the meantime be circumspect to suspend judgement.

4. PRONOMINAL SUFFIXES

The third-person suffixes of Standard (= Tyro-Sidonian) Phoenician appear to be organized in a system of complementary distribution as indicated in the following table. This system is not well described in the Grammars. Col. A shows the situation after sing. and fem. plur. nouns in the nomin. and accus., and verbal forms ending in a consonant; col. B. after sing. and fem. plur. nouns in the genit., masc. plur. nouns, and verbs with vocalic endings. The 1 sing. suffix does not belong to the system, but is included in the table because of its orthographic similarity to the 3 sing. suffixes, which can, in not a few inscriptions, lead to difficulties in interpretation.

	A	B
1 sing.	׳ = [ī]	׳ = [ī] or [yā]
3 masc. sing.	– = [ō]	׳ = [yū]
	(from [á(h)ū])	([y] replacing [h])
3 fem. sing.	– = [ā]	׳ = [yā]
	(from [á(h)ā])	
3 masc. plur.	ם = [ōm]	נם = [nōm]
	(from [–(h)úm(ū)])	(Poenulus *labunom;*
		from [–n(h)úm(ū)]
3 fem. plur.	ם = [ēm]	נם = [nēm]

Examples (from **15** Karatepe unless otherwise stated):
אמי 'my mother' (**28** Eshmunazar 14; nomin.); שמי 'my name' (C iv 18; accus.); שם 'his name' (A iii 14; accus.); יברך 'may he bless him!' (**29** Baalshillem); עד מבאי 'to its (masc.) setting' (A i 5; genit.); לחדי 'alone (fem.)' (A ii 5; genit.); תברכי 'may you bless her!' (**20** Ur box 2); ירדם 'he (I) brought them (masc.) down' (A i 20); שתנם 'I placed them (masc.)' (A i 16); יספננם 'we added them (fem.)' (**28** Eshmunazar 19).

Notes

(a) The above system is not yet fully operative in the 9-cent. Kilamuwa inscr. (**13**), where the 3 plur. masc. suffix is הם, though it seems to work with the 3 sing. masc. suffixes. In Kilamuwa the 1 sing. suffix is also archaic, behaving as in the Byblian dialect (see at 2, 5, and at **25** Yehaumilk 3). In later Tyro-Sidonian (as in the table) this suffix is written ׳ but pronounced [ī] for all cases in sing. (and fem. plur.) nouns, i.e. [ī] has replaced [yá] but the ׳ of the latter is retained, giving a historical spelling (though apparently the older method continues to be followed with prepositions; see at **27** Tabnit 4).

(b) It is not unlikely that prior to the emergence of this system, which clearly betrays vestiges of a case system, suffixes to nouns were added to the appropriate case endings. Presumably this was also the situation in the earliest Byblian inscriptions (**1–10**).

(c) It is not known what connecting vowels were subsequently employed with 2 sing. and plur. suffixes; but there is some evidence that with the 1 plur. suffix the old nomin. [u] was used; see at **16** Seville 4. There is a similar uncertainty about connecting vowels (including those with 3 pers. suffixes) in the later Byblian inscriptions.

(d) The fact that the 3 fem. plur. suffix has [m] rather than [n] as in Hebr. suggests that the independent series was masc. המת = [hŏmat] and fem. המת = [hēm(m)at] (cp. Hebr. [hēnnā]); the latter indeed prob. occurs in **36** Lapethos ii 5.

(e) 3 pers. suffixes with the prepos. ל (originally [la]) behave as in col. A, those with ב (originally [bi]) as in col. B; e.g. ל 'for it' (fem.) (**15** Karatepe iii 16); בנם '(rule) over them' (**28** Eshmunazar 9).

See further on the above matters Ginsberg, 'Ugaritico-Phoenicia', 141 ff.; C. Krahmalkov, *JSS* 15 (1970), 181 ff.; 17 (1972), 68 ff.; *RSF* 2 (1974), 39 ff. On the 3 pers. suffixes of the Byblian dialect, which are substantially different, see the Grammars.

OLD PHOENICIAN INSCRIPTIONS

I

ARCHAIC PHOENICIAN ARROWHEADS

THE bronze arrowheads whose inscriptions are given below form a homogeneous set dating from the late 12 to the early 10 cents. BC. They measure from about 8 to 11 cm. in length and come from various places, known (Ruweiseh, Al-Biqʻah) or unknown, in Lebanon, with the exception of the earliest three from El-Khaḍr near Bethlehem, which if not also of Phoenician manufacture must originate from one of the Canaanite city-states in Palestine in the period of the Israelite Judges. The three from El-Khaḍr were part of a hoard which included 23 uninscribed heads; the others are single finds. One of the Palestinian heads is now in the Museum at Amman, the other two being privately owned; all the Lebanese heads are in the National Museum at Beirut. All the texts have the word חץ followed by a personal name with or without a patronymic or qualifying adjective.

Milik, in one of his studies (1956), draws attention to the fact that several of the names can be paralleled from census-lists of bowmen from 14-cent. Ugarit. From this he concludes that there flourished in the Judges period a hereditary guild of mercenary archers with links that reached back before the collapse of Bronze Age Canaanite civilization brought about by the invasions of the 'Sea peoples'. According to Iwry, on the other hand, the heads were primarily employed for purposes of divination or casting lots and need have had nothing to do with actual warfare; he thinks that חץ means 'good luck' rather than 'arrow' and points out that typologically the El-Khaḍr hoard at least is more accurately described as of javelin heads than of arrowheads; in other words, it was only by chance that some of the objects used happened to be arrows. Cross cleverly combines these two views, emphasizing that the El-Khaḍr weapons must be arrowheads because their number comes within the limits of the average contents of a quiver in antiquity (some 25 to 30 arrows), but arguing that the inscribed ones could have had a special function over and above, perhaps being carried by the archers as a means of assigning tasks in an engagement or of consulting the divine will when decisions had to be made by the guild.

When considering the epigraphic significance of these archaic texts, it is important to remember the awkwardness of writing on such uneven metal surfaces; but due allowance having been made for that, there is no doubt that they provide exceptionally valuable evidence in attempts to trace the early development of the Semitic alphabet or (as some would have it) syllabary. In particular, they considerably reduce the gap between the fully developed Phoenician scripts of the Old Byblian texts (chapter II) and the heterogeneous collection of small enigmatic semi-pictographic inscriptions from Sinai and from Lachish and other Bronze Age sites in Palestine which are usually termed respectively 'Proto-Sinaitic' and 'Proto-Canaanite', and which as our knowledge stands at the moment supply our earliest sure data on experimental 'alphabetic' systems. Cross and others probably exaggerate the importance of the arrowheads by calling them a 'missing link' and by sometimes carelessly extending to them, and to a few other 12- and 11-cent. finds from Syria-Palestine, the title 'Proto-Canaanite', which ought, as Garbini insists, to be confined to the Palestinian Bronze Age texts of the 13 cent. and before. The 12- and 11-cent. texts belong archaeologically to the Iron Age and are in fact more appropriately regarded as archaic Phoen, (the arrowheads from Lebanon and the earliest Byblian inscrs. 1–5) or archaic Hebrew (perhaps the El-Khaḍr arrowheads, and the Manaḥat and Raddana sherds) than as 'Proto-Canaanite'. There are obvious and interesting relationships between the two epigraphic groups, which I try to bring out in the Notes to this chapter; but there is discontinuity as well as continuity, and it is a mistake to assume that there was any direct line of descent from the one to the other.

The remit of our Textbook begins properly then with the arrowheads and the few Old Phoen. and Old Hebr. texts contemporary with them. These texts use a 22-letter writing system which, whatever its remoter ancestry, was beyond doubt formulated in Phoenicia for the Phoenician language. This is established by the exact equivalence of signs in the one with consonantal phonemes in the other, an equivalence that is lacking in the case of Hebrew and Aramaic, the other main languages to employ it. These languages possessed one or more extra distinctive consonantal sounds which, when the system was taken over by them, had to be accommodated within it by making certain letters perform a double role; for details see the Notes on phonology at the beginning of volumes I and II. Another indication that for these languages the system was a borrowed one not ideally suited to them is their having to resort almost immediately to the device of *matres lectionis* or vowel-letters to express the vowels in uncertain positions, a device that was not needed in Phoen. itself for many centuries, and then mainly in the overseas Punic dialect. A third is possibly the fact that whereas word-dividers were rarely used in Phoen. inscriptions after the time of the Old Byblian texts, they were not dispensed with in Hebr. and Aram. until several centuries later.

The introduction, just mentioned, of vowel-letters by Hebrew and Aramaean scribes was a structural innovation in the Phoen. system and is on a par with the theoretical issue, also previously touched on, of whether the system as a whole belongs in the history of writing to the syllabic or the alphabetic type. My own preference is for the syllabic theory described most fully by I.J. Gelb, though it has to be admitted that this has attracted more adherents among general linguists than practising epigraphists (e.g. Segert, Driver). See my article listed in the Bibliography below. Meanwhile it is worth pointing out that formally, as distinct from structurally, there is during the first three centuries or so of the system's existence little divergence between Phoen., Hebr., or Aram. letter shapes on inscriptions that date from the same period, and that it is only from about 800 BC (a little earlier in the case of the Palestinian texts) that we find unmistakable indications of the emergence of local or national variations. It is, interestingly, also around the latter date that the Greeks, using a Semitic model, develop a system that is indubitably alphabetic in structure with discrete signs for all the vowels, though there is evidence in the shape and stance of certain Greek letters that their first acquaintance with Semitic writing should be placed much earlier (Naveh). Structurally, it is important to note the connection between the Greek vowel notation and the Semitic *matres lectionis*, which suggests that room should be made for Aramaean as well as Phoenician influence on the borrowing (Segert).

Select Bibliography

On the 'Proto-Sinaitic' and 'Proto-Canaanite' inscriptions and other problems connected with the origin and early development of the 'alphabet' (e.g. the syllabic theory, the acrophonic principle, the order of the letters, the direction of writing, the shorter and longer 'alphabets', cuneiform adaptations like the Ugaritic script, possible relations with Egyptian, Pseudo-Hieroglyphic, and other writing systems, links with the South Semitic script, the origin of the vowel-letters, the date of Greek borrowing, etc.) see:

W. F. Albright, *The Proto-Sinaitic Inscriptions and their Decipherment* (1969).
Articles on the 'Alphabet' in Bible Dictionaries and *Encyclopaedia Judaica*.
Bange, *Vowel-Letters*, Part I.
Birnbaum, *Scripts*, Part I, 31 ff.
Cross and Freedman, *EHO, passim*.
F. M. Cross, 'The evolution of the Proto-Canaanite alphabet', *BASOR* 134 (1954), 15–24.
F. M. Cross, T. O. Lambdin, 'A Ugaritic Abecedary and the origins of the Proto-Canaanite alphabet', *BASOR* 160 (1960), 21–6.

F. M. Cross, 'The origin and early development of the alphabet', *Eretz Israel* 8 (1967), English section, 8–24.

Diringer, *Alphabet,* Part II, chapter I (and similar works in other languages).

Driver, *Writing,* sections II, III, and supplement, pp. 239 ff.

Dunand, *Byblia Grammata.*

G. Garbini, 'Le iscrizioni "protocanaanaiche" del XII e XI secolo a. C.,' *AIUON* 34 (1974), 584–90.

I. J. Gelb, *A Study of Writing,* rev. ed. (1963), chapters IV–VI.

J. C. L. Gibson, 'On the linguistic analysis of Hebrew writing,' *Archivum Linguisticum* 17 (1969), 131–60.

Inscriptions Reveal: Documents from the time of the Bible, the Mishna and the Talmud (Israel Museum, Jerusalem, 1973), 9 ff.

Lillian H. Jeffery, *The Local Scripts of Archaic Greece* (1961).

P. K. McCarter, 'The early diffusion of the alphabet', *Bibl. Archaeologist* 37 (1974), 54–68.

idem, *Antiquity.*

M. Martin, 'A preliminary report after re-examination of the Byblian inscriptions', *Orientalia* 30 (1961), 46–78.

A. R. Millard, 'The Canaanite linear alphabet and its passage to the Greeks', *Kadmos* 15 (1976), 130–44.

J. Naveh, 'Some Semitic epigraphical considerations on the antiquity of the Greek alphabet', *American J. Arch.* 77 (1973), 1–8.

idem, *Origins of the Alphabet* (1975).

W. Röllig, G. Mansfeld, 'Zwei Ostraka vom Tell Kamid-el-Loz und ein neuer Aspekt für die Enstehung des kanaanäischen Alphabets', *WO* 5 (1970), 265–70.

S. Segert, 'Der Charakter des westsemitischen Alphabets', *Arch. Or.* 26 (1958), 243–7.

idem, 'Die Rolle der Aramäer bei der Vermittlung des westsemitischen Alphabets an die Griechen', *Arch. Or.* 26 (1958), 572–8.

R. R. Stieglitz, 'The Ugaritic cuneiform and Canaanite linear alphabets', *JNES* 30 (1971), 135–9.

J. Starcky, P. Bordreuil, 'Une des plus grandes découvertes de l'humanité: l'invention de l'alphabet', *Les dossiers de l'arch.* 12 (1975), 91–106.

M. Sznycer, 'Quelques remarques à propos de la formation de l'alphabet phénicien', *Semitica* 24 (1974), 5–12.

idem, 'Les inscriptions protosinaïtiques' in *Le déchiffrement des écritures et des langues, Colloque du XXIXe Congrès intern. des Orientalistes,* juillet 1973 (1975), 85–93.

S. Yeivin, 'The Canaanite inscriptions and the story of the alphabet' in B. Mazar (ed.), *The World History of the Jewish People* (1970), 24–34.

[*Note:* many of the above works are richly illustrated.]

On the arrowheads in general see:

S. Iwry, 'New evidence for belomancy in ancient Palestine and Phoenicia', *JAOS* 81 (1961), 27–34.

Cross, loc. cit. *(Eretz Israel),* 13 ff.

On the individual arrowheads (arranged here in chronological order) see:

El-Khaḍr i–iii

  J. T. Milik, F. M. Cross, 'Inscribed javelin-heads from the period of the Judges', *BASOR* 134 (1954), 5–15; fig. 1.

  F. M. Cross, 'A typological study of the El-Khaḍr javelin- and arrowheads', *Ann. Dept. Ant. Jordan* 3 (1956), 15–23.

  KAI no. 21; Taf. I (of iii).

  ANEP no. 805.

  Bange, *Vowel-Letters*, pp. 16–17.

  Inscriptions Reveal etc. (op. cit.), no. 7 (i).

  Driver, *Writing*, fig. 104.

Gerbaal   Fig. 1

  J. T. Milik, 'Flèches à inscriptions phéniciennes au Musée National Libanais', *BMB* 16 (1961), 103–8; pl. I, figs. 1,2.

  Cross, loc. cit., fig. 18.

  Bange, *Vowel-Letters*, p. 18.

  Magnanini, *Iscrizioni*, p. 43 (4).

Rapa'   Fig. 2

  M. F. Martin, 'A twelfth century bronze palimpsest', *RSO* 37 (1962), 175–93; tav. I and figs. 1,2.

  Cross, loc. cit., fig. 4.

Ruweiseh

  P.-E. Guigues, 'Pointe de flèche en bronze à inscription phénicienne', *MUSJ* 11 (1926), 323–8.

  S. Ronzevalle, 'Note sur le texte phénicien …', ibid., 329–58; pl. III.

  R. Dussaud in *Syria* 8 (1927), 185 f.

  Birnbaum, *Scripts*, no. 03.

  KAI no. 20; Taf. I.

  Bange, *Vowel-Letters*, pp. 17–18.

  Magnanini, *Iscrizioni*, p. 40.

  Driver, *Writing*, fig. 55.

Al-Biq'ah

  J. T. Milik, 'An unpublished arrowhead with Phoenician inscription of the 11th–10th century B.C.', *BASOR* 143 (1956), 3–6.

  P. Grelot, 'Sur une pointe de flèche à inscription phénicienne', *Orientalia* 26 (1957), 273–9.

  S. Yeivin, 'Note sur une pointe de flèche inscrite provenant de la Beqaa (Liban)', *RB* 65 (1958), 585–9.

  Milik, 'Flèches …' (loc. cit.), 105 f.; pl. I, figs. 1,2.

  KAI no. 22; Taf. I.

  Yeivin in Mazar, *World History* (op. cit.), fig. 8.

  Bange, *Vowel-Letters*, p. 17.

  Magnanini, *Iscrizioni*, p. 43 (2).

  Driver, *Writing*, fig. 101.

Azarbaal   Fig. 3

  Milik, 'Flèches …' (loc. cit.), 107; pl. I, figs. 1,2.

  Bange, *Vowel-Letters*, p. 18.

  Magnanini, *Iscrizioni*, p. 44.

חץ עבדלבאת	i	El-Khaḍr
חץ עבדלבת	ii	
חץ עבדלבאת	iii	
חץ גרבעל		Gerbaal
צדני		
חץ רפא		Rapa'
בן יחש		
חץ אדא		Ruweiseh
בן עכי		
חץ זכרב]על[		Al-Biq'ah
בן בנען		
חץ ' עזרבעל		Azarbaal
בן ' אדנבעל		

NOTES

Writing. Comparisons are made below with three earlier texts, the 13-cent. 'Proto-Canaanite' Lachish Bowl, Lachish Ewer, and Beth-Shemesh Sherd (see Driver, *Writing*, pls. 42, 43 and the Table of Scripts in this vol.) and with the partly contemporary, partly later Old Byblian inscrs. (chapt. II). The original pictographic shapes of the 'Proto-Canaanite' systems could, as far as we can ascertain, be written either in vertical columns or in horizontal rows, and the horizontal rows could be written either from left to right or (as in the developed Phoen. system) from right to left. The simplifying of the pictographs and the elimination of the vertical and the left to right directions of writing seems to have been a gradual and somewhat haphazard process. Thus sometimes the stance and sometimes the basic shape of some of the letters and sometimes both stance and shape remained essentially the same all through (e.g. ג, ח, כ, מ, ש, ת), whereas in the case of other letters both the 'Proto-Canaanite' and to a lesser degree the earliest Phoen. texts exhibit simplifications of outline not easy to trace and many confusing changes of orientation; e.g.

(1) Vertical writing: Beth-Sh., El-Kh. i, ii, iii
(2) Early letter shapes, semi-pictographic or intermediate:
    א (semi-pict.) Ewer, El-Kh. iii
       (interm.) El-Kh. i, Cone ii (**3**)
    ב Bowl, Beth-Sh., all arrows except Al-Biq., Spat. (**1**) Cones i (**2**), ii (**3**)
    י (semi-pict.) Ewer
    ל Bowl, Ewer, Beth-Sh., El-Kh. i, ii, iii
    נ Ewer, Beth-Sh., Gerb., Rapa', Ruw., Al-Biq., Cone i, Spat.
    ע (semi-pict.) Beth-Sh., El-Kh. ii, Ahir. (**4**; possibly twice)
    ר Beth-Sh., Rapa', Azarb.

(3) Left to right stance:
  א El-Kh. iii, Rapa'
  ב Beth-Sh., El-Kh. ii, iii, and (partially) Shipit. (9), Abda (10)
  ד El-Kh. ii, iii
  ל Bowl, Ewer, El-Kh. i, ii, iii
  מ Ewer, Cones i, ii
  נ Gerb.
  פ Rapa'
  צ El-Kh. i, ii, iii
(4) Shifts in stance of 90° or thereby clockwise or anti-clockwise:
  ב Bowl
  ג Gerb., Spat., Ahir.
  ז Beth-Sh.
  ח El-Kh. i, ii, iii
  י Gerb., Rapa'
  ל Beth-Sh., El-Kh. i, ii, iii
  נ Beth-Sh.
  צ Gerb., Rapa', and (partially) Al-Biq., Yehim. (6)
  ש Bowl, Ewer

An especially interesting letter is צ on El-Kh. i–iii, which has a simplified form not particularly close to the later shape, which has been thought to represent a surviving [ẓ] sound; cp. Ugar. ḥẓ. There are no certain earlier examples of this letter, however, and until one turns up it is advisable to suspend judgement.

On the basis of the above features the inscrs. may be arranged chronologically in the following order:

late 12 cent. BC:	El-Khaḍr arrows
early 11 cent:	Gerbaal and Rapa' arrows
mid-11 cent.:	Ruweiseh arrow
	Azarbaal spatula (1)
	Byblos cones (2, 3)
late 11 cent.:	Ahiram and Ahiram graffito (4, 5)
early 10 cent.:	Al-Biq'ah and Azarbaal arrows

None of these inscrs. can themselves be securely dated, and the arrangement is based on the dates assigned to Abibaal and Elibaal (7, 8), where there is external evidence placing them in the late 10 cent.; see introd. to 4 Ahiram.

The word חץ. There are two bases, ḤSS and ḤSY, both of which give nouns meaning 'arrow' and 'good luck, fortune'; Ugar. ḥẓ 'arrow' and ḥẓt 'good luck'; Hebr. [ḥēṣ] and [ḥēṣi] 'arrow', plur. only [ḥiṣṣīm]; Arab. [ḥaẓẓu] 'luck, portion', [ḥiẓatu] and [ḥuẓwatu] 'regard, favour', [ḥaẓwatu] 'small arrow, rod'. There is undoubtedly a semantic connection between these bases, but it is significant that in both Ugar. and Arab. the two meanings are distinguished formally, and Ugar. in particular would lead us to expect a fem. form in Phoen. for the meaning 'good luck'. Iwry's citation of passages from the Bible (e.g. Ezek. xxi 26) and other ancient sources attesting the use of arrows for divination or the casting of lots does not cancel out that fact. Translate therfore 'Arrow of so-and-so'.

The personal names. The names on the El-Kh. and Ruw. arrows are paralleled in the Ugar. census-lists of archers already mentioned (Gordon, *Ugaritic Textbook*, text 321, ob. 41, rev. 37, 38). עבדל[א]ת = ['abd labīt] with syncope of ['], 'servant of the lioness', thought to be a title of the goddess Anat, well known from the Ugar. myths for her warlike qualities; perhaps she was patroness of the archers' guild. גרבעל 'client of Baal' (Benz, *Names*, p. 298). The mention of Sidon as his home town is interesting; Sidon and Byblos were the first Phoen. cities to recover after the attacks of the 'Sea peoples' (Albright in *Cambr. Anc. Hist.*, 3rd edit., II, part 2, 518 f.). Note that there is no article with the gentilic adject.; this is as expected in so early a period (see at **6** Yehimilk 2). רפא; cp. רפאל 'El has healed' (1 Chron. xxvi 7). יחש is unattested; perhaps from the same base as Biblical חושי. The Rapa' arrow is technically a palimpsest, as faint traces of another name underneath are visible (see Martin, loc. cit.); this is an indication that a special importance was attached to the inscribed arrows, as an ordinary arrow would hardly have been handed down from one archer to another. אדא is prob. hypocoristicon of a fuller name beginning with אדן 'lord'. עכי is perhaps a gentilic used as a proper name; Acco, south of Tyre, was often disputed between Israel and Tyre (2 Sam. xxiv 7 1 Kgs. ix 11). זכר followed by ב; we have to assume either that ב is a mistake or that the arrow tip had been broken and resharpened leading to the final two letters of an original בעל being effaced or cut off (Cross); note the squatness of the tip in comparison with the other arrowheads. Yeivin thought he could see traces of these letters, but the first editor (Milik) denied this in his subsequent article. The name זכרבעל is attested as that of a king of Byblos in the early 11 cent. (the Egyp. Wen-Amon report; *ANET* p. 26). בנען: ען was the masc. counterpart of the goddess Anat and is now well attested in Ugar. names, though he does not appear in the myths; otherwise we may restore with Yeivin בנענ[ת]. עזרבעל; the same name as on the spatula inscr. (**1**); 'Baal has helped' (cp. Hebr. Azariah) or 'Baal is helper' (partic.; cp. the transcription 'Οζερβαλος) or 'Baal is help' (cp. Hasdrubal); see Benz, *Names*, p. 375. אדנבעל; a very common name in Phoen. and Punic inscrs. (Benz, *Names*, p. 56). Note the word-dividers on this arrowhead.

II

INSCRIPTIONS IN THE OLD PHOENICIAN DIALECT OF BYBLOS

1 Azarbaal Spatula

THE small bronze triangular object containing the Phoen. inscr. on one side was first published by M. Dunand in 1938. It measures 96 × 96 × 56 mm., and is now in the National Museum at Beirut. There are traces of Pseudo-Hieroglyphic writing (or, more accurately, according to Martin, of a developed mid-2 millenn. form of this) both on the side with the Phoen. inscr. and on the reverse side. A number of similar objects, some inscribed with (normal) Pseudo-Hieroglyphic signs and some uninscribed, were also found in the excavations. Most of them have a tapering corner to which perhaps a wooden handle had been attached, suggesting that the objects may originally have been used for some workaday spreading purpose. We do not know why they were also used for writing texts in Pseudo-Hieroglyphic, but it is unlikely that even if we did it would help us to understand the purpose of the Phoen. inscr., which is several centuries later than the inscrs. underneath and behind it. The contents seem to be jejune enough, and concern some kind of message from an unknown person to one called Azarbaal. The details are cryptic and obscure, however, and many different interpretations have been offered, none of which has convinced more than a few scholars. No translation is attempted below, but my own preference is for the older view that the inscr. records a simple money transaction or a request for a debt to be repaid rather than the more recent and more complicated suggestions of Iwry, according to whom it deals with a process for resolving a quarrel by casting lots (cp. Albright), or of McCarter and Coote, according to whom it is a sharp reply by a superior to a subordinate seeking compensation to which he was not entitled, or of van den Branden, according to whom it is an ultimatum to make peace or else resume hostilities. The script prob. belongs with that of the two short inscrs. on clay (**2, 3**) to around the middle of the 11 cent.; see further in the Notes to the previous chapt. and the introd. to **4** Ahiram. The text is much too uncertain to supply any dialectal data.

Bibliography

M. Dunand, 'Spatule de bronze avec épigraph phénicien du XIII s.', *BMB* 2 (1938), 99–107; and in *Fouilles de Byblos* I (1939), p. 28.

W. F. Albright, 'A Hebrew letter from the Twelfth Century B.C.', *BASOR* 73 (1939), 9–13.

J. Obermann, 'An early Phoenician political document with a parallel to Judges 11:24', *J. Bibl. Lit.* 58 (1939), 229–42.

W. F. Albright, 'The copper spatula of Byblus and Proverbs 18:18', *BASOR* 90 (1943), 35–7.

Dunand, *Byblia Grammata,* 155 ff.

H. Torczyner in *Leshonenu* 14 (1946), 158 ff. (in Hebrew).

Albright, 'Inscriptions', 158 f.

A. Dupont-Sommer, 'L'Inscription phénicienne de la spatule dite d'Asdrubaal', *Arch. Or.* 17 (1949), part I, 158–67.

EHO p. 13.

S. Iwry in *JAOS* 81 (1961), 32–34 (see Bibliogr. to chapt. I).

M. Martin in *Orientalia* 30 (1961), 60 ff. (see Bibliogr. to chapt. I).

KAI no. 3.

Bange, *Vowel-Letters,* p. 28.

Magnanini, *Iscrizioni,* p. 32.

P. K. McCarter, R. B. Coote, 'The spatula inscription from Byblos', *BASOR* 212 (1972), 16–22.

A. van den Branden in *RSF* 2 (1974), 138 ff.

Illustrations

Fouilles de Byblos I, Atlas (1937), pl. XXXII; Byblia Grammata, pl. XIII; Birnbaum, Scripts, no. 02; Martin, loc. cit., fig. 4 and tab. VIII–XI; Driver, Writing, pl. 53,2. Sketches in Dupont-Sommer, loc. cit.; Diringer, Alphabet, fig. 107,3; KAI Taf. I; McCarter and Coote, loc. cit.

1]י לעזרבעל [--]

2 תשעם ' שלם [כ]סֹף

3 נשבת ' אם נחל

4 תנחל ' מפֿשתך

5 עלך ' ומפֿשת

6 עֹלי

NOTES

1. עזרבעל; the same name as on one of the bronze arrowheads studied in chapt. I (q.v. Notes). If the lacuna contained a name, it may have been a hypocoristicon ending in [ay] (cp. כלבי, **10**) or perhaps a gentilic used as a proper name (cp. עכי, Ruweiseh arrowhead). Torczyner restores [על]י; cp. עלך (5). Dupont-Sommer [לאח]י, 'To my brother.'

2. תשעם is most obviously taken as the numeral 90. Van den Branden thinks of a verb and cites Arab. [ša'ama] 'to reconcile'. Albright's suggestion that it comes from Š'Y 'to gaze' (Hebr.), 'to behold, look for, aim at' (Akkad.) with enclitic [m] (thus, 'Do you seek reconciliation (שלם)?') is hardly to be accepted until the presence of this enclitic, which is common enough in Ugar. poetry (*CML*[2] p. 150) is more securely established in Phoen. prose (see at **42** Pyrgi 10–11). שלם may be an imper. Piel 'pay, make restitution!' or a noun meaning 'peace, compensation', or the like. The last word was formerly read as כסף, but the reading סג[1] is now generally preferred. The traces before ס do not seem sufficient for word-divider plus כ, and פ does not usually have so sharp a point at this early date. However, this reading is attractive along with שלם 'pay', and is defended by Martin in his re-examination of the inscription. סג has been interpreted as imper. or partic. from SWG 'to backslide, turn back' (Albright, McCarter and Coote) or a noun meaning 'strife, refractoriness' (Iwry). Van den Branden reads סף 'destruction' (SWP) and takes נשבת (3) as Niph. perf., though with future meaning 'shall be at an end'.

3. נשבת is, however, more prob. 1 plur. imperf. (or jussive) Yiph. 'we shall (let us) bring to an end, settle' (Albright, Iwry). Less likely is a derivation (Torczyner, Dupont-Sommer) from a putative NŠB related to Aram. NSB 'to take', e.g. 'I have received'. McCarter and Coote find traces of a little upraised ע after ב and read נשבעת 'I have sworn'; Teixidor, after examining the original, denies that it is there ('Bulletin' for 1975, p. 280). נחל 'to possess, inherit' or (Iwry) 'to share by casting lots' or, as argued by McCarter and Coote on the basis of Ugar. economic documents, 'to receive a grant'; thus 'I have sworn, You shall by no means receive a grant'. This interesting argument is weakened by the fact that only a nominal form *nhl* occurs in the Ugar. texts in question, but their rendering at least gives weight to the nuance of the infin. absol., which seems rather inappropriate in a conditional clause. Note that in the imperf. as in Hebr. [n] does not assimilate to the pharyngal [ḥ]. Van den Branden 'If on the contrary you choose (sc. combat)' is based very doubtfully on Arab. NHL.

4. מגשת is now for the reason given in 2 preferred to מפשת, though we cannot be certain. No etymology for either immediately suggests itself. מפשת may be connected with the word for 'flax' (Torczyner; Hebr. פשת) or with the base NPŠ, Akkad. *napāšu* 'to breathe, be broad, numerous', Arab. [nafīsu] 'numerous (goods)', suggesting a meaning like 'wealth, possessions' (Dupont-Sommer, *KAI*). מגשת may come from NGŠ 'to draw near', thus 'offering(s)' (Albright), 'divining implement' (Iwry; cp. 1 Sam. xiv 18 xxiii 9), 'combat' (van den Branden), or from NGŚ = Hebr. NGŚ 'to oppress, exact', thus 'obligations' (McCarter and Coote).

5. עלך = ['alēkā] or the like. The meaning could be 'incumbent upon' or perhaps better, if the context is one of settling a debt, 'owed by' (cp. II **27** Hermopolis papyrus ii 9). Van den Branden 'for your part'. In the noun the suffix [ī] is unwritten; see Note on phonology and grammar.

6. It is difficult to decide whether ע should be restored as in the previous line (עלך); the ל in this line is slightly nearer the edge. עלי = ['aláyyā] or the like.

2, 3 Inscriptions on clay cones

The two inscrs., consisting of the prepos. ל followed by a proper name, were published by Dunand in *Fouilles de Byblos* II (1950) (see Atlas pl. CXLIV), where they are given the numbers 7765 (2) and 11687 (3); their present numbers in the Beirut Museum are B1473 and B1462. It is not certain what use the cone-like objects on which they are incised were put to. The writing seems to me slightly to pre-date 4 Ahiram and makes them with the Azarbaal spatula (1) the oldest Phoen. inscrs. so far known from Byblos; see the Notes to chapt. I. See also the studies by F. M. Cross and P. K. McCarter, *RSF* 1 (1973), 3–8 and by J. Teixidor, *BASOR* 225 (1977), 70–1, both illustrated.

לעבדחמן 2

לאחאם בבד 3

NOTES

The name on 2 is attested on another Phoen. inscr. and in Akkad. transliteration (*Abdiḥimunu*); Benz, *Names*, p. 312; see further on עבדאמן (29 Baalshillem). It should not, in view of the absence of בעל, be too readily linked with the deity Baal-Hammon (13 Kilamuwa i 16). The first name on 3 was read by Cross and McCarter as אחאש, giving an example of an archaic ש with upright rather than horizontal stance but giving also an unparalleled structure; the correct reading, as Teixidor points out, is מ (facing, however, from left to right), which gives a structure 'brother of the Mother (goddess)', attested in Akkad. *Aḥi-um-me-a* (Tallqvist, *Assyrian Pers. Names*. 14, 18) and comparable with Hebr. Ahab, 'brother of the Father (god)'. בבד; with the assimilation of [n] of בן to the first letter of the patronymic cp. ביחמלך (8 Elibaal 1) and בכלבי (10 Abda); a phonetic feature, therefore, of the Old Byblian dialect, though note that it does not occur before a laryngeal (בן אחרם, 4 Ahiram 1); cp. תנחל (1 Azarbaal spatula 4). בד; hypocoristicon consisting of the prepos. phase 'by the hand of' or 'from the hand(s) of' with the deity's name omitted; it was pronounced [bōd] as many Greek and Latin trascriptions show (Benz, *Names*, pp. 283 ff.)

4 Ahiram

The famous inscr., the oldest connected and readable text in Phoen., was discovered in 1923. The longest part (*l.* 2) is carved on one side of the lid of a decorated limestone coffin, but the inscr. begins (*l.* 1) on the upper rim of the sarcophagus itself, remarkably a little way in from the edge; Martin, in his careful re-examination of the original, has suggested that the mason was trying to avoid a previous inscr. in a later semi-linear form of the so-called Pseudo-Hieroglyphic writing. The coffin is dated by its archaeological context in the 13 cent., and presumably the inscr. detected by Martin recorded the burial of an earlier occupant who died at that time. The date of its re-use by Ahiram has consequently to be decided solely by the Phoen. writing, which (see below) I would place in the latter part of the 11 cent. BC. The inscr. is the first in an interesting and valuable series of royal inscrs. covering roughly the 10 cent. BC, which with the earlier Report of Wen-Amon in Egyptian (first half of the 11 cent.; *ANET* pp. 25 ff.) supplies evidence of a quick recovery by Byblos after the incursions of the 'Sea peoples' and the attainment of a reasonably high level of literacy. The sarcophagus is now housed in the National Museum in Beirut.

Writing

The scripts of this and the next inscr. (**5** Ahiram graffito) share with those of the Azarbaal spatula (**1**) and the Byblos cones (**2, 3**) a number of features which do not reappear on Yehimilk and the other early inscrs. from the city (**6–10**); e.g. the peculiar א (**1, 4**), the upright stance of ג, the horizontal cross-bars of ח, the (mostly) shorter ז, the archaic ע (twice on **4**). Inscrs. **6–10** can be dated on the basis of external evidence (see at **7** Abibaal and **8** Elibaal) to the mid- and late 10 cent., which suggests somewhere in the latter half of the 11 cent. for inscrs. **1–5**. We cannot go much higher than that if we are to make room in the late 12 and early 11 cent. for the still more archaic features seen on some of the arrowhead scripts (see the discussion in the Notes to chapt. I). Garbini does not take account of the arrowheads (or of Martin's article) in his recent attempt to reinstate the inscr. in the 13 cent., to which, because of the date of the coffin, it was automatically assigned by the first commentators. Word-dividers are used on all the Old Byblian inscrs., a practice which was abandoned by most Phoen. scribes after the 9 cent. See further on the writing McCarter, *Antiquity,* 31 ff.

Style. see the final paragraph in the introd. to **13** Kilamuwa i.

Bibliography

First publication: R. Dussaud, 'Les inscriptions phéniciennes du tombeau d'Ahiram, roi de Byblos', *Syria* 5 (1924), 135–45.
For other early studies see P. Montet, *Byblos et l'Égypte* (1928), p. 238 and Harris, *Grammar,* p. 158.
Further:
Albright, 'Inscriptions', 155 f.
K. Galling in *WO* 1/5 (1950), 421–5.
EHO pp. 13–14.
J. H. Winnikov in *Vestnik Drevnej Istorii* 42 (1952), 141–52 (a Russian article not available to me).

H. Donner, 'Zur Formgeschichte der Aḥīrām-Inschrift', *Wiss. Z.d. K.-Marx-Univ., Leipzig, Gesellsch. und sprachw. Reihe,* Heft 2/3 (1953–4), 283–7.

A. van den Branden, 'Inscription sur le sarcophage d'Ahiram', *Al-Mashriq* 54 ((1960), 732–6.

M. Martin in *Orientalia* 30 (1961), 70 ff. (see Bibliogr. to chapt. I).

KAI no. 1.

ANET p. 661.

M. Metzger in *Ug.-Forsch.* 2 (1970), 157–8.

M. Chéhab, 'Observations au sujet du sarcophage d'Ahiram', *MUSJ* 46 (1970–1), 107–17.

H. Tawil, 'A note on the Aḥiram inscription', *JANES* 3 (1970–1), 33–6.

Bange, *Vowel-Letters,* pp. 29 f.

Greenfield, 'Scripture', 254–7.

Magnanini, *Iscrizioni,* p. 29.

Teixidor, 'Bulletin' for 1973, item 113.

G. Garbini, 'Sulla datazione dell' iscrizione di Aḥiram,' *AIUON* 37 (1977), 81–9.

Illustrations

RB 34 (1925), pls. VI–VIII; *Byblos et l'Égypte,* pls. CXXXVIII–CXL and figs., pp. 236–7; *ANEP* nos. 456–9; Diringer, *Alphabet,* fig. 108, 1; Birnbaum, *Scripts,* no. 01; *KAI* Taf. I; Harden, *Phoenicians,* fig. 34 and pl. 15 (sarcophagus); Moscati, *Phoenicians,* pl. 11 (sarcophagus); Driver, *Writing,* pls. 51 (2), 52.

1 ‏ארן' זפעל' [א]תבעל' בן אחרם' מלך גבל' לאחרם' אבה' כשתה'‏
‏בעלם'‏

2 ‏ואל' מלך' במלכם' וסכן' בס‹כ›נם' ותמא' מחנת' עלי' גבל'‏
‏ויגל' ארן' זן' תחתסף' חטר' משפטה' תהתפך' כסא' מלכה'‏
‏ונחת' תברח' על' גבל' והא' ימח ספרה' לפף' שבל‏

1. Coffin which Ittobaal, son of Ahiram, king of Byblos, made for Ahiram, his father, when he placed him in 'the house of eternity'.

2. Now, if a king among kings or a governor among governors or a commander of an army should come up against Byblos and uncover this coffin, may the sceptre of his rule be torn away, may the throne of his kingdom be overturned, and may peace flee from Byblos! And as for him, may his inscription be effaced ....!

NOTES

1. ז; cp. Hebr. [zū], [zō], [zē] (Massor. [ze]) as relatives; Aram. [dī], Ugar. ḏ, Arab. [ḏū]. אתבעל; cp. the name of the king of Tyre and father of Jezebel in 1 Kgs. xvi 31, Massor. Hebr. ['etba'al] but Josephus *Ἰθωβαλος* (Benz, *Names*, p. 281), i.e. in Standard (Tyro-Sidonian) Phoen. ['ittōba'l], 'Baal is with him'. Elsewhere in this inscr. the 3 sing. masc. suffix is ה, though in other Old Byblian texts it is ו, giving a diphthong; the form here suggests that the change was already taking place and that in this position in the middle of a proper name the diphthong has further reduced, giving [ō] as in Standard or some other vowel, depending on the connecting vowel after the preposition. בן with [n] unassimilated before a following laryngal; see Notes to **2, 3** Byblos cones. אחרם = ['hīrōm], 'my brother (god) is exalted', with [ō] from stressed [ā]; the spelling Ahiram is kept here for convention's sake. A shortened form [ḥīrām], [ḥīrōm] is found as the name of a king of Tyre and contemporary of Solomon (1 Kgs. v 15 ff. 2 Chron. ii 2 ff.); cp. Phoen. חרם (**17** Baal Lebanon *a*), a king of Tyre and Sidon; Akkad. transcription *Ḥi-ru-um-mu* (Benz, *Names*, p. 232). גבל; Hebr. [gbal]; Akkad. *Gubli*. אבה prob. = ['abīhū], the noun being genit.; later, when the original function of the connecting vowel was fogotten, [ū] may have been usual as in Aram. אבוהי; Dan. v 2); cp. Latin *labunom* (Segert, *Grammar*, p. 117). כ שתה = [kī šōtáhū]; cp. ŠYT in Hebr. (Ps. xii 6 lxxxviii 7) and Ugar. (of the burial of Aqhat, **19** 112). There is no need to assume a missing letter, thus Dussaud and Albright כש<ב>תה 'as his abode in eternity'; a letter is missing in בס<כ>נם at the beginning of **2**, but that is a repeated word. בעלם; Tawil's arguments seem to me persuasive that ב is an abbreviation of בת with the prepos. ב omitted, as often in Hebr. before this word (e.g. Gen. xxiv 23 I **13** Arad C 9). The prepos. ב is not found with עלם elsewhere in the Canaanite or Aram. languages, whereas an abbreviation בי for בית is well known in the Aram. of the papyri (*DISO* p. 35) and later. A particularly instructive example is בי עלמא 'cemetery' in a Syriac inscr. (Nöldeke, *ZA* 21 (1908), 158); cp. also בת עלם in Punic in the sense of 'tomb' (*DISO* p. 35).

2. אל; cp. Hebr. ['illū] (Eccles. vi 6 Esth. vii 4) and ['ūlay] (Gen. xviii 24, 28 Hos. viii 7) (i.e. here ['ūlē]). מלך במלכם etc.; cp. **15** Karatepe A iii 12 f. סכן; cp. Hebr. [sōkēn] (Isa. xxii 15) and Ugar. *skn* (**17** i 27), both 'steward'; Tell-Am. *zukini* (*EA* 256, 9) 'commissioner, ambassador' and Phoen. סכן 'minister' (in a small text from Cyprus published in Masson and Sznycer, *Recherches*, 69 ff.). Here, however, and in **17** Baal Lebanon, the meaning is 'governor', of which the Hebr. equivalent is סגן. Both forms are prob. loanwords from Akkad. *šakēnu, šaknu* 'governor, administrator', that with [g] being a later borrowing; see further Lipiński, *Ug.-Forsch.* 5 (1973), 191–207. תמא; Punic תמיא; the derivation is unknown; Gevirtz, *JNES* 26 (1971), 15–16, proposes a connection with Greek *ταμίας* 'steward, overseer' (*Il.* iv 84). מחנת = [maḥnōt] (from [maḥnāt]) or possibly [maḥnūt]; see further at II **5** Zakir A 5. עלי = ['alay(a)], later ['alō] (Punic עלא), followed by the direct object as frequently in Hebr. (e.g. Gen. xlix 4 Ruth iv 1), although these examples do not have the sense 'go up against'. With the perf. in the protasis of a conditional sentence of this type cp. Deut. xxxii 41 and Job ix 16, 30, three examples where as here (ויגל) there is a second verb in the protasis. This is in Deut. xxxii 41 an imperf. with ordinary *Waw*, in Job ix 16 a '*Waw* consecutive' imperf., and in Job ix 30 another perf. with *Waw*. The first and third of these seem to me to reflect Hebr.

usage better and I am inclined to question the Massoretic pointing in the second (and in the not quite similar example in Ps. cxxxix 11). It is, therefore, more suitable to regard the tense of יגל as imperf. [yiglē] (cp. Friedrich, *Grammatik*, p. 266, note) and to conclude that in contradistinction to the perfs. (עלי) the diphthong formed by the original [y] has reduced in the imperfs. of verbs final weak than to argue for a 'Waw consecutive' form in an environment where it would look peculiar even in Hebr., which has developed 'Waw consecutive' constructions much more than any other Semitic language. This view is given added weight by the fact that no certain example of a 'Waw consecutive' imperf. in a normal narrative position has so far been discovered in Phoen., though a number of 'Waw consecutive' perfs. with future or precative meaning are attested (see at **15** Karatepe A iii 2). See also at II **5** Zakir A 11 ff., where I question the appropriateness of the term 'Waw consecutive' for a number of 'imperfects' with past meaning in an Old Aram. dialect. זן; cp. Zenjirli זן (II **14** Panammu 22 has זנה), Aram. [dēn], [dnā]; note that the noun does not have the article, as it usually has in later Phoen. texts. תחתסף and תהתפך; verbal forms with infixed [t] on the pattern of the Ugar. Gt conjugation. The form survives in I **16** Mesha 11 (as a reflexive) but is not certainly found in any later Phoen. or other Canaanite source. The first is prob. to be connected with Arab. [ḥasifa], 'sank, became emaciated' but also 'sunk (a well), humbled, tore off' (cp. Ugar. ḥsp, **19** 31) or Arab. [ḥasafa] 'picked, culled', form VII 'to be smashed', rather than with Hebr. ḤŚP and apparently (see *CML²* p. 140) Ugar. ḥsp, 'stripped off, skimmed'. With the second cp. HPK in II **7** Sefire i C 21. The whole imprecation is closely paralleled in Ugar. (**6** vi 28–29)

> lyhpk. ks'a. mlkk
> lytbr. ḥṭ. mṭpṭk

Cp. also חטר חלבבה (II **13** Hadad 3) and Isa. xiv 5 Jerem. xlviii 17 Ps. lxxxix 45. Note that the nouns in Phoen. are apparently fem.; so *kussū* (and *ḥaṭṭu*) in Akkadian. Alternatively, the verbs have been regarded as masc. with [t] prefix, though ימח later in the line has the normal [y]; for possible examples of such a form in Hebr. see van Dijk, *VT* 19 (1969), 440 ff. משפטה prob. at this early period = [mišpaṭēhū] (< [ihū]), the noun being in the genit.; cp. [lmīnēhū] (Gen. i 12). נחת = [nōḥat] < [nawḥat], lit. 'rest' (sc. from enemies); cp. Hebr. מנוחה in 1 Kgs. viii 56 1 Chron. xxii 9. A similar form *nḫt* occurs in Ugar. (**3** D 47 **16** vi 24) in a conventional passage in parallelism with *ks'i mlkh*, on the basis of which some have argued for a metaphorical meaning here, '(royal) authority' or the like, lit. the 'rest' or seat on which the king sat. But in the present context the word describes something happening to Byblos, not, like the previous phrases, something happening to those attacking it. With על 'from' cp. Ps. iv 7 lxxxi 6 Job xxx 2; this meaning is also found in Ugar. (*CML²* p. 154) and in Moabite (I **16** 4). ימח = [yimmaḥ], jussive Niph. from MḤY where, as in Hebr., one expects the end vowel to be dropped; cp. Ps. cix 13 and with the sense Exod. xxxii 32 Ps. lxix 29 **15** Karatepe A iii 13. ספר; cp. **13** Kilamuwa i 15 II **7** Sefire i C 17 **8** ii C 2. לפף שבל; no satisfactory rendering has been so far advanced. The ל prob. describes the agent following the passive verb. פף may be a reduplicated form of פ 'mouth'; cp. the plur. Hebr. form פיפיות (Isa. xli 15). שבל could then be the name of some kind of erasing instrument; cp. Hebr. לפי חרב 'by the edge of a sword'. For some other suggestions see *DISO*, pp. 139, 288–9.

5 Ahiram graffito

The graffito with its warning against grave robbers was found scratched on the shaft of the tomb containing Ahiram's coffin; it was clearly, from its writing, put there at his and not the previous burial. See the Bibliography to **4** and further *KAI* no. 2; Magnanini, *Iscrizioni*, p. 29. Illustrations in Montet, *Byblos et l'Égypte,* fig. p. 216 and pl. CXXVI; Diringer, *Alphabet,* fig. 108, 2; Driver, *Writing,* fig. 54.

1 לדעת '

2 הן יפד לך '

3 תחת זן

Beware! Behold, there is disaster for you under this!

NOTES

לדעת lit. 'to know'. יפד = [yūpōd] < [yupād(u)], passive Qal impersonal construction from PWD/PYD; cp. Hebr. [pīd] 'ruin, misfortune'; Arab. [fāda], imperf. in [u] or [i], 'died, passed away'.

6 Yehimilk   Fig. 9

The inscr., found in 1929, consists of seven lines of Phoen. writing superimposed upon a previous (late) Pseudo-Hieroglyphic inscr., which was divided into registers. According to Martin, the stone which had contained the earlier inscr. was broader than the broken-off and partly worn portion (35 × 70 × 45 cm.) later used for the Phoen. inscr.; this is now housed in the Beirut Museum. The fact that Yehimilk does not give his parentage and (*ll.* 6–7) emphasizes his legitimate right to the throne makes one suspect that he was the founder of a new dynasty and prob. a usurper (cp. II **5** Zakir A 1). Yehimilk is the father of Elibaal, whose inscr. (**8**) belongs to 914 BC or shortly afterwards; if, as is commonly suggested but is not certain, he is also the father of Abibaal, whose inscr. (**7**) is a decade or two earlier, his own inscr. may be placed around 950–940. See further on the writing in the introd. to **4** Ahiram.

Bibliography

First published by P. Montet in *CRAIBL*, 1929, 250.
See further:
M. Dunand, 'Nouvelle inscription phénicienne archaïque', *RB* 39 (1930), 321–31.
idem, *Fouilles de Byblos* I (1939), p. 30.

Albright, 'Inscriptions', 156 f.
EHO pp. 14–15.
M. Martin in *Orientalia* 30 (1961), 63 ff. (see Bibliogr. to chapt. I).
KAI no. 4.
ANET p. 653.
Bange, *Vowel-Letters*, pp. 30–1.
Magnanini, *Iscrizioni*, pp. 30–1.
Avishur, 'Stylistic features', 7–8, 12–13.

Illustrations

Dunand, *Fouilles* I, Atlas (1937), pl. xxxi; Birnbaum, *Scripts*, no. 04; Martin, op. cit., fig. 6 and tab. XII, XIII; Driver, *Writing*, pl. 53, 1.

1 בת' זבני' יחמלך' מלך גבל

2 הֹאת' חוי' כל' מפלת' הבתם

3 אל' יארך' בעלשממ' ובעל\<ת\>

4 גבל' ומפחרת' אל גבל

5 קדשמ' ימת' יחמלך' ושנתו

6 על גבל' כ מלך' צדק' ומלך

7 ישר' לפן' אל גבל' קֹדֹשֹם ['הא]

1. Temple which Yehimilk king of Byblos (re-) built;
2. he it was who restored all the ruins of these
3. temples. May Baalshamem and the Mistress of
4. Byblos and the assembly of the holy gods of
5. Byblos prolong the days and years of Yehimilk
6. over Byblos! For [he is] the legitimate and rightful
7. king in the sight of the holy gods of Byblos.

NOTES

1. בת; prob. 'temple' but perhaps simply 'building'. ז; relative; see at **4** Ahiram 1. בני with [y] retained; see at **4** Ahiram 2 (עלי). יחמלך 'Milk lives'; cp. Hebr. יחיאל, יחיה; the Akkad. transcription *Ia-ḫi-mil-ki* (of a king of Tyre; Benz, *Names*, p. 309) suggests a vocalization [yhīmilk], though with the Phoen. base being ḤWY and not as in Hebr. ḤYY one might expect [yḥūmilk] with the short imperf. (jussive) in [ū]. Milk here is prob. a title of El, the chief god in the Byblian triad of El, Baalat, and Adonis (Moscati, *Phoenicians*, 31). Baal, who does not appear in this triad, was also an important deity at Byblos, as the presence of his name as an element in the kings' names in inscrs. **7–9** shows.

2. האת; a longer pronominal form related to Ugar. *hwt*, fem. *hyt*, though the

latter are restricted to oblique cases (nomin. *hw, hy*); it is not found in later Phoen.; Bibl. Hebr. has only הוא, though a longer הואה appears in the Dead Sea Scrolls. חוי = [ḥiwway(a)]; Piel; cp. Hebr. [ḥiyyā] in 1 Chron. xi 8 Neh. iii 34. The use of this word suggests that בני should be given the meaning 'rebuilt' as in I **16** Mesha 9, 21 ff. and frequently in Hebrew. מפלת; cp. Isa. xxv 2 Ezek. xxxi 13. הבתם; the earliest occurrence of the definite article in Phoen., used when a demonstrative follows (אל). As in Moabite (I **16** Mesha 3), the demonstr. does not itself take the article. The article is lacking, however, with קדשם (5), an adjective qualifying a definite noun; in later Phoen. it would normally be used in such a position. We may have evidence here of its gradual introduction into the language. It is entirely missing from **4** Ahiram, as it is from the earliest Hebr. inscr. (I **1** Gezer).

3. אל = ['ëllē]; cp. Neo-Punic אלא, Poenulus *ily*. יארך = [ya'rēk] or the like; Yiphil jussive; cp. **25** Yehaumilk 9 II **19** Nerab ii 3 1 Kgs. iii 14 Prov. iii 2. בעלשמם; Akkad. *Ba-al-sa-me-ma*; Aram. בעלשמין. The problem of the origin and identity of this deity has not yet been satisfactorily solved. Here he ought from his position at the head of a list of deities to be equated with El, the leading god of Byblos, though in several texts from other places the title seems to refer to Baal (II **5** Zakir A 3 and below **15** Karatepe A iii 18). בעלת; comparison with **7** Abibaal 2 **8** Elibaal 2 **9** Shipitbaal 3–4 makes the correction to a fem. very likely; the female member of the Byblian triad corresponding to Astarte at Tyre and Sidon; she may be meant here also, but if Baalshamem is El, an equation with Athirat, the consort of El in the Ugar. myths, is more probable. See most recently on these matters R. A. Oden in *CBQ* 39 (1977), 451 ff.

4. מפחרת; cp. Ugar. *mpḫrt bn 'il* (in non-mythological texts) and *pḫr bn 'ilm* (**4** iii 14). אל; constr. plural.

5. ימת; the later Byblian inscr. of Yehaumilk has a masc. plur. form (**25** 9); the Standard dialect also has the two forms (**13** Kilamuwa i 12 **15** Karatepe A i 5 iii 1); the masc. form predominates in Hebr., but a fem. form is occasionally found (Deut. xxxii 7). שנתו with ו for the earlier ה (**4** Ahiram 1); prob. to be vocalized [šnōtaw] < [šnōtáhu], the noun being in the accus. case. Fem. plur. nouns in Phoen. add suffixes in the same way as sing. nouns, against the practice in Hebrew.

6. כ; **4** Ahiram 1; comparison with **25** Yehaumilk 9 suggests that הא is to be restored at the end of *l*. 7, which is badly worn; there seems to be just room for it. צדק and ישר (7) prob. refer to Yehimilk's claim to the throne and are used in the same sense as Ugar. *'att ṣdqh* and *mtrḫt yšrh*, 'his lawful wife', 'his rightful spouse' in the Keret epic (**14** 12–13); cp. צדק **25** Yehaumilk 9, **36** Lapethos ii 11, and in Hebr. Jerem. xxiii 5. With the parallelism cp. Deut. ix 5.

7 Abibaal
Fig. 4

The incomplete inscr. was the first Old Byblian text to be published (in 1905), though it was not successfully deciphered until much later owing to unfamiliarity with the archaic writing. It is incised on a large fragment of the base of a statue of Sheshonk (Biblical Shishak), an early Pharaoh of the Twenty-second dynasty, who reigned (in Albright's chronology) *c*.935–914 BC, and whose invasion of Palestine is recorded in 1 Kgs. xiv 25 ff.; there is no evidence that he reached beyond this and subjugated Byblos (see *ANET* pp. 263–4). The writing is later but not much later than on **4** Ahiram (q.v. introd.) and the inscr. was prob., therefore, carved on the statue (which on one interpretation of the text was brought by Abibaal from Egypt) during Sheshonk's lifetime. It is not clear why a monarch of Byblos should employ a Pharaoh's statue for a dedication to the Mistress of Byblos and a pious prayer that his own reign may be a long one. If it was an act of homage from a vassal to his superior, we should have expected some acknowlededgment of this relationship in the text. It is in fact more likely that Abibaal was given it as a present on a visit to Egypt and placed it in the goddess's shrine on his return as a testimony to his own power and renown. If Abibaal is a son of Yehimilk that visit was prob. made well on in Sheshonk's reign and the inscr. should be dated *c.*925–920, with his brother Elibaal's inscr. (**8**) being placed a decade or two later. An equally acceptable sequence, however, is given by Moscati (*Phoenicians,* 11), viz. Abibaal 940 (he uses a slightly higher chronology than Albright for the Egyptian kings), Yehimilk 920, Elibaal 900, and Shipitbaal 880. On this interpretation Abibaal is the last king of Ahiram's dynasty and the usurping of the throne by Yehimilk took place on his death.

Bibliography

First publication by Ch. Clermont-Ganneau, *Recueil d'archéologie orientale* 6 (1905), 74–8.
See further:
R. Dussaud in *Syria* 5 (1924), 145 ff. (see Bibliogr. to **4** Ahiram).
B. Maisler in *Leshonenu* 14 (1946), 174 ff. (see Bibliogr. to **9** Shipitbaal).
Albright, 'Inscriptions', 157 f.
EHO p. 15.
W. Herrmann, 'Der historische Ertrag der altbyblischen Inschriften', *Mitt. d. Inst. f. Orientf.* 6 (1958), 14–32.
S. Yeivin in *Jewish Qu. Rev.* 50 (1959–60), 214.
KAI no. 5.
J.-G. Février in *Africa* 1 (1966), 13 ff. (see Teixidor, 'Bulletin' for 1968, item 66).
Bange, *Vowel-Letters,* 32
Magnanini, *Iscrizioni,* p. 28

Illustrations

Syria 5 (1924), pl. XLII; Diringer, *Alphabet,* fig. 108, 3; Birnbaum, *Scripts,* no. 05

1 [......ב' גבל] מלך' אבבעל' זי]בֿא' מש]

2 גבל' בעלת' תארך' אדתו' גבל' לבעל[ת' במצרם' גבל] מלך]

על גבל [' ושנתו' אבבעל' ימת

1. [Statue which] Abibaal king of [Byblos son of ....]
2. [king of] Byblos brought from Egypt for the Mistress [of Byblos, his lady. May the Mistress of Byblos prolong the days and years of Abibaal] over Byblos!

NOTES

1. מש; this troublesome word which appears in Punic as מאש and which, from the contexts in which it is found, seems mostly to mean 'statue' or 'image', is discussed further at **36** Lapethos ii I; it should prob. be distinguished from Phoen. מאש 'gift' in **32** Umm el-'Amed xiii 2. This and most of the other restorations are made on the basis of **8** Elibaal (where the word is in fact uncertain) and **9** Shipitbaal, whose formulas are very similar; cp. also **6** Yehimilk. יבא; Yiphil perf. (Albright). The ב is uncertain and the verb is rare in Phoen.; but the only other verbs ending in א that are used in votive or dedicatory inscrs. are יטנא (Yiph.) 'erected' and נשא 'offered', and the faded letter is more like ב than it is like either נ or ש. The meanings of these verbs, moreover, do not fit with the most obvious rendering of במצרם in 2 as 'from Egypt'. אבבעל; Benz, *Names*, p. 257. At the end of the line restore perhaps ביחמלך; see the introduction.

2. The meaning 'from' for ב is common in Ugar. (*CML*[2] p. 143) and not infrequent in Hebr. (e.g. Ps. xviii = 2 Sam. xxii 9 Job v 21, etc.); other examples in Phoen. are **15** Karatepe A iii 14 (בשער) and **29** Eshmunazar 6 (במשכב). The first of these examples precedes [š], so the explanation of Friedrich (*Grammatik,* p. 21) and others that [b] is by dissimilation for [m] in the vicinity of another [m], i.e. that ב = מן, is not possible. מצרם is most easily taken as the place-name 'Egypt', especially since the inscr. is written on a statue of a Pharaoh. In view of the fragmentary state of the text, however, the suggestion of Février that the word be rendered '(in) distress' (cp. Hebr. מצרים in Lam. i 3) cannot be entirely dismissed. This interpretation is based on the phrase נצב מלכת במצרם on a votive inscr. *CIS* i 198, 4–5. מלכת there is prob. a fem. or a plur. form of the technical sacrificial term מלך and means, therefore, 'offering(s)' (from the Yiph. of the verb 'to go'). As far as we can tell מלך usually refers to the widespread Phoen. and Punic practice of child-sacrifice; but though the formula of CIS i 198 is similar to those of many מלך inscrs., מלכת cannot have that precise meaning there but must signify some other kind of offering, since it is made on behalf of a certain Adonibaal. The phrase in question may, therefore, be translated 'stele of an offering (or offerings) (made) in (time of) distress'. See further on the מלך sacrifice at **21, 22** Malta, where bibliogr. is given. אדתו prob. = ['dattēw] (<[ihu]) after a genit. noun; note assimilation of [n] (masc. אדן). על גבל: these final words are visible on the other side of the design, suggesting that the long second line encircled it.

8 Elibaal   Pl. II, 1

The inscr. of Elibaal son of Yehimilk was written on a statue of Osorkon I (914–874 BC). Three fragments of this statue were acquired from a private source by the Louvre and the part of the inscr. which they contained was published by Dussaud in 1925. Further fragments were discovered in the excavations at Byblos, enabling some letters to be added to the text, though it is still incomplete. The statue seems to have been made (פעל, 1) in Egypt at Elibaal's request, perhaps because he wished to enhance his status by having those who read his inscr. think he was an equal of the Pharaoh; see further in the introd. to **7** Abibaal. The writing is not greatly different from that on Yehimilk **(6)** and Abibaal, making a date early rather than late in Osorkon's reign the more likely.

Bibliography

R. Dussaud, 'Dédicace d'une statue d'Osorkon I par Eliba'al, roi de Byblos', *Syria* 6 (1925), 101–17.

For other early studies see P. Montet, *Byblos et l'Égypte* (1928), p. 54, and Harris, *Grammar,* p. 159.

For the fragments see M. Dunand, *Fouilles de Byblos* I (1939), p. 18 and fig. 7.

Further:

Albright, 'Inscriptions', 158.

EHO p. 15.

KAI no. 6.

Bange, *Vowel-Letters,* pp. 32–3.

Magnanini, *Iscrizioni,* p. 30.

Illustrations

Syria 6 (1925), pl. XXV; Montet, op. cit., pls. XXXVI–XXXVII and fig. 16, p. 52; Birnbaum, *Scripts,* no. 06; Harden, *Phoenicians,* pl. 38.

1 מ֝ש ׳ זפעל ׳ אלבעל ׳ מלך ׳ גבל ביח[מלך ׳ מלך ׳ גבל]

2 [לב]עלת ׳ גבל ׳ אדתו ׳ תארך ׳ בעלת [׳ גבל]

3 [ימת ׳ א]לבעל ׳ ושנתו ׳ על [׳ גבל]

1. Statue which Elibaal king of Byblos, son of [Yehimilk king of Byblos], had made
2. [for] the Mistress of Byblos, his lady. May the mistress of [Byblos] prolong
3. [the days] and years of Elibaal over [Byblos]!

NOTES

1. מש; the word, it should be noted, is not clear; see at **7** Abibaal 1. פעל here must mean 'commissioned the making of' or the like. אלבעל; cp. Hebr. Elijah; *EA Ilimilku* (Benz, *Names,* p. 267). ביחמלך for בן יחמלך with assimilation of [n]; contrast בן אחרם (**4** Ahiram 1) and בן אלבעל (**9** Shipitbaal 2); see further Notes to **2, 3** Byblos Cones (כבד).
2. Cp. **6** Yehimilk 3, 5–6 and **7** Abibaal 2.

9 Shipitbaal

The inscr. of Shipitbaal son of Elibaal was discovered in 1935 near the remains of a wall associated with the part of the acropolis at Byblos occupied by the temples of Hathor (the deity with whom the Egyptians equated Baalat Gebal) and Hershef. This wall is presumbaly the one which Shipitbaal built (or rebuilt); it is much later than the temples, which were founded in the late 3 millenn. BC when Egypt was in control of Byblos, and was prob. designed to shore up the ground between them where it sloped downwards towards a well, which seems to have served as the city's water supply (Dunand). The inscr., which is now in the National Museum in Beirut, is to be dated around 900 BC or shortly afterwards. Note ב with the foot turned outwards, an indication that some scribes (the form is also found in the next inscr.) were even at this late date uncertain about its proper stance; see further in the Notes to chapt. I.

Bibliography

First publication: Dunand, *Byblia Grammata*, 146–51.
Further:
B. Maisler, 'The Phoenician inscriptions from Gebal and the evolution of the Phoenico-Hebrew alphabetic script,' *Leshonenu* 14 (1946), 165–81 (Hebrew).
W. F. Albright in *BASOR* 103 (1946), 14–15.
idem, 'Inscriptions', 158.
KAI no. 7.
Bange, *Vowel-Letters*, p. 33.
Magnanini, *Iscrizioni*, p. 35.

Illustrations

Byblia Grammata, pls. XVb, XV1; Diringer, *Alphabet*, fig. 107, 2; Birnbaum, *Scripts*, no. 07; Harden, *Phoenicians*, fig. 34; *KAI* Taf. II; Driver, *Writing*, pl. 50, 2.

1 קר ' זבני ' שפטבעל ' מלך

2 גבל ' בן אלבעל ' מלך ' גבל

3 ביחמלך ' מלך ' גבל ' לבעלת

4 גבל ' אדתו ' תארך ' בעלת גבל

5 ימת ' שפטבעל ' ושנתו ' על ' גבל

1. Wall which Shipitbaal king of
2. Byblos, son of Elibaal king of Byblos,
3. son of Yehimilk king of Byblos (re-)built for the Mistress of
4. Byblos, his lady. May the Mistress of Byblos prolong
5. the days and years of Shipitbaal over Byblos!

NOTES

1. קר; Hebr. קיר; Moabite קר (I **16** Mesha 11) is 'city'. שפטבעל 'judgement of Baal'; a second king of this name is known from Akkad. sources of the 8 cent. (*Si-pi-it-ti-bi-'-il*); and a recently discovered fragmentary inscr. of about 400 BC mentions a third (see Bibliogr. Notes); cp. Hebr. שפטים 'acts of judgement' and the personal name Shiphtan (Num. xxxiv 24); Benz, *Names*, pp. 423 f. For 3–5 see the previous inscriptions.

10   Abda

The inscr., now in the Beirut Museum, was found in the same excavations and dates to the same period as the previous inscr. (cp. ב). Written on two fragments which belonged to the cylindrical neck of a large vessel, it was incised before firing and according to the accepted restoration preserves the name of the potter from whose workshop the vessel originated.

Bibliography

Dunand, *Byblia Grammata*, 152–55.
Maisler, op. cit. (see Bibliogr. to **9** Shipitbaal).
Albright, 'Inscriptions', 158.
KAI no. 8.
Bange, *Vowel-Letters*, pp. 33–4.
Magnanini, *Iscrizioni*, p. 35.

Illustrations

Byblia Grammata, pl. XVa; *Fouilles de Byblos* II (1954), pl. CXLIV; Diringer, *Alphabet*, fig. 107, 1; Birnbaum, *Scripts*, no. 08; *KAI* Taf. II; Driver, *Writing*, pl. 51, 1.

עבדא' בכלבי ' הי[צר]

NOTES

1. Maisler and Albright restore ל before the name on the analogy of similar inscribed jars from Palestine, e.g. Hazor and Gibeon (vol. I **5, 14**), but there the prepos. indicates ownership of the jar or its contents, whereas the usual restoration at the end suggests that the name is the signature of the craftsman. עבדא = ['abda'] with final ['] prob. still pronounced; hypocoristicon of a name like Hebr. עבדאל; cp. עבדא (Samaria ostr. lvii); in most later Biblical names this ending, which takes the place of the theophorous element, is expressed by the vowel-letter ה. The transcription 'Aβδου (Benz, *Names*, p. 372) reflects a later pronunciation [ō] [< [ā]). An ending like [ō] in Hebr. שלמה (Solomon) would not have been expressed in writing. בכלבי for בן כלבי; see Notes to **2, 3** Byblos Cones (כבד). With [kalbay] cp. Ugar. *klby;* hypocoristicon of a name like כלבאלם (Benz, *Names*, p. 131). היצר; note the definite article, the first occurrence in normal usage with a noun (in **6** Yehimilk 2 a demonstrative follows).

III

INSCRIPTIONS IN OLD STANDARD (= TYRO-SIDONIAN) PHOENICIAN

11 Nora (Sardinia)   Pl. II, 2

THE famous stone (1.05 m. high by 57 cm. broad), when discovered in 1773, was serving as part of the wall of a vineyard belonging to a religious order at the village of Pula near the ancient site of Nora. It was transported in 1830 to the museum at Cagliari. The top of the stone is quite irregular, as if a portion had been broken off. Its left edge, on the other hand, has been carefully chiselled, perhaps when it was used to build the wall, so that the letters now come hard against it; none of them is damaged or cut off, however, and it may therefore be that, apart from a line or two at the beginning, the inscr. is complete, though the rather large size of the letters in comparison with the stone as we have it tells strongly against such a conclusion.

The writing suggests a date in the early or mid-9 cent. before the Kilamuwa inscrs. from Zenjirli (**13, 14**) and around the same time as the old Cyprus inscr. (**12**), though one can never be other than tentative about comparing scripts from places so far apart; cp. particularly the partially upright מ (it is rather more upright in old Cyprus); the squat א and (not in old Cyprus) צ; the ו with the downward stroke descending from the middle of the curve (though old Cyprus has also the later upturned 'h' shape). See further McCarter, *Antiquity,* 39 ff. We may assume, therefore, that it belongs with the latter to the earliest phase of Phoen. colonization and that both represent the dominant Tyro-Sidonian dialect; but though, in the absence of Old Phoen. inscrs. from the mother cities themselves, the two inscrs. may well be our oldest texts in that dialect, the interpretation of both is so uncertain that they cannot safely be used for dialectal study. Only with the Kilamuwa i inscr. (**13**) do we have a long and reliable enough text to allow investigations of that kind to begin.

Though on the excellent photographs of Guzzo Amadasi and Delcor the text is not in doubt, I find it impossible to give a translation. The notes below list examples of the kind of interpretations which have been offered; these have been mainly of two types, seeing the inscr. either as a building inscr. (בת) or, more imaginatively, as having to do with military expoits involving Tarshish

(תרשש) as well as Sardinia (שרדן). None of them carries much conviction and most suffer from the assumption that the inscr. is complete or almost so as it stands.

Bibliography

CIS i 144 (earlier studies are mentioned there).

NSE p. 427.

NSI no. 41.

KI no. 60.

W. F. Albright, 'New light on the early history of Phoenician colonization', *BASOR* 83 (1941), 17–22.

A. Mentz, 'Beiträge zur Deutung der phönizischen Inschriften', *Abh. f. d. Kunde d. Morgenl.* 29, 2 (1944), 15–24.

A. Dupont-Sommer, 'Nouvelle lecture de l'inscription phénicienne archaïque de Nora,' *CRAIBL*, 1948, 12–22.

J.-G. Février, 'L'Inscription archaïque de Nora', *RA* 44 (1950), 123–6.

A. van den Branden, 'L'Inscription phénicienne de Nora', *Al-Mashriq* 56 (1962), 283–92.

KAI no. 46.

B. Mazar, 'The Philistines and the rise of Israel and Tyre', *Isr. Ac. of Sc. and Hum.*, *Proceedings* 1, 7 (1964).

J. Ferron, 'La pierre inscrite de Nora', *RSO* 41 (1966), 281–8.

Guzzo Amadasi, *Iscrizioni*, pp. 83–7.

M. Delcor, 'Reflexions sur l'inscription phénicienne de Nora', *Syria* 45 (1968), 323–52.

F. M. Cross, 'An interpretation of the Nora stone', *BASOR* 208 (1972), 13–19.

B. Peckham, 'The Nora inscription', *Orientalia* 41 (1972), 457–68.

Teixidor, 'Bulletin' for 1973, item 137.

Illustrations

CIS i tab XXXII; *NSE* Taf. II, 3; *KAI* Taf. II; Mazar, loc. cit.; Guzzo Amadasi, *Iscrizioni*, tav. XXVII; Delcor, loc. cit.

1 בתרשש

2 וגרשהא

3 בשרדנש

4 למהאשל

5 מצבאם

6 לכתנבן

7 שבננגד

8 לפמי

NOTES

1-2. Dupont-Sommer and Delcor divide בת רש ש נגר, 'temple of the headland of Nogar which is in Sardinia'. Apart from רש for ראש and ש for אש, both remarkable in so early a text (though cp. עבדלבת, El-Khaḍr arrow ii), this is unacceptable because of the meaning 'of' given to ש(א), a sense not found elsewhere in Phoen., early or late. Février and van den Branden render 'principal temple which Naggar, who is from Sardinia, completed', which is better syntactically, though the phrase 'who is from Sardinia' in an inscr. from the island is to say the least superfluous. These interpretations take the first letter in 2 as נ, whereas Delcor's photo shows that it is clearly ו with an open cup at the top. Other commentators read the place-name Tarshish in 1, thus Albright (who is one of the few in recent times to insist that the inscr. is incomplete), '... in Tarshish ... and [that] man shall be banished ... from Sardinia'; Peckham, 'From Tarshish he was driven out' (he regards the ו as analogous to the Hebr. *Waw apodosi*); Cross, 'He fought with the Sardinians at Tarshish and he drove them out'. The verb is גרש; cp. I **16** Mesha 19. The meaning 'from' for ב is well attested in Ugar. and not unknown in Hebr.; see at **7** Abibaal 2. Tarshish is usually located in Spain (Tartessos), but there was another Tarshish in Cilicia (Ezek. xxvii 12) and some on the evidence of this inscr. think there may have been one in Sardinia also; we may compare the several Phoen. settlements called Carthage or 'new city'; **17** Baal Lebanon.

3-5. In favour of the inscr. being more or less complete are the similar phrases, both spread over two lines, שלם הא and שלם צבא; thus Dupont-Sommer, 'Prospère soit-il! ...'; Peckham, 'In Sardinia he found refuge, his forces found refuge'. However, neither of these renderings of שלם sounds at all right. A reference (Février, van den Branden) to the consruction of a building, e.g. 'it was, has been completed' (Qal or Pual) or 'he completed it' (Piel) is more obviously in accord with Semitic usage (cp. Neh. vi 15   1 Kgs. ix 25). The suffix with the Piel verb and with צבא would be vocalic [ō] and therefore unrepresented in the orthography; see the discussion in the Note on phonology and grammar. צבא 'army' goes well with נגד 'commander' in 7. I am more attracted, however, to Ferron and van den Branden's comparison of צבא מל(א)כת with צבא העבודה 'work of service' (Num. viii 25). מלכת, which they connect with the actual building of the temple, is suspect for the same reason as רש in 1 (and of course if the inscr. is incomplete neither it nor שלם is in fact there); but צבא on its own could very appropriately refer to arrangements for the service of the new sanctuary, this being its sense in Numbers. Followed by מקדש?

6-8. There is a gap sufficient for one letter after בן in 6, suggesting that if the inscr. is incomplete, the line ended at that point. In that case בן may be part of the verb 'to build'. If, on the other hand, the inscr. is complete, בן could be 'son of' and 6-8 contain the name of the temple official responsible for the building or, if one prefers Cross and Peckham's interpretation, the general of the army (צבא). נגד is found in Hebr. with both these senses (Jerem. xx 1 1 Chron. ix 11 2 Chron. xxxii 21). Thus e.g. 'MLKTN son of ŠBN, overseer to (or commander of) PMY'. מלכתן is, however, a very strange formation (for מלכיתן?), and it seems safer to regard only שבן as a proper name, since it can be paralleled in Hebr. שבנא (Isa. xxii 15; it is prob. a shorter form of שבניהו; I **8** Siloam tomb 1). The final name פמי is known as that of a deity, though only from personal names (Benz, *Names,* p. 391); see further at **18** Carthage pendant; but especially if the inscr. is complete, it can hardly be such here, as it is inconceivable that so important a feature as the name of the god to whom the inscr. was dedicated would be held over to the very end (Teixidor). It is much more likely to be a hypocoristic form, the name possibly belonging to the ruler of the district, preceded in the missing portion of the inscr. by a date formula 'in such and such a year of' (ל). He may have been mentioned with his full title earlier in the inscription.

My own view, for what it is worth, is that we possess only the bottom right corner of a much larger inscr., perhaps no more than a quarter or a sixth of the whole, the original stone having been cut up into slabs for use in other construction work around the buildings of the religious order. The words בת and צבא suggest that its purpose was to celebrate the building of a temple, and the inscr. seems to conclude with the name of the temple official responsible for carrying out the task and a note of the date when it was completed; more than that it is not possible to say.

12   Grave inscription (Cyprus)   Pl I, 3

Of unknown provenance, the inscr. was discovered in the Cyprus museum at Nicosia and published by A. M. Honeyman in 1939. The stone, which is a grave inscr., measures 40 cm. in height and from 44 to 47 cm. in breadth. We possess parts of the final seven lines, but a portion containing the name and lineage of the deceased and perhaps more details about him is missing from the top. The edges are damaged; it seems from the restorations required by the sense in *ll.* 2 and 4 that a substantial piece is missing from the right edge, though only a letter or two need be missing on the left. The part we have contains an imprecation against anyone tampering with the grave, which may usefully be compared with the imprecations on other grave inscrs., Hebr. and Aram. as well as Phoenician. The writing places the inscr. along with **11** Nora (q.v. introd.) in the early or mid-9 cent.; but like it, it is much too incomplete to be used for dialectal study. The one unusual form is זא for the masc. demonstrative pronoun 'this'. Words are separated by little strokes as on the Aram. Zakir stele (II 5); after the 9 cent. word-dividers are rare on Phoen. inscriptions.

Bibliography

A. M. Honeyman, 'The Phoenician inscriptions of the Cyprus Museum', *Iraq* 6 (1939), 104–8.
W. F. Albright in *BASOR* 83 (1941), 14–17 (see Bibliogr. to **11** Nora).
A. Dupont-Sommer, 'Une inscription phénicienne archaïque de Chypre', *RA* 41 (1947), 201–11.
KAI no. 30.
Masson and Sznycer, *Recherches,* 13–20.
Magnanini, *Iscrizioni,* p. 134.

H.-P. Müller, 'Die phönizische Grabinschrift aus dem Zypern-Museum und die Formgeschichte des nordwestsemitischen Epitaphs', *ZA* 65 (1975), 104–32.

J. Teixidor, 'Early Phoenician presence in Cyprus: Analysis of epigraphic material' in *The Archaeology of Cyprus, Recent Developments* (ed. N. Robertson) (1975), 121–8.

Illustrations

Honeyman, loc. cit.; *KAI* Taf. III; Masson and Sznycer, op. cit., pls. II, III; *Bibl. Archaeologist* 37 (1974), fig. 2 at p. 62.

‏[‎– ‏אש‎ ‏והֿאש‎ ‏מפת‎ ‏אי‎ ‏אי‎ ‏הֿא‎]‏	1
‏[‏זא‎ ‏הגבר‎ ‏על‎ ‏כֿ‎ ‏זא‎ ‏לקבר‎ ‏מ‎]‏–	2
‏אש‎]‏הא‎ ‏אית‎ ‏זאֿ‎ ‏[ספר‎]‏ה‎ ‏ויאבד‎ ‏שי‎]‏	3
‏[‏ובֿ]‏ן‎ ‏אדם‎ ‏יד‎ ‏ובֿן‎ ‏בעל‎ ‏יד‎ ‏בֿן‎]‏	4
‏[‏ל‎ ‏יֿ‎––‏ל‎ –––––– ‏אלם‎ ‏בֿר‎]‏ח‎	5
‏ש‎]‏––––––––––––– ‏אית‎ ‏––‎]‏	6
‏נֿי‎ ‏––––––––‏י‎––‏מֿ‎‏שֿ‎–[‏	7

1. .... there is nothing of note. And as for the man who .....
2. .... (and comes upon) this grave, if (he should open what is) over this man
3. (and) .... his ....., and should destroy this [inscription], (that) man
4. .... (be it) by the hand of Baal or by the hand of man or by (the hand)
5. .... (the whole) company of the gods ....
6, 7. ....

NOTES

1. The ה of הא is very uncertain; ב is a possibility. אי is the negative used as in 27 Tabnit 4 ('they did not gather silver for me') and I 12 Lachish ii 6; cp. also I 8 Siloam tomb 1 (אין) and II 19 Nerab ii 6–7. With מפת cp. Hebr. אנשי מופת (Zech. iii 8), 'men of note' or perhaps better 'good omen'; the word means lit. 'wonder' or 'sign'. For האש the older reading was ראש; Müller retains this and renders the first line, 'If (there is) any notable or prince who ...', comparing Hebr. [hē] and Aram. [hā], both lit. 'behold!', Hebr. אי (Prov. xxxi 4 Qere), and Ugar. 'ay 'any' (*CML²* p. 141); and for the formula ואל מלך etc. 4 Ahiram 2. The letter in question seems to me, however, to lean too far to the left to be ר; cp. also the restored האש in 3.

2. Restore a verb construed with ל and meaning 'come upon' or the like. אז (masc.) is an anomalous (perhaps archaic) form which has been compared to Arab. [ḏā] (fem. [ḏī]), 'this' of something near at hand, which is the sense required here. The regular Tyro-Sidonian form is ז for both masc. and fem. (with a different vowel), which in the later inscrs. from Cyprus usually appears as אז with prosthetic [']. כ = [kī] 'when, if'; the latter sense is not, as far as I know, found elsewhere in Phoen., but note that in the Hebr. examples the subject often precedes the conjunction; thus אדם כי (Lev. i 2 xiii 2 Mic. v 4 etc.). על recalls the phrase פתח עלתי 'open (what is) over me' of **27** Tabnit 4; cp. **28** Eshmunazar 4. זא הגבר refers to the deceased.

3. שי—; prob. part of a noun, genit. sing. or plur., with the 3 sing. masc. suffix י (Tyro-Sidonian) referring back to גבר. Müller thinks of לבש 'clothing'; cp. II **19** Nerab ii 7. יאבד with perhaps הספר following; cp. II **8** Sefire ii C 4 and with a different verb **13** Kilamuwa i 15. אית = ['iyyāt] or the like, the regular Phoen. form of the object marker, also known in Old Aram. (II **5** Zakir B 5 **8** Sefire ii C 5), whence the shortened imperial form ית; it is not certain whether the shorter forms את (Poenulus *yth*) and ת (Poenulus *th*) are reduced from אית or are related to an alternative form like Hebr. ['ēt]. הא 'that', referring back to האש in 1 is required at the end (or at the beginning of 4).

4. A long restoration would seem to be needed, e.g. '(may the gods destory) that man (and may he die) by the hand of …!'; cp. the curses in II **7** Sefire i C 21 and in **25** Yehaumilk 15 **28** Eshmunazar 6 ff. etc. בן יד 'between the hands of' or since this prepos. (Hebr. בין) is not found elsewhere in Phoen., better 'by the hand, agency of' or '(may they deliver him) into the hands of'. בן is therefore the prepos. ב with the ending [n]; Ugar. *bn;* see further at **13** Kilamuwa i 14. The phrase is equivalent to Hebr. ביד; Ugar. *bd* (*CML*[2] p. 143). אדם is thought by some to be in this position a divine name; cp. the lists of deities in the curses in **15** Karatepe A iii 18 ff. II **5** Zakir B 23 ff. etc. However, cp. 2 Sam. xxiv 14.

5. חבר 'company' is restored by Honeyman, a variant of e.g. כל דר (**15** Karatepe A iii 19), though the word is not otherwise attested in descriptions of the divine assembly.

13   Kilamuwa i (Zenjirli)   Fig. 10

The inscr. is carved on a large orthostat (1.30 × 1.54 m.) found in 1902 during the German excavations at Zenjirli at the entrance to a vestibule leading into the royal palace. The top left corner of the stone is occupied by a relief of the king, who is pointing with his right hand to certain symbols which fill up much of the space in the first two lines; his left hand hangs by his side and holds a flower. The text is divided by a line after *l.* 8. The monument like Kilamuwa ii (**14**) and the later Aram. inscrs. of Hadad and Panammu (II **13, 14**) is housed in the Staatliche Museen, Berlin.

Historical circumstances and date

The inscr. prob. celebrated the dedication of the palace where it was found, though it makes no explicit reference to building operations and is largely taken up with an account of the king's internal and external achievements. Four kings covering three generations preceded Kilamuwa, the third of whom, his father חיא (Akkad. *Ḥani, Ḥaiani*), is mentioned twice in the annals of Shalmaneser III (858–824 BC) as having offered tribute in the course of his expeditions early in his reign against the Aramaean coalition organized by Barhadad of Damascus (*ANET* pp. 277, 278). The dynasty had prob. been founded by Kilamuwa's great-grandfather around 900 BC; his name (גבר) suggests he was an Aramaean adventurer whose clan seized power in this predominantly Neo-Hittite area, though in deference to the majority element in the population most of his successors were given Anatolian names. The succeeding dynasty of Panammu and Barrakkab, to judge by its founder's name (קרל; II 13 Hadad 1), was native Neo-Hittite by race. The first part of the inscr. records Kilamuwa's successful defence of his kingdom against the ambitions of surrounding rulers, notably the king of the Danunians (דננים), a predecessor of the Cilician monarch known from the Karatepe texts (15). He acknowledges the assistance of Shalmaneser (7–8), but not in terms that remotely imply a relationship of suzerain and vassal; nor is any such expedition against Cilicia mentioned in Shalmaneser's records, which suggests that from the Assyrian point of view it may not have been particularly fruitful. We may therefore date the inscr. around 830–825 BC towards the end of Shalmaneser's reign, when Assyrian power was lessening and the empire was on the point of entering upon one of its recurrent periods of retrenchment. Not till after Adadnirari's succession in 810 was Assyria again active in the west. The latter part of the inscr. is concerned with Kilamuwa's attempts to improve the lot of the indigenous population and to establish better relations between them and the newer Aramaeans, among whom the royal family itself had originated. It closes with the usual imprecations.

Script and orthography

The script fits neatly enough into the period between the Nora and Cyprus stones and the 8-cent. Phoen. inscrs.; see the discussions in the introd. to 11 Nora and 15 Karatepe. A wider comparison, bringing in the roughly contemporary Palestinian script of Mesha (I 16) and the later Aram. scripts of Zenjirli (II 13, 14 Hadad, Panammu) as well as the Phoen., makes, however, for a more balanced picture. Kilamuwa emerges as almost the last representative of the undifferentiated script used by all the dialects in the earliest period, lacking the individual features both of the Palestinian group, the first to separate itself from the parent stock (cp. ג, כ, ת), and of the later Aram. (cp. ז, ק) and Phoen. (cp. י, מ) groups. I have the impression that the stance of the letters (particularly ר) is slightly more Aram. than Phoen., but it is no more than an impression. Words are divided by dots. See further J. Naveh, *The Development of the Aramaic Script*, 7 ff.

The orthography is Phoen. 'consonantal' with no indication of the vowels, except in the case of the royal names, where in addition to the use of the Aram. word for 'son' (בר) the Aram. practice of final *matres lectionis* is adopted; thus במה, חיא, and prob. כלמו itself, which should therefore properly be transliterated Kilamū as in the case of Panammū in the later Aram. inscriptions. The form Kilamuwa is, however, kept here out of convention. In the next inscr. (Kilamuwa ii) the Aram. dialect of the area is employed, but confusingly the Phoen. orthography is retained and is even extended to one of the royal names (חי for חיא of the present text), though Kilamuwa's own name still has the final vowel-letter.

Language

The inscr. is written in the so-called Standard Phoen. derived from the dialect of Tyre and Sidon, who together (under Sidonian overlordship at first) formed the leading Phoen. power in the period of colonial expansion. The language, which is also used in the Karatepe inscrs. from the same general region, would be introduced to this corner of Asia Minor and northern Syria by Phoen. traders, probably based on a hitherto undiscovered colony or staging-post on the southern Cilician coast founded around the same time as the colonies on Cyprus and in the western Mediterranean. Doubtless, as was the case with Aramaic a little later in the time of the Assyrian empire, it commended itself to the Neo-Hittite states chiefly because its script was much more manageable than their own cumbersome hieroglyphic system. We are not, however, to think of a widespread use of Phoen. as a *lingua franca* on the Aram. model. To that extent the title 'Standard' could be misleading. It is above all the fact of Tyro-Sidonian foundation of most of the Phoen. colonies that imparts their similarity to all the Old Phoen. texts treated in this chapter. Where non-standard features occasionally appear, especially phonetic ones, as in the inscrs. from Cyprus, we can usually put them down to influence from the indigenous non-Semitic tongues, though we have not to forget the possibility that a different home dialect may sometimes be involved (see at **36** Lapethos ii). In this inscr. the few signs of local influence are in fact Semitic, reflecting the spoken Aram. dialect of the Zenjirli area (e.g. the form נבש for נפש); see further on that dialect in II, pp. 62 ff.

The present inscr. is particularly valuable in that it gives us an idea of the Tyro-Sidonian dialect at an early stage in its development, though most of the features commonly cited as archaic are in fact on fuller investigation found not to be so.

Style

The inscr. has an almost metrical structure, and much of it can easily be divided up into short couplets or triplets showing a rough parallelism of lines, each with three or four main stresses. It is not regular poetry, but it has a distinct poetic flavour. No Phoen. epics, myths, or hymns having survived, it is perhaps the clearest instance in Phoen. of the influence of the Canaanite poetic tradition known from the epics of Ugarit and the poetic parts of the Hebrew Bible. A similar influence can be detected less directly in the vocabulary and phraseology of this and most of the other royal inscrs. both in Phoen. and Aramaic. The flow of rhetoric, often spilling over into bombast, prob. owes much to the example of generations of court minstrels and prophets skilled in the composition of oral poetry and the art of eulogy. It is obvious from the excellent if rather flowery Phoen. of this inscr. that professionals of this nature must have been employed in the court of Zenjirli.

Bibliography

First publication: F. von Luschan, *Ausgrabungen in Sendschirli* 4 (1911), 374–7.
The early study I have most consulted is H. Bauer, 'Die KLMW Inschrift aus Sendschirli', *ZDMG* 67 (1913), 684 ff.; 68 (1914), 227 ff.
Other early studies are listed in *EHO* p. 11, n. 3.
See further:
EHO pp. 15–19.
S. Herrmann in *Orientalistische Literaturzeitung*, 1953, 295 ff.
KAI no. 24.
ANET p. 654.
T. Collins, 'The Kilamuwa inscription — a Phoenician poem', *WO* 6 (1970–1), 183–8.
Bange, *Vowel-Letters*, pp. 35–41.
Magnanini, *Iscrizioni*, pp. 45–7.
Lipiński, 'Miscellanea', 49–50.
A. van den Branden in *RSF* 2 (1974), 140–1.
Avishur, 'Stylistic features', 11, 15, 17 f.
M. O'Connor, 'The rhetoric of the Kilamuwa inscription', *BASOR* 226 (1977), 15–30.

Illustrations

Von Luschan, op. cit., Abb. 273; Birnbaum, *Scripts*, no. 014; *KAI* Taf. XXVII.

1 אנך. כלמו. בר. חי[א]

2 מלך. גבר. על. יאדי. ובל. פ[על]

3 כן במה. ובל̇. פעל. וכן. אב̇. חיא. ובל. פ̇על. וכן. אח

4 שאל. ובל. פעל. ואנ[ך]. כלמו. בר. תמֿ–. מאש. פעלת

5 בל. פעל. הלפניהם. כן. בת אבי. במתכת. מלכם. אד

6 רם. וכל. שלח. יד ללֿ[ח]ֿם. וכת. ביד. מלכֿם כם אש. אכלת

7 זקן. ו[כם.] אש. אכלת. יד. ואדר עלי מלך. ד[נ]נים. ושכר

8 אנך. עלי. מלך אשר. ועלמת. יתן. בש. וגֿבר. בסות. ‖

9 אנך. כלמו. בר היא. ישבת. על. כסא. אבי. לפן. המ

10 לכם. הלפנים. יתלנֿן. משכבם. כם. כלבם. ואנך. למי. כת. אב. ולמי.
   כת. אם.

11 ולמי. כת. אח. ומי. בל חז. פן. ש. שתי. בעל. עדר. ומי. בל חז. פן.
   אלף. שתי. בעל

12 בקר. ובעל. כסף. ובעל. חרץ. ומי. בל. חז. כתן. למנערי. ובימי. כסי.
   ב

13 ץ. ואנך. תמכת. משכבם. ליד. והמת. שת. נבש. כם. נבש יתם. באם.
   ומי. בבן

14 י אש. ישב. תחתן. ויזק. בספר ז. משכבם. אל יכבד. לבעררם. ובערר

15 ם. אל יכבד. למשכבם ומי. ישחת. הספר ז. ישחת. ראש. בעל. צמד.
   אש. לגבר

16 וישחת. ראש. בעל חמן. אש. לבמה. ורכבאל. בעל. בת. ‖

1. I am Kilamuwa, the son of Hayya.
2. Gabbar became king over Y'DY, but accomplished nothing.
3. There was BMH, but he accomplished nothing. Then there was my father Hayya, but he accomplished nothing. Then there was my brother
4. Š'L, but he accomplished nothing. But I Kilamuwa, the son of TM-, what I accomplished
5. not (even) their predecessors accomplished. My father's house was in the midst of powerful kings,
6. and each put forth his hand to eat it; but I was in the hand(s) of the kings like a fire that consumes
7. the beard or like a fire that consumes the hand. The king of the Danunians lorded it over me, but I

8. hired against him the king of Assyria. He gave a maid for the price of a sheep, and a man for the price of a garment.
9. I Kilamuwa, the son of Hayya, sat upon my father's throne. In face of the former
10. kings the MŠKBM used to whimper like dogs. But I — to some I was a father, and to some I was a mother,
11. and to some I was a brother. Him who had never seen the face of a sheep I made owner of a flock; him who had never seen the face of an ox, I made owner
12. of a herd, and owner of silver and owner of gold; and him who had never seen linen from his youth, in my days they covered
13. with byssus. I grasped the MŠKBM by the hand, and they behaved (towards me) like an orphan towards (his) mother. Now, if any of my sons
14. who shall sit in my place does harm to this inscription, may the MŠKBM not honour the B'RRM, nor the B'RRM
15. honour the MŠKBM! And if anyone smashes this inscription, may Baal-Ṣemed who belongs to Gabbar smash his head,
16. and may Baal-Hammon who belongs to BMH and Rakkabel, lord of the dynasty, smash his head!

NOTES

1. כלמו contains the Anatolian ending [muwa], prob. reduced to [mū] as had clearly happened in the case of פנמו (II **13** Hadad 1) less than a century later. The use of Aram. בר suggests that with the names Aram. orthographic practice is being followed; the final letters in חיא (3, 9) and במה (3) are therefore also *matres lectionis*. The pronounciation of חיא is known from the fuller form *Ḥaiani* in the Assyrian annals (*ANET* p. 278); he is called there son of Gabbar, although as this inscr. makes clear he was his grandson, the founder's name being used as frequently among the Aramaeans to identify the dynasty as a whole. Only the names גבר (cp. 1 Kgs. iv 19 Ezra ii 20) and possibly שאל (4) look Semitic; the dynasty by choosing Anatolian names for most of its monarchs was clearly trying to keep on good terms with its majority of Neo-Hittite subjects. Later and for a similar reason, as the Aramaean element increased, the next dynasty, which was Neo-Hittite, began to use Aram. names (Barṣur, Barrakkab; see at II **14** Panammu 1).

2. מלך; 3 sing. masc. perfect. יאדי (with perhaps final vowel-letter); the indigenous name of Kilamuwa's state, its Semitic name being שמאל 'the north (country)' (II **5** Zakir A 7   II **15** Barrakkab i 2; Akkad. *Samalla*). It does not appear in Assyrian sources, where (*kur*) *Ia-u-da-a-a* seems always to refer to Judah; see further at II **13** Hadad 1. The pronunciation is unknown.

3. כן = [kōn] < [kắna]; 3 sing. masc. perfect. במה is doubtless Anatolian; Lipiński prefers to read בנה (with some justification here, less in 16), a Semitic structure, 'He created him', with ה as an (archaic) suffix. אב = ['abī]; the noun is nomin. and the vocalic suffix is unwritten; This is an older form, since in later Tyro-Sidonian ' (= [ī]) does duty for all cases in

sing. nouns; here it is restricted to the genit. (see at אבי, 5); see further Note on phonology and grammar. Similarly in אח, making שאל an older brother of Kilamuwa; a rendering 'his brother' (*KAI*), making him his uncle, is prob. illegitimate, as אחי = ['aḥūyū] would be expected for this, with י following the vocalic ending [ū] (nomin.).

4. שאל is just as likely to be Anatolian (cp. Lycian Σαλας, Σελλις) as Semitic (Hebr. Saul; Aram. שאילא, *NSE* p. 460). –תמ(תמת?) is prob. the name of Kilamuwa's mother, used here to distinguish him from שאל, who may have had a different mother. מאש is formed from מ 'what' (= [mō] from an original [mah]; Ugar. *mh*) and the relative אש; cp. in Hebr. Eccl. i 9 and possibly Isa. xlvii 13 (מאשר).

5. הלפניהם. The basic form is לפני, an adj. formed from the prepos., with the termination [īy], the [y] being still pronounced, as is clear from לפנים (10) = [lipnīym], [lipniyyīm], or the like. A similar form with suffix as here is possibly to be read in Job xxi 8, 'their ancestors'. The middle ה here, however, is usually explained as a mason's error, since otherwise we have to account not only for the archaic suffix הם (later מ, נם; see Note on phonology and grammar) but for an anomalous definite article. The latter may have been kept because the adj. is based on a prepos.; we may compare in Hebr. העליה 'that which is upon it' (1 Sam. ix 24), not exactly parallel, but it shows the article fulfilling a similar relative function. In the light of this, I prefer to retain the text as it is, though the reference is to kings previous to his own dynasty rather than as in 2–4 to Kilamuwa's immediate predecessors. Vocalize therefore [lipnīyēhōm] or the like. A different explanation is offered by *EHO* (cp. Lipiński), viz. ה + לפני + הם, 'the ones who before me (were) they', i.e. 'my predecessors'; but against this is the normal free-standing pronominal form המת (13). אבי = ['abīyā]; the noun is genit.; it is not a regular noun, but the presence of י coupled with its absence in אב (3) suggests that regular nouns at this stage added this suffix as in Byblian and not as in later Tyro-Sidonian; see at **25** Yehaumilk 3. מתכת is usually taken as a fem. noun equivalent to Hebr. תוך 'midst'; but since the form is not found elsewhere, there is something to be said for van der Branden's etymology from TKK (cp. Hebr. [tōk] 'oppression'), i.e. 'was under the domination of'. The powerful kings (Ps. cxxxvi 18) were prob. monarchs of the surrounding Neo-Hittite states like Commagene, Gurgum, and Carchemish.

6. כל; Gen. xvi 12. יד; Hebr. usage (Judg. v 26 1 Sam. xxii 17 xxiv 7) suggests a suffix, i.e. [yadō] < [yadá(h)ū]; cp. ראש (15) where a suffix is definitely required. ללחם; infin. with ל and perhaps unwritten suffix [ō]; the verb LHM 'to eat' does not occur again in Phoen. and it is rare in Hebr., but it is not uncommon in Ugar. (*CML*[2] p. 150). There is no need to emend to ל<ה>לחם, Niph. infin. 'to make war (on it)', especially as this verb has not been found in Phoen. either. Herrmann neatly lowers the awkward ה from הלפניהם directly above, but why should a mason make so strange a mistake? כת = [káttī] from KWN. ביד מלכם referring to the kings already mentioned and therefore definite; this is the kind of example where according to Lambdin we should assume syncope of [h] of the article; see Note on phonology and grammar. כם אש = [kmō 'ēš]; cp. כאש (II **7** Sefire i A 25) and כם in *ll*. 10, 13. This is the straightforward solution, especially in the light of the Hebr. phrase אש אכלת 'a devouring fire', said of Yahweh's glory or presence (Exod. xxiv 17 Deut. iv 24 ix 3), giving a nice rhetorical touch; cp. the Engl. metaphor 'singe the king of Spain's beard'. Reading כמאש (כם + the relative; Hebr. כאשר) (so *KAI*), i.e.

'as if I had eaten my beard ...' yields an equally extravagant metaphor, but it is an imprecise one; it also makes the statement an abject admission of the treatment Kilamuwa had received at the hands of the kings and squares ill with his boasting elsewhere. אכלת = ['ōkalt]; fem. partic., אש being fem. as is usual in Hebrew.

7. זקן; normal Hebr. usage would have the article, here perhaps omitted because of the poetic style. אדר; verbal form. עלי = ['aláyyā], later prob. reduced to ['alay] as in Hebr.; the same form occurs in 8 for 'against him', i.e. prob. ['alōyū] < ['aláyhū] with [y] replacing [h]. דננים; see the discussion in the introd. to **15** Karatepe and the Note to A i 2. שכר אנך; the verb is prob. to be regarded as 3 masc. sing. perf., used neutrally in this peculiar construction, rather than (as e.g. J. M. Solá-Solé, *L'Infinitif sémitique,* 1961, 110 ff.) as infinitive absoute. The construction, found also in **15** Karatepe, is common in Ugar. verse, not only with *'ank* but with a fem. noun as subject, e.g. *šmḫ rbt 'aṯrt ym,* 'Dame Athirat of the sea rejoiced' (**4** ii 28–29). This suggests that it belongs properly to the domain of oral narrative and that it survives in the Phoen. royal inscrs. due to the influence of the bards or singers of tales attached to the courts of the monarchs concerned. The significant factor which precludes its being taken as an infin. absol. (unless we are willing to give this another name and rewrite the rules) is that both in Phoen. and in Ugar. it can be followed by a suffix. Thus in Ugar.

>ngš 'ank · 'al'iyn b'l
>'dbnn 'ank 'imr bpy (**6** ii 21–22)
>'I it was who confronted mightiest Baal,
>I who made him (like) a lamb in my mouth.'

Examples at Karatepe are וישב אנך (A i 11) with unwritten suffix [ō]; ירדם אנך (A i 20). Distinguish אנך ... ענתנם (19), where the emphatic pronoun comes first; this construction is found in Mesha (I **16** 2, 21 ff.) and occurs also in Zakir (II **5** B 3–4). The Assyrian king whose help was sought on one of his many expeditions beyond the Euphrates was doubtless Shalmaneser III, with whom Kilamuwa pretends to be on equal terms. Shalmaneser himself might have described the relationship differently, but Kilamuwa's tone contrasts sharply with the fawning terms in which Panammu and Barrakkab later describe their dependence on Tiglathpileser (II **14** 7 ff. II **15** 3 ff.) Illustrate from Deut. xxiii 5 2 Kgs. vii 6 Isa. vii 20.

8. יתן refers prob. to the king of the Danunians, who had to settle with Kilamuwa on a loser's terms. With the *Beth pretii* cp. II **14** Panammu 6 2 Kgs. vii 1; see further at **21** Malta 1, where the meaning of the construction is discussed in more detail. The expression here may be proverbial. According to Rosenthal (*ANET*), the subject is the king of Assyria and Kilamuwa is boasting of the good bargain he had made in enlisting his aid so cheaply. Röllig (*KAI*) in line with his interpretation of 6–7 thinks the phrase is parenthetical — 'one had to give ...' — describing the heavy tribute Kilamuwa had to pay to the Assyrians to be rescued from his enemies.

9. ישבת; cp. 1 Kgs. ii 12.

10. יתלנן; Yithpolel imperf. (with [ūn]) against the jussive יכבד (14; with [ū]), from LWN II 'to murmur (people), to howl (dog)'; cp. Ps. lix 16 (Hiphil). The imperf. has a frequentative nuance as in II **13** Hadad 3 ff. The first נ is dubious, having a head not unlike ו, though the tail slopes distinctly to the left. If ו is read, some form of LWY 'to turn, twist' is indicated, perhaps Yithp. 'to turn oneself, curl up, cringe' or similar. משכבם; prob.

Yuph. partic.; cp. 2 Kgs. iv 32 (of being laid out for burial) and 2 Sam. viii 2 (Hiph., of making defeated enemies prostrate themselves). The name prob. reflects a native Aram. form and is a designation of the conquered indigenous population, who had been held in subjection by Kilamuwa's predecessors but were now to be given more rights and allowed to share in the growing prosperity of the country. In that case בעררם (14; prob. = [ba'rīrīm] 'savage, cruel ones'; cp. Syriac) may refer to the dominant but minority Aramaean element, being perhaps a Semitic rendering of a title given by the natives to the small clan of Gabbar which had seized power several generations before. If it described wilder Aramaean tribes who had more recently arrived, one would have expected some mention of steps being taken to curb their activities. Note that neither term has the article, perhaps because as sociological terms they are tantamount to gentilics but possibly reflecting the original Aram. forms, the Zenjirli dialect not possessing an emphatic state (II, p. 63). למי; lit. 'for someone, whomever', a peculiar usage of the interrogative. מי should be vocalized [miyyā] or the like at this early stage; EA mi-ia; later [mī] (Poenulus mi). אב; Isa. xxii 21; cp. also 15 Karatepe A i 3.

11. חז = [hazō] < [hazay(a)]. פן = [pnē]; dual construct. שתי = [šattīyū]; 1 sing. perf. Qal with suffix.

12. בעל כסף etc.; cp. II 14 Panammu 11, II 15 Barrakkab i 10–11, and below 15 Karatepe A iii 7 ff. כתן = [kittōn] 'linen' (Aram. [kittānā]) rather than 'tunic' (Hebr. כתנת; Aram. [kittūnā]; Syr. [kuttīnā]). נערי = [n'ūrōyū] or the like; see at 7. למן; for this prepos. see 15 Karatepe A i 4 and in Hebr. 2 Sam. vii 6 Jerem. vii 7 etc. Cp. also Job xxxi 18. בימי = [byammáyyā] or the like; see also at 7; cp. II 13 Hadad 9, 10; 15 Karatepe A i 5 ii 1, 5. Note the resumptive ו; cp. II 8 Sefire ii C 10. כסי is best taken as Piel 3 sing. or plur. masc. perf. (indefinite) with suffix, i.e. [kissōyū] or [kissúyū]; the original [y] of the base would hardly be kept in a perf. passive form (Pual) when it has already become vocalic in the active (חז, 11). בץ 'byssus', a fine flaxen fabric.

13. תמך with direct object as in Prov. iii 18 ('lay hold of'); in Hebr. it is usually followed by ב (Isa. xlii 1) 'support, uphold'. The ל in ליד perhaps indicates the agent, i.e. 'with (my) hand' rather than 'by (their) hand'. With the sentiment cp. Ugar. 'the hungry she grasped by the hand' (15 i 1–2), said of Huray, Keret's future wife. המת = [hōmat] (masc.). נבש; the form with ב is due to the Aram. dialect, appearing in all the Zenjirli inscrs., including Barrakkab ii (II 16 7), which is written in the imperial Aram. dialect. The lack of the article or of a suffix is again suggestive of the poetic style. The sense has to be filled out, 'they made (their) soul (with me) like ....' ומי בבני; the final imprecation formulas begin here; cp. II 13 Hadad 15, 20 II 9 Sefire iii 17.

14. ישב תחת; cp. 1 Kgs. i 30. תחתן; if the Massoretic tradition is to be trusted we have here a rare instance of the 'verbal' suffix [nī] used with a prepos.; thus [tahténī] as in 2 Sam. xxii 37. But perhaps the form (in Hebr. as in Phoen.) is more properly linked with Hebr. suffixed forms like איננו 'he is not', i.e. [tahta/in + ī] and with the [n] in Ugar. prepos. forms like bn, ln, 'mn (see CML² Glossary), which can occur both free and with suffixes. Cp. also Phoen. בן יד (12 Old Cyprus 4) and (all with suffixes) בן (15 Karatepe A ii 18 28 Eshmunazar 5 36 Lapethos ii 13) and לן (27 Tabnit 4). Both these explanations of תחתן involve adding either the 'verbal' suffix or the termination [a/in] to a sing. base; such a base is occasionally used elsewhere in Hebr. and in Old Aram. (II 7 Sefire i A 6 9 iii 7), whereas normally in

Hebr. and Aram. and apparently also in Phoen. (**28** Eshmunazar 9) a plur. base תחתי is used. יזק; Yiph. imperf. from NZQ; Bibl. Aram. Haph. (Ezra iv 13, 15, 22); in Phoen. construed with ב, lit. 'to cause hurt against'. יכבד; plur. jussive (Piel) with [ū] against [ūn] of the imperf. (10). בעררם; see at 10.

15. ישחת is prob. Piel or Yiph. as in Hebr. (Piel, Hiph.) 'to ruin, destroy'; the same verb is used in the sense of 'ruin (a person)' in II **13** Hadad 27 ff. (where, as in Aram., the form is prob. Peal). ראש = [ra'šō] or [rōšō]. Cp. the Ugar. imprecation in **16** (Keret) vi 54 ff. בעל צמד; a title of Hadad (Baal), the chief god of the Aramaeans of Zenjirli (II **13** Hadad 1, 2, 8, etc. II **14** Panammu 2), meaning 'lord of the mace'; cp. Ugar. ṣmd, a weapon used by Baal in his victory over the sea-god Yam (**2** iv); Hebr. צמד is 'yoke'. The strange phrase 'belongs to Gabbar' prob. means that his official worship at Zenjirli began in Gabbar's time.

16. בעל חמן was the chief god of Carthage; the occurrence of his name here shows, however, that he must have been Phoen. or Canaanite in origin. He was identified in the classical world with Kronos and Saturn, i.e. the Semitic El, who appears after Hadad in II **13** Hadad 1. The name is usually explained as meaning 'lord of the incense-altar' (Hebr. [ḥammān]) or 'lord of (Mt.) Amanus' (Akkad. Ḫamanu), the latter suggestion localizing him in the area of Zenjirli, since Amanus was the mountain range on the western border of Sam'al separating Syria and, Asia Minor. But perhaps more simply he should be identified with אל חמן of **32** Umm El-'Amed xiii 1 (q.v.), a title 'god (or El) of Hammon' given to the deity Milkashtart. Hammon was the ancient name of Umm El-'Amed, a place a little to the south of Tyre, and is prob. the same as the town mentioned in Josh. xix 28. Milkashtart is a fusion of El ('the king') and Astarte, the two being worshipped together in the local temple at that late period (3–2 cents. BC). It seems reasonable to assume that Hammon was particularly associated with El at a much earlier period and that בעל חמן was a title by which he was commonly known in the area of Tyre in the early 1 millenn., being transferred from there both to Carthage and (via the putative Phoen. trading-post in Cilicia) to Zenjirli. See further at **21** Malta 3–4. The reference to BMH will then indicate that it was in his reign that the title was first introduced. רכבאל was the patron deity of the royal houses of Gabbar and QRL (see further at II **13** Hadad 2 **14** Panammu 22, where as here he follows Baal-Hadad and El in sequence). The name means 'rider' (Phoen. [rōkēb], Aram. [rākēb]) or 'charioteer' ([rakkāb]) of El, and may be an epithet of Baal in his aspect as 'rider on the clouds' (Ugar. rkb 'rpt). בעל בת; II **14** Panammu 22; prob. taken over from the Zenjirli dialect and therefore lacking the article, unless we are to assume syncope of [h].

14 Kilamuwa ii (An Aramaic inscription with Phoenician orthography)   Fig. 5

The letters of the inscr. were punched into two panels on a tiny sheath (6.7 cm. long) made up of soldered gold wire and little gold plates, which was prob. once fitted over the handle of a staff or sceptre. Now in Berlin with the other inscrs. from the same site, it was found in the royal palace of Zenjirli. It is a problematic inscr., which was not translated in the original publication. Much of the argument has centred upon the language used, *KAI,* following Friedrich, *Grammatik,* classifying it as Phoen., although most commentators, correctly in my view, regard it as having been composed in the Aram. dialect employed in the later inscrs. of Hadad and Panammu (II **13, 14**). The orthography, however, is not Aram. but (with the possible exception of Kilamuwa's own name) pure Phoen. 'consonantal'. We therefore have a unique pairing of an Aram. dialect with a Phoen. orthography. Because of the controversy surrounding it, I did not include it in vol. II, where strictly speaking it belongs. For 'mixed' texts of a rather different kind see **23, 24** Arslan Tash i, ii.

Bibliography

First published in *Ausgrabungen in Sendschirli* 5 (1943), 102.

A. Dupont-Sommer, 'Une inscription nouvelle du roi Kilamou', *RHR* 133 (1947–8), 19–33.

K. Galling, 'The scepter of wisdom: Notes on the gold sheath of Zendjirli and Ecclesiastes 12:11', *BASOR* 119 (1950), 15–18.

J. J. Koopmans, *Aramäische Chrestomathie* (1962), 16–18.

KAI no. 25.

ANET p. 655.

Magnanini, *Iscrizioni,* pp. 47–8.

Ginsberg, 'Ugaritico-phoenicia', 146–7.

Illustrations

Ausgrabungen, Abb. 124 and Taf. 47 f–g; Galling, loc. cit.

1 סמר ז קן	5 יתן לה ר
2 כלמו	6 כבאל
3 בר חי	7 ארך חי
4 לרכבאל	

Nailed ornament which Kilamuwa son of Hayya fashioned for Rakkabel. May Rakkabel grant him long life!

NOTES

1. סמר; perhaps 'object nailed on' and connected with Hebr. מסמרות, מסמרים 'nails'; cp. סמרת (**36** Lapethos ii 13) and Mishn. Hebr. סמר 'to nail on'. Others cite Akkad. *asmara* 'lance', thinking of the finished pole or staff. On the basis of this inscr. Galling suggests the translation 'sceptre' for משמרות in Eccles. xii 11, 'like sceptres which are set up by the masters of assemblies', but to accommodate this rendering he has to tamper with the word order. ז; since סמר lacks the article, 'this' is not possible; if the inscr. is Phoen. ז would have to be a relative with the noun in the construct

before the relative clause. Such a relative is, however, attested in Phoen. only for the Byblian dialect (**4** Ahiram 1); Kilamuwa i has שא. ז therefore = ז ([ḏī]), the relative of Zenjirli Aram. (II **13** Hadad 1). 'This' in Zenjirli Aram. is זן. קן = [qanō] with Phoen. vocalization, [qnā] with Aram. vocalization; perhaps 'obtained, procured' rather than 'created, fashioned', a meaning occurring elsewhere only with a god as subject (Ugar., Hebr., Arabic).

2. כלמו; it is hardly likely that the names of Kilamuwa and his father have a different pronunciation in this and the previous inscr.; חי (3) therefore = [ḥayyā] or the like as does חיא in i 3. It seems that in the case of the reigning monarch's name the standard (Aram.) spelling is adhered to (Kilamū), whereas the strict Phoen. orthography is used in the case of a former monarch's name. See further at i 1.

4. רכבאל; i 16.

5. יתן; II **13** Hadad 23 (with לה). *KAI* explains לה here as Phoen. [lắhū] with penultimate accent, but in i the 3 sing. masc. suffix behaves exactly as in the later Tyro-Sidonian inscrs.; if the language had been Phoen., we should therefore have expected ל = [lō]; cp. **15** Karatepe A iii 16. Vocalize [lēh] as in Aramaic.

7. ארך חי; cp. **15** Karatepe A iii 5 ('days') Ps. xxi 5. יי = [ḥayyī]; oblique plur. ending as in Zenjirli Aram.; if the text is Phoen., we have to assume that the מ of חים had been left out owing to lack of space.

15   **Karatepe** (Cilicia)   Figs. 11–14(A)

The bilingual inscr. in Phoen. and Hieroglyphic Hittite (HH; the name given to the writing system used for the Luwian dialect of the Neo-Hittite states) was discovered in three exemplars in 1946–7 at Karatepe in eastern Turkey in the area known in classical times as Cilicia. It celebrates the building (or rebuilding) of a city on the site. The last Phoen. exemplar to be discovered is the best preserved, and is printed below with (following *KAI*) the designation A; it was apparently set up in one of the gates of the city and comprises three columns of text (i–iii) distributed over four orthostats and the base of a fifth uninscribed one, ending with three lines (iv) carved on the body of a stone lion. Exemplar B, the most incomplete, is also a gate inscr.; it begins on a stone lion and is continued on two orthostats. Exemplar C, which has some sizable lacunas, though hardly any full line is missing, occupies four sides (i–iv) of a great statue of Baal, with six or so extra lines (v) on the pedestal; the statue was prob. installed in the city temple. For the most part exemplars B and C are identical with A, and it is sufficient to indicate minor differences of text in an apparatus; but the final imprecations of C, being directed against interference with the statue and not, as in A and B, with the gate (or gates), diverge considerably from the parallel section of A and are printed separately after it. The (relatively) complete versions A and C are by a substantial margin the longest texts so far found in Phoenician.

Writing

The Karatepe script is difficult to date precisely. It is clearly later than the 9 cent.; cp. מ which already has the distinctive later Phoen. shape with separately formed bar; but some letters, e.g. ת, ק, ו have alternative shapes, one of which often reminds us of early forms, one of later. Particularly interesting letters are כ, which is very similar to the Kilamuwa ii (**14**) and Zakir (II **5**) shapes, and י, which leans slightly to the left, but not so far as on the Carthage pendant (**18**) or Praeneste bowl (**19**); it thus marks the beginning of a Phoen. process which by the time of the Ur box inscr. (**20**) has the letter more or less fallen on its face. It is noteworthy that the old Seville inscr. (**16**) still has the upright י, as has the Baal Lebanon inscr. (**17**). I would tend on the basis of this feature to place Seville and Baal Lebanon in the early 8 cent., though there is some external evidence to suggest a rather lower date for the second of these (see **17** introduction). The other Old Phoen. inscrs. mentioned would then follow these two in this order: Karatepe, Carthage pendant, Praeneste bowl, Ur box. If, on the other hand, we take מ as the most significant letter, the movement is from the 'saw-toothed' vertical form to the horizontal shape, which does not become firmly established until the 7 or even the 6 cent., and the inscrs. group themselves in this sequence: Carthage pendant, Seville, Baal Lebanon, Praeneste bowl, Ur box, and last Karatepe. Depending on which feature is highlighted, therefore, Karatepe could be dated at any time between *c.*760–750 BC and the early 7 cent. For historical reasons (see below) I prefer the highest of these dates, and would tentatively (for it is wise to remember that the texts we are comparing come from all over the Mediterranean and beyond) arrange the inscrs. as follows:

> Seville (early 8 cent.)
> Baal Lebanon (mid-8 cent.)
> Karatepe (mid-8 cent.)
> Carthage pendant (mid-8 cent.)
> Praeneste bowl (late 8 cent.)
> Ur box (early 7 cent.)

See for further discussion Peckham, *Scripts,* chapt. IV; F. M. Cross, *HTR* 64 (1971), 193 ff.; McCarter, *Antiquity,* 39 ff.

As on most Phoen. inscrs. dating from the 8 cent. or later, *scriptio continua* is employed; cp. in Aram. the Sefire inscrs. (II **7–9**). This can lead to some uncertainty about word division, especially in contexts where the interpretation is difficult. However, there seems to me to be a definite tendency (more so than in the case of e.g. **28** Eshmunazar) for spaces to appear between words, as if the masons were not unacquainted with the use of dots or strokes. Thus on a rough count (using Bossert's sketches) I found 89 spaces in inscr. A, of which only

17 occurred within words; I estimate that if spaces had been used regularly to separate words (as for convenience's sake they are used in the transcripton below), some 350 would have been required. More investigations of this kind, using, of course, good photographs rather than sketches, could yield valuable and perhaps surprising results. See further vol. I, pp. 34, 72, vol. II, pp. 99–100, and my article in *Archivum Linguisticum* 17 (1969), 131 ff.

In contrast to the Sefire and Hadad inscrs. (see vol. II, pp. 20, 62), there are very few mason's errors, which suggests masons well used to the language, and could be made an argument in favour of the Phoen. versions being primary rather than the HH. See the apparatus and the Notes to A i 17   ii 17   C iv 3, 14   v 6.

Historical circumstances

Next to nothing is known of the history of Cilicia in the early 1 millenn. BC apart from these inscrs., an allusion to דננים in the Kilamuwa i inscr. from neighbouring Sam'al (**13** 7), and a few references in the Assyrian annals, where the area is called Que or Kue (*ANET,* Index). Their chief·purpose is to commemorate the building (or rather rebuilding) of a city on the site now called Karatepe; it is given the name of the person who commissioned the inscrs., one Azitiwada, arrangements are made for regular sacrifices to be offered in its temple, and there are the usual concluding blessings and curses. But before he describes the building, Azitiwada gives a long preamble, in which he rehearses his achievements in bringing peace and prosperity to the plain of Adana (עמק אדן), to the people called the Danunians, and to the royal house of Mopsos (בת מפש). The name Que does not appear. Azitiwada speaks like a king (e.g. 'the kings who were before me', A i 19), yet he does not in the opening sentence give himself the title king, but acknowledges that he owes his high position to a certain Awarku, who is the one called 'king of the Danunians'. He also states (A i 11) that he enabled the 'root, or scion, of my lord' to succeed to the throne. The best way to make the details cohere is, it seems to me, to assume that Azitiwada was either a high official of Awarku's court or a prince of the royal blood, that he had lands in the region of Karatepe, and that after Awarku's death he acted as regent while his son was still a minor. The rebuilding of the main town in the area of his estates marks his increased status and wealth as regent, and gives him a chance to boast of his achievements as if he were a king and as if his ducal seat were capital of the whole country (the actual capital was פער, A i 6). On the grounds of the pre-Assyrian architectural style of the gateway the inscrs. have been dated in the late 9 cent., presumably following the war in which the Danunians had been worsted by Kilamuwa of Sam'al (**13** 7); but the late features of the writing (see above) make such a high dating most improbable. Most commentators, making an equation between the recently deceased Awarku of the inscrs. and the Urikki of Que, who along with Panammu of Sam'al offered tribute to Tiglathpileser in 738 BC (*ANET* p. 283), date the text around 730. At this period, however, the whole of Syria and eastern Anatolia was fast collapsing before the Assyrian advance, whereas the expansionist and confident tone of the inscrs. seems to me to demand a date rather earlier in the 8 cent., when the west had peace from imperial interference, in the same period, that is, which is reflected in the Zakir inscr. (II **5**) and the opening lines of the Hadad inscr. (II **13**), and which farther south in Israel and Judah saw the long and prosperous reigns of Jeroboam and Azariah. The Awarku of the inscrs. will therefore be the father (or the grandfather) of the one who paid tribute to Tiglathpileser. The architecture is not so immovably dated that it could not be half a century or so later, nor is the writing so developed that it could not be a few decades earlier than 730. Considering all the issues, a date around 760–750 BC is indicated.

Ethnic situation

It is impossible at the present moment either to dismiss or to make complete sense of the Greek tradition that Cilicia was colonized by Mycenaean Greek adventurers in the aftermath of the Trojan war; but there must be some connection between the מפש (HH *Mukas-s*), who according to these inscrs. was the founder of the Danunian royal house and Mopsos, the seer of Greek legend who defeated Calchas in a contest of divination at Clarus near Colophon and later moved to Cilicia where he set up a new oracle, and between both of these and a certain Mukshush, who according to Hittite records was an ally of the Achaeans (Hitt. *Aḫḫiyawa*) in their invasion of western Asia Minor in the late 13 cent. BC. I am not, however, inclined to go further than this and on the grounds of the ethnic term Danunians in these inscrs. name the adventurers led by Mopsos or Mukshush as Danaoi, a Mycenaean people from Argos whose strong links with the east are stressed in Greek legend and whose name was used by Homer as a general designation of all the allies of Agamemnon at the siege of Troy, though it is not improbable that the 'Sea people' who were called Denyen by the Egyptians and who took part in the great ethnic migrations that engulfed Anatolia and Syria around 1200 BC are to be related to the Danaoi. There is a reference to a land of Danuna north of Ugarit in a 14-cent. Amarna letter which takes us back well before the period of Mopsos and suggests that the Danunians had already been present in the Cilician region for over a century when he arrived to seize power. If there is any connection between them and the

Danaoi and Denyen, it must then be as ancestors rather than as descendants. Whether the name Danunians is, as most commentators seem to assume, derived from that of the city אדן (the present-day Adana), which is known as *Ataniya* in Hittite records as early as the 16 cent., or whether, as I suspect, the resemblance between them is fortuitous, is not possible to decide with any certainty. Astour in his book *Hellenosemitica* argues that the Danunians were a Canaanite people who had been settled in Cilicia from at least the early 2 millenn. and that by the time of the Karatepe inscrs. the region had long been thoroughly Semitized. I find this theory impossible to accept because of its implication that the language of the inscrs. is an independent development out of an old Canaanite dialect, when it is in fact Tyro-Sidonian Phoen. and must, together with such evidence of Phoen. civilization as the inscrs. supply, have reached Cilicia as a result of Phoen. colonization and trade. Much more plausible is Goetze's theory based on a study of the proper names of Awarku and some earlier known kings of the region (though not Azitiwada) that the Danunians were originally of Hurrian extraction. Be that as it may, it is prob. that by the 8 cent. they spoke a Luwian dialect and that their culture and religion had been largely accommodated to those of their Anatolian neighbours, though even here it is important to emphasize that apart from the Luwian version of these inscrs. no HH remains have been found in Cilicia; this could mean that HH no less than Phoen. was a foreign medium, and should give us pause before arguing straight from the Luwian version to native Danunian practice and belief. Add to this the fact that the HH writing and the Luwian language are still very imperfectly known (I rely below on Meriggi's renderings), and it will be clear that some of the problems raised by the Karatepe texts are likely to be intriguing scholars for many years. An essential first step in reaching firmer conclusions is the appearance of the long-awaited official volume on the excavations and a definitive edition of the texts in both languages with clear and usable photographs.

Bibliography

Initial publications and illustrations:
(A) H. Çambel, *Oriens* 1 (1948), 162, Taf. 1.
    H. T. Bossert, U. B. Alkim, *Die Ausgrabungen auf dem Karatepe* (1950), Taf. XIV, 70.
    H. T. Bossert, *Türk Tarih Kurumu Belleten* 17 (1953), figs. 1–6.
(B) H. T. Bossert, loc. cit., figs. 12–13.
(C) H. T. Bossert, U. B. Alkim, *Karatepe: Second preliminary report* (1947), pls. XXIX–XXXI, XL–XLIV.
    H. T. Bossert, loc. cit., pp. 143–9 and figs. 7–11.

A useful list of early studies is given in J. M. Solá-Solé, *L'Infinitif sémitique* (1961), pp. xxv–xxvii; I found the following most helpful:

G. Levi della Vida, 'Observazioni all'iscrizione fenicia di Karatepe', *Acc. Naz. dei Lincei, Rend.* 4 (1949), 273–90.

R. T. O'Callaghan, 'The great Phoenician portal inscription from Karatepe', *Orientalia* 18 (1949), 173–205.

M. J. Mellink, 'Karatepe: More light on the dark ages', *Bibl. Or.* 7 (1950), 141–50.

A. Dupont-Sommer, 'Études du texte phénicien des inscriptions de Karatepe', *Jahrb. f. kleinas. Forsch.* 1 (1950–1951), 216–306; 2 (1952–3), 189–200.

A. Alt, 'Die phönikische Inschriften von Karatepe', *WO* 1 (1947–52), 272–87; 2 (1954–9), 172–83.

E. Laroche, 'Adana et les Danouniens', *Syria* 35 (1958), 263 ff.

See further:

A Goetze, 'Cilicians', *J. Cuneiform St.* 16 (1962), 48–58.

M. J. Dahood, 'Karatepe notes', *Biblica* 44 (1963), 70–3.

KAI no. 26.

A. van den Branden, 'Les inscriptions phéniciennes de Karatepe', *Melto* 1 (1965), 25–84.

M. Astour, *Hellenosemitica* (1967), chapt. I.

P. Meriggi, *Manuale di Eteo geroglifico,* II Testi (1967), 69–100.

ANET pp. 653 f.

M. Haran, '*zbḥ ymm* in the Karatepe inscriptions', *VT* 19 (1969), 372–3.

A i

1 אנך אזתוד הברך בעל עבר

2 בעל אש אדר אורך מלך דננים

3 פעלן בעל לדננים לאב ולאם יחו אנך אית

4 דננים ירחב אנך ארץ עמק אדן לממצא ש

5 מש וער מבאי וכן בימתי כל נעם לדנני

6 ם ושבע ומנעם ומלא אנך עקרת פער ופע

7 ל אנך סס על סס ומגן על מגן ומחנת על

8 מחנת בעבר בעל ואלם ושברת מלצם

9 ותרק אנך כל הרע אש כן בארץ ויטנא אנך

10 בת אדני בנעם ופעל אנך לשרש אדני נעם

11 וישב אנך על כסא אבי ושת אנך שלם את

A i 7 C: ... מגן] ל[ע]ן וֹפֹ   8 C: אל[ם   וב[עבר

D. Ussishkin, 'The date of the Neo-Hittite enclosure in Karatepe', *Anatolian St.* 19 (1969), 121–3.

W. Weippert, 'Elemente phönikischer und kilikischer Religion in den Inschriften vom Karatepe', *ZDMG* Suppl. 1 (1969), 191–216.

E. Olávarri, 'El calendario cúltico de Karatepe y el Zebaḥ Hayyamym en 1 Sam.', *Est. Bibl.* 29 (1970), 311–25.

F. Steinherr, 'Zu einige Probleme von Karatepe', *WO* 6 (1970–1), 166–82.

Greenfield, 'Scripture', 265–8.

Teixidor, 'Bulletin' for 1971, items 97, 98; 1973, item 121.

Ginsberg, 'Ugaritico-phoenica', 134–41.

Magnanini, *Iscrizioni,* pp. 51–7.

Lipiński, 'Miscellanea', 45–9.

W. Röllig in *NESE* 2 (1974), 3.

F. Bron, 'Phénicien RŠ'T = vieillesse', *AIUON* 37 (1975), 545–6.

Cambridge Ancient History, 3rd edit., vol. II, part 2 (1975), chapts. by Stubbings (338 ff.), Barnett (359 ff.), Albright (507 ff.).

Avishur, 'Stylistic features', 9 ff., 14, 16.

Lipiński, 'North Semitic texts', 240 ff.

J. D. Harkins, A. M. Davies, 'On the problems of Karatepe; The Hieroglyphic text', *Anatolian St.* 28 (1978), 103–19.

Illustrations

Initial publications (see above): O'Callaghan, loc. cit.; Harden, *Phoenicians,* pl. 37.

A i

1. I am Azitiwada, blessed by (or, vizier of) Baal, servant of

2. Baal, whom Awarku, king of the Danunians, made powerful.

3. Baal made me a father and a mother to the Danunians. I revived

4. the Danunians. I extended the land of the plain of Adana from the rising of the

5. sun to its setting. And in my days the Danunians had everything (that was) good,

6. and plenty (of grain), and fine food; and I filled the granaries of Pahar. And I

7. acquired horse upon horse, and shield upon shield, and army upon

8. army, by the grace of Baal and the gods. And I shattered dissenters,

9. and I drove out every evildoer who was in the land. And I put

10. the house of my lord into good order; and I acted kindly towards the scion of my lord,

11. and I set him on his father's throne. And I made peace with

9 C: ‏ותר‎[‏ק‎‏ת‎ B: ‏ויטנאנת‎ C: ‏את‎[‏נ‎]‏ויט‎

12 כל מלך ואף באבת פעלן כל מלך בצדקי ו

13 בחכמתי ובנעם לבי ובן אנך חמית ע

14 זת בכל קצית על גבלם במקמם באש כן

15 אשם רעם בעל אגדדם אש בל אש עבד

16 כן לבת מפש ואנך אזתוד שתנם תחת פעם

17 י ובן אנך חמ֗ית במקמם המת לשבתנם דנן

18 ים בנחת לבנם ועך אנך ארצת עזת במבא

19 שמש אש בל עך כל המלכם אש כן לפני וא

20 נך אזתוד ענתנם ירדם אנך ישבם אנך

21 בקצת גבלי במצא שמש ודננים

A ii

1   ישבת שם וכן בימתי בכל

2   גבל עמק אדן לממצא שמש

3   ועד מבאי ובמקמם אש כן

4   לפנם נשתעם אש ישתע אדם ללכת

5   דרך ובימתי אנך אשת תך לחד

6   י דל פלכם בעבר בעל ואלם

7   וכן בכל ימתי שבע ומנעם ושבת

8   נעמת ונחת לב לדננים ולכל עם

9   ק אדן ובן אנך הקרת ז ושת

10   אנך שם אזתודי כ בעל ורשף

11   צפרם שלחן לבנת ובני אנך ב

12   עבר בעל ובעבר רשף צפרם ב

12. every king, and indeed every king treated me as a father because of my righteousness,

13. and because of my wisdom, and because of my goodness of heart. And I built

14. strong fortresses in all the remote areas on the borders, in the places where there were

15. wicked men, leaders of gangs, not one of whom had been a subject

16. of the house of Mopsos; but I Azitiwada placed them under my feet.

17. And I built fortresses in these places so that the Danunians might dwell in them

18. with their minds at peace. And I subdued strong lands at the rising

19. of the sun, which none of the kings who were before me had been able to subdue; but

20. I Azitiwada subdued them. I brought them down; I settled them

21. on the edge of my borders at the setting of the sun; and I settled

A ii

1. Danunians (up) there. So in my days they were on all

2. the borders of the plain of Adana from the rising of the sun

3. to its setting, even in the places which were

4. formerly dreaded (and) where a man was afraid to walk

5. on a road — but in my days a woman could walk by herself

6. with (her) spindles, by the grace of Baal and the gods.

7. And throughout my days the Danunians and the whole plain of Adana

8. had plenty (of grain), and fine food, and a gracious life, and peace of mind.

9. And I (re-) built this city, and I

10. called its name Azitiwadiya; for Baal and Resheph

11. of the he-goats had commissioned me to build it. And I (re-) built it by

12. the grace of Baal, and by the grace of Resheph of the he-goats, with

A ii 6 C: ובעבר אלם   8–9 B omits ונחת .... אדן   9–10 C: וש>ת אנך ש<ם   11 B: צנרם (error)

13 שבע ובמנעם ובשבת נעמת ובנחת

14 לב לכני משמר לעמק אדן ולב

15 ת מפש כ בימתי כן לארץ עמק א

16 דן שבע ומנעם ובל כן מתם לדנני

17 ם לל בימתי ובן אנך הקרת ז שת

18 אנך שם אזתודי ישב אנך בן

19 בעל כרנתריש וילך זבח לכל

A iii

1 המסכת זבח ימם אלף 1 וב[עת ח]רש

2 ש 1 ובעת קצר ש 1 וברך בעל כר[נ]

3 תריש אית אזתוד חים ושלם

4 ועז אדר על כל מלך לתתי בעל כרנתריש

5 וכל אלן קרת לאזתוד ארך ימם ורב

6 שנת ורשאת נעמת ועז אדר על כל מל

7 ך וכן הקרת ז בעלת שבע ותרש ועם

8 ז אש ישב בן יכן בעל אלפם ובע

9 ל צאן ובעל שבע ותרש וברבם ילד

10 וברבם יאדר וברבם יעבד לאז

11 תוד ולבת מפש בעבר בעל ואלם

12 ואם מלך במלכם ורזן ברזנם אם א

13 דם אש אדם שם אש ימח שם אזתו

14 ד בשער ז ושת שם אם אף יחמד אי

15 ת הקרת ז ויסע השער ז אש פעל א

16 זתוד ויפעל ל שער זר ושת שם עלי

16: From this point the C text is printed   19–iii 2   B omits
1 ש .... וילך   A iii 9:   B breaks off after בעל

13. plenty (of grain), and with fine food, and with gracious living, and with peace

14. of mind, so that it might be a protection for the plain of Adana and for the

15. house of Mopsos; for in my days the land of the plain of

16. Adana had plenty (of grain) and fine food; and the Danunians never had

17. night in my days. So I (re-) built this city; I

18. called its name Azitiwadiya; I made Baal

19. KRNTRYŠ dwell in it. Now let people bring a sacrifice for all

A iii

1. the images, the yearly sacrifice of one ox, and at ploughing [time]

2. one sheep, and at harvest time one sheep! And may Baal KRNTRYŠ

3. bless Azitiwada with life and health

4. and powerful strength above every king! May Baal KRNTRYŠ and all

5. the gods of the city give to Azitiwada length of days, and many

6. years, and a pleasant old age, and powerful strength above every king!

7. And may this city be owner of plenty (of grain) and new wine; and may

8. this people who dwell in her be owners of oxen, and owners

9. of sheep, and owners of plenty (of grain) and new wine; and may they bear many (children),

10. and as they grow many become powerful, and as they grow many serve

11. Azitiwada and the house of Mopsos, by the grace of Baal and the gods!

12. Now, if a king among kings, or a prince among princes, or

13. any man who is a man of renown, effaces the name of

14. Azitiwada from this gate and puts up his own name, or more than that, covets

15. this city and pulls down this gate which Azitiwada

16. made, and makes another gate for it and puts his own name on it,

אם בחמדת יסע אם בשנאת וברע יסע 17

השער ז ומח בעלשממ ואל קן ארץ 18

ושמש עלם וכל דר בן אלם אית הממלכת הא ואית המלך הא ואית 19

A iv

אדם הא אש אדם שם אפס 1

שם אזתוד יכן לעלם כם שם 2

שמש וירח 3

Ciii

. . . .

ובל כן 13

מתם לל בימתי לדננים ובן אנך ה 14

קרת ז ושת אנך שם אזתודי וישב 15

אנך האלם ז בעל כרנתריש וברך 16

בעל כרנתריש אית אזתוד בח 17

ים ובשלם ובעז אדר על כל מלך 18

לתתי בעל כרנתריש לאזתוד 19

ארך ימם ורב שנת ורשאת נעמת 20

C iv

ועז אדר על כֹל מלך 1

וזבח אש יֹ[לך --ל]אלם 2

כל המסכת ז 3

ז זבח יֹ[מם] א[לף 1 ו]ב 4

עת חרש [ש 1 ו]בעת קֹצֹר 5

ש 1 וכן [ה]קֹרת ז בעלֹֹ[ת] 6

שבע ותרש ועֹם ז א[ש] 7

ישב בן יכן בעלֹ [א]לפם ו 8

17. whether it is out of covetousness or whether it is out of hatred and malice that he pulls down
18. this gate — then let Baalshamem and El-Creator-of-Earth
19. and the eternal Sun and the whole generation of the sons of the gods efface that kingdom and that king and

A iv

1. that man who is a man of renown! Only

2. may the name of Azitiwada last for ever like the name

3. of the sun and the moon!

C iii

. . . .

13. . . . . and

14. the Danunians never had night in my days. So I (re-) built

15. this city, and I gave it the name of Azitiwadiya, and I

16. made this god Baal KRNTRYŠ dwell (in it). So may Baal

17. KRNTRYŠ bless Azitiwada with life

18. and with health, and with powerful strength above every king!

19. May Baal KRNTRYŠ give to Azitiwada

20. length of days, and many years, and a pleasant old age,

C iv

1. and powerful strength above every king!

2. And the sacrifice which [a man shall bring for] all

3. the images of this god is

4. this: the [yearly] sacrifice of [one] ox, [and] at

5. ploughing time [one sheep, and] at harvest time

6. one sheep. And may this city be owner of

7. plenty (of grain) and new wine; and may this people who

8. dwell in her be owners of oxen, and

9 בעל צאן ובעל שבֿ[ע ו]תר[ש]

10 וברבם ילדֿ וברבֿם [י]אדר

11 ובר[ב]ם יעבד לאזתוד ול

12 בת מֿ[פ]ש בעבר בעל ובעבר אֿלם

13 וא[ם] מלך במלכם ורזן ברזֿנם

14 {ם} [א]ֿם אדם אש אדם שם אש יֿא

15 מ[ר] למחת שם אזתוד בסמל

16 אֿ[ל]ֿם ז ושת שם אם אף יחמד

17 אֿ[י]ת הקרת ז ויאמר אפעל

18 סמל זר ושת שמי עלי ואי

19 ת סמל האלם אש פעל אזתוֿדֿ

20 בעל כרנתריש אש בבא מלֿח ב

21 נֿנֿחֿֿל אם אט–לֿ –– אל ––––

C v

1]רנב –– ר]   [   ]

missing 2–4

5 מ]   ]ר [אפס שם]

6 אזתוד}י{ יכן לעלם כם שם

7 שמש וירח

9. owners of sheep, and owners of plenty (of grain) [and] new wine;

10. and may they bear many (children), and as they grow many become powerful,

11. and as they grow many serve Azitiwada and the

12. house of Mopsos, by the grace of Baal and by the grace of the gods!

13. Now, if a king among kings, or a prince among princes,

14. or any man who is a man of renown, gives

15. orders for the name of Azitiwada to be effaced from the statue

16. of this god, and puts up his own name, or more than that, if he covets

17. this city and says, I will make

18. another statue and put my own name on it, and the

19. statue of the god which Azitiwada made, (that of)

20. Baal KRNTRYŠ, which is at the king's entrance in(to)

21. ....

C v

1. ....

2–4. ....

5. .... [Only may the name]

6. of Azitiwada last for ever like the name

7. of the sun and the moon!

NOTES

A i

1. אזתוד; a name of Hittite or Luwian type (Goetze); HH *Asitiwata*. For בעל HH has *Tarhui*, the name of the Weather-god who was the chief deity of the Neo-Hittite states. הברך בעל; there are two possible interpretations. (1) 'The blessed one of Baal', with the article attached to the first member of the construct relation; cp. ברוך יהוה (Gen. xxiv 31 xxvi 29). The anomalous usage may be compared with הלפניהם in **13** Kilamuwa i 5 and perhaps more accurately with the Hebr. phrases in Jerem. xxxviii 6 ('the pit of Malchiah') and Lam. ii 13 ('the daughter of Jerusalem'), in both of which the second member is a proper name as here. There may be another example in **42** Pyrgi 10–11 (q.v.). (2) 'Grand vizier of Baal', in which the ה equates with the א in Hebr. אברך, a title of ultimate Sumerian origin given to Joseph in Gen. xli 43; Akkad. *abarakku*. It is not clear why a chief minister of Awarku should be called 'vizier of Baal' (i.e. of *Tarhui* or a local Danunian Weather-god) rather than 'vizier of the king'; but as Lipiński points out, there are a number of interesting parallels between the roles of Azitiwada and those of Joseph, e.g. their provision of food for the people (i 6; Gen. xli 48), which makes this solution attractive. The HH version has 'man (illuminated by) the Sun-god' or possibly 'man of the Sun', i.e. of the king ('the Sun' being a common epithet of Hittite kings); it does not equate directly with the Phoen. and is itself uncertain, so it cannot safely be used to decide Azitiwada's status.

2. אדר; Piel. אורך; HH *Awarku*, a name of Hurrian type (Goetze); to be equated with Akkad. *Urikki*, a king of Que in the time of Tiglathpileser III (*ANET* p. 283) or more prob. (see introd.) a previous king of the same name. The phrase 'king of the Danunians' must go with his name and not with Azitiwada's, for otherwise we would have a minor king Azitiwada's patron or suzerain introduced without a title. Que or Kue (1 Kgs. x 28; II **5** Zakir A 6) is a name used in the Assyrian annals for the eastern part of the classical Cilicia, the western part being called *Hilukka*, whence the classical name (*ANET* p. 277). In earlier Hittite and Egyptian sources the region is called Kizzuwatna and (prob. related) Qode or Kode (*ANET* pp. 205, 206, 235, 262). דננים; HH has *Atanyana* 'inhabitants of Adana'. See introd. for a discussion of the ethnic situation. On the philological level the facts as I see them are (1) the word can be regarded as being formed from a base DNN with the gentilic termination [īyīm] or [iyyīm]; (2) it can thus be related directly to the 14-cent. land of *Danuna* (*EA* 151, 52); (3) it can only be related to the 13-cent. ethnic terms *Denyen* (Egyp.) and *Danaoi* (Greek) if we assume that Danuna was itself originally an ethnic term formed from a weak base containing the letters DN with a termination [una] and that דננים has in effect a double ethnic ending (a not unattested phenomenon); (4) it is virtually impossible to relate either Danuna or דננים to the name of the ancient (16-cent.) city Adana, which universally retains the first syllable in Hitt. (*Ataniya*), Phoen. (אדן), HH (*Atanya*), and in modern Turkish; this would have given as a gentilic in Phoen. אדנים, as in the contemporary HH it gave *Atanyana*. There seems to me to be no escape, therefore, from the conclusion that Danunians and Adanites were originally two distinct gentilics which came by chance to have much the same reference.

3. פעלן = [p'alánī]. אב; cp. Isa. xxii 21 **13** Kilamuwa i 10. יחו = [yiḥwō] < [yiḥway(a)]; Yiph. 3 masc. sing. used as a neutral form; see on this construction at **13** Kilamuwa i 7. אית; **12** Cyprus grave 3.

4. ירחב; Yiph.; cp. Exod. xxxiv 24 Amos i 13. למֹמצא; prepos. למן as in **13** Kilamuwa i 12. שמש; perhaps with syncope of [h] of the article. There are other possible instances in constructs זבח ימם (A iii l), אלן קרת (A iii 5), קן ארץ (A iii 18), שם שמש (A iv 2); after 'and' ואלם (A i 8 ii 6 iii 11), וירח (A iv 3); after כל (A i 14); after על (A i 14); after the object marker אית אדם (A iii 19). See the Note on phonology and grammar. There are similar phrases with שמש in Isa. xlv 6 Mal. i 11 Ps. 11 cxiii 3.

5. מבאי with suffix [í/ēyū]; the noun is genitive. בימתי = [b(a)ymōtī]; by this time י = [ī] is used for all cases; in A iii 1 the form is masc. (ימם); Hebr. also has both forms. Cp. **13** Kilamuwa i 12.

6. שבע; cp. Gen. xli 29 ff.; referring mainly to grain and perhaps actually to be so rendered in Prov. iii 10 and in A iii 7 (where it is parallel with מנעם (תרש. lit. '(every) dainty'; sing. after כל; cp. Ps. cxli 4. מלא; Piel 3 masc. sing. perfect. עקרת; the context and the parallel of Gen. xli 47–9 suggests 'granaries, storehouses'; HH 'i granai di Pahar' (Meriggi); Arab. ['aqāru] 'landed property, estate' does not bring us particularly close; Lipiński connects the word with Akkad. *ekurru*, plur. *ekurrāti*, lit. 'temples'. פער; a Phoen. rendering of the name of the capital of Que; HH *Pahar*; Akkad. *Paḥri*. It is perhaps to be located on the site of the later Greek city of Mopsuestia (see at 16). פעל; for the meaning 'acquire' cp. Prov. xxi 6.

7. סס; cp. 1 Kgs. x 28, confirming that Cilicia was renowned for its horses; the מצרים of the Massor. text prob. refers not to Egypt but to a land *Muṣri* in southern Anatolia (*ANET* p. 279). מחנת = [maḥnōt], sing.; cp. **4** Ahiram 2 II **5** Zakir A 5.

8. בעבר; either 'for the sake of, in the cause of' (Ps. cxxxii 10) or 'thanks to, as a result of' (Exod. xiii 8). Note that the prepos. is not repeated before the second noun, though it is in C (i 14). אלם; here and in A ii 6 iii 11 'the (other) gods' in general; contrast אלן קרת (iii 5), 'the (specific) gods of the city'. In C iii 16 iv 2, however, אלם seems to be used in a sing. sense characteristic of later Phoen. and Punic inscriptions. ושברת; the normal inflected 1 sing. perf. used without אנך for variety. In C the next two verbs are given in this form; stylisticly one would prefer ושברת followed by ותקרת, since both clauses deal with the same subject (the removal of evildoers), with the אנך construction instead of ויטנאת (C). But cp. the narrative poetry of the Ugar. epics, where there seems to be no difference of meaning implied by the bewildering interchange of *ktb* and *yktb* (e.g. in the story of Keret's campaign, **14** 154 ff.). מלצם; Yiph. partic. plur.; cp. Hebr. LYṢ 'scorn, deride' with nuances of arrogance in Isa. xxviii 22, of causing dissension in Prov. xxii 10, of treachery in Hos. vii 5.

9. תרק; otherwise unknown; perhaps cognate with Akkad. *tarāku* 'to beat, strike' or better Aram. תרך, Pael, 'drove out' (Targum Gen. iii 24). With the sense cp. Ps. lxxii 4 ci 8 (of the Davidic king) Prov. xx 8 II **13** Hadad 9 Keret **16** vi 30–1, 47–8. יטנא; Yiph.; a figurative usage, normally of erecting a stone or statue.

10. נעם; **25** Yehaumilk 8. שרש; **36** Lapethos ii 16 II **5** Zakir B 28 II **7** Sefire i C 24 Isa. xi 1, 10 (of the Messianic prince).

11. ישב = [yōšībō]; 3 masc. sing. Yiph. perf. (neutral form) with vocalic suffix unrepresented in the orthography; HH as rendered by Meriggi supports this interpretation. Cp. II **14** Panammu 19 II **15** Barrakkab i 5 1 Kgs. ii 24. *Ll.* 8–11 prob. speak of Azitiwada's containment of the internal strife that followed the death of Awarku and that seems to have threatened the

succession of the legitimate heir, who must have been a minor. Cp. the opening lines of the Panammu inscr. (II **14**), which similarly deal with the crushing of a coup on the death of a king; cp. also the position of King Eshmunazar (**28**), who ruled as a minor with the help of his mother. אבי = ['abīyū] (genit. noun) or with this word possibly ['abūyū], with the old nomin. termination acting as connecting vowel; cp. Latin *labunom* (Segert, *Grammar*, p. 117) with [ū] before the 3 plur. masc. suffix. שת = [šōt]; cp. Hebr. שים שלום (Num. vi 26 Ps. cxlvii 14).

12. כל מלך; there is perhaps here a suggestion that Azitiwada, preoccupied with internal troubles, reversed the warlike policy of previous kings; cp. **13** Kilamuwa i 7–8, which speak of Danunian ambitions in Sam'al. באבת; *Beth essentiae* with plur. of 'majesty' (['abōt]); cp. בעזרי (Ps. cxviii 7) and Gen. lv 8 (Joseph as 'father' to Pharaoh); Ahiqar 55 (the sage as 'father'). The plur. of 'majesty' אבות may occur in Hebr. in Ps. cix 14 (‖ אמו, sing.). Lipiński, 'among the fathers (advisers)'. בצדקי; II **14** Panammu 1, 11, 19 II **15** Barrakkab i 4–5 II **19** Nerab ii 2.

13. חכמתי; Gen. xli 39 (Joseph) II **14** Panammu 11. בן = [banō] < [banay(a)]. חמית = [hōmiyyōt] or the like, lit. 'walls'; sing. presumably [hōmīt] (*EA ḥu-mi-tu*); the Hebr. forms are [hōmā], plur. [hōmōt]. Cp. I **16** Mesha 21. A plur. of Phoen. type should perhaps be read (ח for ה) in Prov. i 21 'on (from) the top of walls'.

14. קצית = [qṣiyyōt] or the like, sing. קצת (21) = [qṣīt]; Hebr. [qaṣā], plur. [qaṣōt], and [qṣāt] (sing. only), all lit. 'end, border'. מקמם; Hebr. usually מקמות. באש; Hebr. would prefer ב .... אשר. כן = [kōnū].

15. אשם רעם; cp. 1 Sam. xxx 22; contrast Hebr. plur. אנשים. בעל אגדדם; cp. Hebr. גדודים שרי 'captains of marauding bands' (2 Sam. iv 2 1 Kgs. xi 24). The א is prosthetic before the initial two-consonant cluster of [gdūd], a feature particularly common in Cyprian Phoen., but found occasionally also in Standard. בל אש; cp. Ugar. *blmt* 'immortality'. עבד is prob. a noun and not forming with כן a pluperfect as in Arabic, though a verbal form with ל is used in A iii 10–11; cp. the sequence כן נדר (*CIS* i 93, 5 from Cyprus), which is usually taken as a pluperfect, but is more satisfactorily explained by Dotan ('Stress position', 90 ff.) as the verb 'to be' followed by the 'passive' partic. [nadūr] describing a state as Hebr. ידוע (Isa. liii 3), i.e. the donor 'was (when he died) in a state of having vowed'.

16. מפש; a legendary ruler of Que to be compared with King Keret of the Ugar. epic rather than with Gabbar or QRL in neighbouring Sam'al, who were heads of families and founders of historical dynasties; HH *Mukas-s*. He appears in Greek legend as a seer called Mopsos, who lived in Lydia (Colophon) and who moved later to Cilicia, where his name survives in that of the Greek city of Mopsuestia, east of Adana (this is quite likely to have been built on the same site as Awarku's capital Pahar). The HH form (with [k] for Greek [p] as often in Anatolian languages) allows a further equation with a freebooter of western Asia Minor called Mukshush, who was a thorn in the flesh of the last Hittite rulers; see further in the introduction. The historical Mopsos emerges then as a Lydian adventurer who in the unsettled conditions of the late 13 cent. BC carved out a kingdom for himself among the Danunian people who had settled in Cilicia at least a century and a half previously. As our knowledge stands at the moment it would be unwise to use his career as evidence one way or the other of the Danunians' own ethnic affiliation. שתנם = [šattīnōm] with 'heavy' suffix following [ī]. תחת פעמי; cp. Ugar. *tḥt p'ny* (**19** 109) 2 Sam. xxii (Ps. xviii) 39 Ps. viii 7 xlvii 4.

17. חמית; the middle bar of מ seems to be missing, so that the letter looks more like a broad נ; clearly a mason's error. המת = [hōmat]; cp. the Hebr. longer form [hēmmā], accommodated in its vowel to the fem. [hēnna]; in Phoen. the fem. is apparently also המת = [hēm(m)at] (**36** Lapethos ii 5), accommodated in its consonant to the masculine. לשבתנם = [lšibtinōm] with נם after the connecting (genit.) vowel [i]. The suffix refers back to מקמם with the usual prepos. omitted (as frequently after the partic. in Hebr.);. or it is prospective, i.e. 'that they might dwell, namely the Danunians'; cp. A iii 4 **28** Eshmunazar 9–10 Ezek. x 3 xlii 14.

18. בנחת לבנם; cp. A ii 7–8 **4** Ahiram 2 Ps. cxvi 7 Isa. xxxii 18. Cp. also Ps. lxxii 7 (of life under the Davidic king). ענ = ['innō]; Piel; cp. I **16** Mesha 5,6, where the original [w] of the base is retained. במבא שמש (with syncope?); the mountainous region west of the Cilician plain; the phrase is omitted in B, as is the similar one in 21, making the reference less precise.

19. אש כן לפני; cp. **13** Kilamuwa i 1–5.

20. ענתנם = ['innītīnōm]. ירדם = [yōrīdōm] with 'light' suffix after the uninflected form. ישבם = [yōšībōm]. On the significance of these suffixed forms, showing that the verbs cannot be infins. absol., see at **13** Kilamuwa i 7. Azitiwada's practice of resettling disaffected groups may be compared with the well-known Assyrian policy (cp. II **14** Panammu 14).

21. קצת; see at 14 above. The conquered tribes were transplanted to the eastern border towards Sam'al.

A ii

1. ישבת = [yōšábtī]; cp. I **16** Mesha 13. שם; i.e. in the western uplands. כן = [kōnū] with the Danunians as subj.; apart from the ו before במקמם in 3, the syntax of 1–6 is very similar to i 13–16; I therefore take the ו in the sense of 'even'.

3. אש here and in 4 is equivalent to באש in i 14; cp. אשר in Gen. xxxv 13.

4. לפנם; cp. 1 Sam. ix 9 Ruth iv 7 etc. נשתעם; Niph. partic. from ŠTʻ 'to fear, be in dread'; Ugar. ttʻ (**6** vi 30); Hebr. only Isa. xli 10,23. ישתע; imperf. Qal with frequentative force.

5. דרך without prepos. after the verb 'to go'; cp. Num. xx 17 Isa. xxxv 8. אנך; with the strengthening use of the pronoun cp. שם אנך (**25** Yehaumilk 12); šmk 'at (Ugar. **2** iv 11); in Hebr. 1 Kgs. xxi 19. תך לחדי; this division of the words was suggested independently by Ginsberg and Röllig (*NESE*) on the basis of the HH version, which speaks of women walking, and of the occurrence of לחדי '(I) alone' on a recently published fragmentary inscr. from Byblos. תך is imperf. fem. of the verb 'to go' and may be compared to the irregular Aram. imperf. יהך (= [yhāk], Ezra. v 5); presumably both come from an alternative base ḤWK, with Phoen. dropping the [h]. לחדי = [lhōdáyyā] or the like with fem. suffix added to a plur. stem as in Aramaic.

6. דל 'with' as in **25** Yehaumilk 14; the etymology is unknown. The picture is of women going peaceably about their everyday work in the village or surrounding countryside; Ginsberg cites Dalman's photograph of a Bedouin woman spinning as she walks with a spindle (Hebr. פלך) in her right hand; *Arbeit und Sitte in Palästina*, 5, appendix of illustrations, no. 8. Cp. Prov. xxxi 13, 19, and, for a similar picture of women working, Ugar. **14** 111–4. ואלם; see at A i 8.

7. שבת נעמת; Ps. xvi 6, 11 Job xxxvi 11.

9. בן; since the gods of the city are mentioned (A iii 5), it is not a completely new foundation, and the meaning is prob. 'rebuilt' as in I **16** Mesha 9. ז = [zō], fem.; cp. Hebr. זה, זו for the usual זאת; it is distinguished from זא (fem. of זז) in the Byblian dialect, and therefore prob. has a different origin. שת אנך; this phrase is carelessly omitted in the C text (iii 7–8); cp. **25** Yehaumilk 12–13.

10. שם = [šmā] with fem. suffix; cp. Hebr. שים את שמו (Judg. viii 31). Contrast A iii 14.

11. צפרם 'he-goats' (Hebr. [sapīr]) rather than 'birds' (Hebr. [sippōr]) as a divine 'stag' corresponds to this god in the HH version (Lipiński); Resheph was the Syrian god of pestilence, very popular on Cyprus, where he was equated with the Greek Apollo, but here standing prob. for some Anatolian deity as the name Baal does for the local Weather-god. שלחן; cp. II **13** Hadad 13–14. לבנת; perhaps with objective suffix [ō] in contrast to the subjective suffix in לכני (14). בני = [banōyū]; cp. כסי (**13** Kilamuwa i 12).

14. לכני = [lkūni/ēyū] or the like.

16. מתם 'always'; cp. Zenjirli Aram. מת 'ever, always' (II **13** Hadad 12 ff.); Syr. [me(m)mtōm] 'from everlasting, aforetime' and with negative 'never'; Akkad. *lā-matē-ma* 'never'. Zenjirli מת, however, may be related to Ugar. *mt, 'imt* 'indeed' (*CML²* p. 152).

17. לל 'night'; cp. II **13** Hadad 24 Ps. xci 5 Job xxxvi 20 Isa. lx 20 Revel. xxi 25. There is nothing corresponding to this portion in the HH text, and the C text (iii 13–14) changes the sequence of words to ובל כן מתם לל בימתי לדננים. Many commentators, dissatisfied with the peculiar adv. מתם, prefer to follow this order and emend here to read מתמלל. This is a drastic solution which raises more difficulties than it resolves. Suggestions include 'none speaking against, insulting' the Danunians (Avishur following Dahood; cp. Aram. Pael 'to speak'; Hebr. [millā], 'by-word'); 'none languishing' among the Danunians (Friedrich, *Arch. f. Orientf.* 21 (1966), 83 f.; cp. Hebr. Hithpoel in Ps. lviii 8); 'none discontented' among the Danunians (Lipiński; cp. Arab. V form 'be weary, restless'); see further *DISO*, p. 155. For the first of these suggestions there is no comparable verbal form in the cognate languages (Aram. Ethpa. is passive) and the other two have to render ל in a way that cannot easily be paralleled. שת; C had ושת, also וישב (18).

18. ישב; Yiph.; cp. **28** Eshmunazar 17 II **13** Hadad 19. בן = [binnā] or the like (< [binhā]) with fem. suffix; cp. **28** Eshmunazar 5; Ugar. *bn;* see further at **13** Kilamuwa i 14.

19. בעל; referring prob. to the statue containing inscr. C (see at C iii 16). כרנתריש is obviously non-Semitic, perhaps a place-name (the former name of the city?), suggesting that this deity was a form of the Anatolian Weather-god. He may already have been the chief local deity. וילך; Yiph. from HLK/YLK. Azitiwada may be the subject, in which case the verb is perf. and אנך had been carelessly omitted. But as the C text, which is in a slightly different position (see C iv 2–6), makes clear, this section is not describing what Azitiwada did, but is giving instructions about sacrifice at the city shrine where the molten images of the god were set up (and apparently also the statue on which the C text was inscribed). Take therefore as a 3 sing. or plur. (indefinite) imperf. or jussive, 'One shall bring', or 'Let one, them, bring!', or possibly perf. after ו like וברד (iii 2). This section about the sacrifices is missing in the B text.

A iii

1. מסכת; Num. xxxiii 52 Deut. ix 12 Isa. xxx 22. Note plur. ימם (also in 5) against ימת eslsewhere in the inscription. The HH version has a word meaning 'year', thus confirming that the זבח הימים of 1 Sam. i 21 ii 19 xx 6 is the Canaanite name of an important yearly pilgrimage, which in the Biblical references is prob. the feast of Ingathering (אסיף) celebrating the vintage (cp. 1 Sam. i 14–15, where Eli suspects that Hannah is drunk), or, as it was later called, Tabernacles. That it here refers to the same agricultural occasion is likely, since the other two occasions for which prescription is made are ploughing (חרש) and reaping or grain harvest (קצר). Danunian and not Canaanite festivals must be meant, however, for Canaan knew no celebration at ploughing time. The vintage is put first because as in Israel it was the most important and joyous occasion of the farmer's year. There is no possible allusion to official New Year rites in which Azitiwada as king took part; for the Hittite (and therefore presumably other Anatolian) New Year celebrations occurred like the Mesopotamian not at the vintage (where the putative Jerusalem New Year festival is placed), but in the spring; and moreover, the sacrifices prescribed are too small to be a royal or state contribution, and must (like Elkanah's in the Bible) have been offered by individuals. The main purpose of the new (or refurbished) shrine was therefore, as the inscr. shows, to serve the needs of the local population, not to be a centre for great state occasions. This is not unexpected if Azitiwadiya is simply a town rebuilt and renamed after a high official or nobleman, but would be much harder to explain if, as some have claimed, Azitiwada was a king setting up a new capital. חרש = [harīš]; קצר (2) = [qaṣīr]; Gen. xlv 6 Jerem. l 16. The top left corner of the stone containing two letters from this line and one from the end of 2 has been chipped off, the final two letters of this line being carried over on to the uninscribed fifth stone (cp. 4).

2. וברך is best explained as a 'Waw consecutive' perfect in initial position in place of a jussive (cp. Amos v 26). It is followed in the list of blessings in 2–11 by another 'Waw-consecutive' perf. (וכן, 7) or when the subject comes first, by a jussive (יכן, 8; ילד, 9; יאדר, יעבד, 10). There is a similar 'Waw consecutive' perf. with precative sense in 18, which begins the apodosis of a conditional sentence (ומח). In the complicated protasis of that sentence (12 ff.), which includes a number of clauses joined by ו, we have an imperf. to begin with (ימח, 13) followed twice by ושת (14, 16); however, in 15–16 there is twice an ordinary imperf. directly after ו (ויסע, ויפעל); Hebr. would not normally vary the tenses in such a situation. The only other place where 'Waw consecutive' perfects are certainly found is in the Punic tariffs from Marseilles and Carthage (CIS i 165, 167 = KAI nos. 69, 74). The 'Waw consecutive' perf. construction then did exist in Phoen., though the evidence could be interpreted to suggest that it was confined to the more formal kind of discourse like blessing formulas and priestly legislation. There is, on the other hand, no definite evidence that Phoen. knew the 'Waw consecutive' imperf. construction so characteristic of Hebr. narrative; if it had, one would have expected to find some trace of it in the lengthy historical sections of this inscr. or of 13 Kilamuwa i; see further the discussion at 4 Ahiram 2 (ויגל). Note that ברך is followed by two objects, direct and indirect, against C iii 17, which has ב 'with'.

3. For the juxtaposition of life and peace (health), see Mal. ii 5; II 27 Hermopolis papyrus iii 5.

4. לתתי; a peculiar construction, the sense being parallel to rather than resulting from the preceding clause; cp. Hebr. Gen. xix 19 1 Sam. xiv 33. The suffix is prospective, referring forward to Baal KRNTRYŠ (see at A i 17). The final letters of this line transgress upon the fifth orthostat.

5. אלנם (Poenulus *alonim*) is dubiously connected with Ugar. *'ilnym* (*CML*² p. 142), who figure only along with *rp'um* as deities of the underworld; it only occurs in the plur. and is prob. a new formation in Phoen. with the termination [ōn] added to אל 'god'; it seems gradually to have replaced the older plur. form אלם (except in bound phrases as in A i 8) as the latter became restricted to a sing. sense 'god' or 'goddess' (as in C iii 16 iv 2). There is undoubtedly some kind of vague parallel between אלם in this sense and Hebr. אלהים, usually 'God' but occasionally 'gods', though it would be unwise to make too much of it; see at C iii 16. ארך ימם; Deut. xxx 20 Ps. xxi 5 Prov. iii 2. רב שנת; Job xxxii 7.

6. רשאת; Bron compares Ethiopic [reš'at] 'old age', which gives excellent sense; the equivalent base would be in Hebr. RŠ', but it is not attested. The usual rendering is 'authority', but the base cited in support is in Hebr., which does not confuse verbs final ['] and [y, w], RŠY ([rišyōn], Ezra iii 7 and verbal forms in Post-biblical Hebrew). The only suitable base which could be RŠ' originally is that reflected in Syriac ['aršī], Aphel, 'to give, confer' and Akkad. *rašū* 'to obtain, take, possess', *maršītu*, 'property, possessions' (particularly of cattle), i.e. here a form meaning '(fine) property' or the like. See further the discussion in II **13** Hadad 27 (ירשי).

7. כן = [kōnā]; fem. perfect. בעלת in the basic sense of 'possessor'; cp. **13** Kilamuwa i 12 and references there. שבע ותרש; see at i 6.

8. בן; see at A ii 9.

9. ברבם 'as, consisting of many', an example of what Hebraists call *Beth essentiae,* here as secondary subject, in A i 12 (באבת) as secondary predicate; cp. Ps. lv 19 'in great numbers they are (arrayed) against me'. ילד; this reading is preferable to ילע; the final letter, being last in the line, is unclear, but on Bossert's drawing it has a slight tail, and I would say this was even more prominent in the photograph of this portion in O'Callaghan (fig. 4). In the C text (iv 10) the letter is drawn as ד, though it is scored over as uncertain. It gives excellent sense (cp. Isa. xlix 20 ff.), whereas no appropriate base for ילע immediately suggests itself (Hebr. LW' or L'Y 'to talk wildly'; L'' 'to gush, overflow' (Dahood, *Biblica* 43, 1962, 225); Zenjirli L'Y 'to be weary' (?); Arab. LW' 'to be anxious').

10. עבר 'to serve' usually has a direct object in Hebr., but occurs occasionally with ל 'to work for'; 1 Sam. iv 9 2 Sam. xvi 19.

11. בעבר is retained before אלם in C (iv 12); see above A i 8.

12. The final imprecation begins here. מלך במלכם; cp. **4** Ahiram 2. רזן; Ps. ii 2 Prov. viii 15 xiv 28.

13. שם אדם; either 'man of note' (cp. Gen. vi 4) or rather awkwardly syntactically, 'a man whose name is (just) a man', with unwritten suffix on the nomin. שם, i.e. an ordinary man without titles (cp. **25** Yehaumilk 11 **28** Eshmunazar 4, 20 I **6** Nimrud 2). ימח; see **4** Ahiram 2 and references there.

14. בשער = [bašša'r]. For ב 'from' see Note to **7** Abibaal 2. ושת etc.; see at A iii 2. שם = [šmō] with vocalic suffix; cp. 2 Kgs. xxi 4, 7. אם אף 'if indeed, moreover' is more likely to introduce a new alternative protasis than to begin a subordinate one tacked on to the previous clause (i.e. 'even if, although'); cp. אף אם in **28** Eshmunazar 6 introducing a completely new

conditional sentence. חמד; prob. 'covet, have designs upon' as in Exod. xxxiv 24 (Avishur) rather than 'esteem, have good intentions towards' (Rosenthal, Lipiński etc.).

15. ז (fem.); A ii 9. יסע; imperf. Qal from NS'; cp. Judg. xvi 3.

16. ל = [lā], i.e. 'the city'. זר lit. 'strange'; cp. II 13 Hadad 30, 34 Job xix 27 Prov. xiv 10. עלי = ['alōyū] or the like; see at 13 Kilamuwa i 7.

17. אם בחמדת etc.; cp. II 13 Hadad 25–6; Hebr. ארץ חמדה חמדה (Jerem. iii 19 Zech. vii 14).

18. ומח; plur.; see at A iii 2. בעלשמם; HH has here 'Tarhui (Weather-god) of heaven', which looks like a straight translation, Tarhui being the Neo-Hittite counterpart of Phoen. Baal. We might compare the list of deities in the similar imprecation in II 5 Zakir B 23 ff., which suggests that a Syrian formula is being adopted, though that fact also does not prove that the deities in question are genuine Phoen. deities rather than equations with Neo-Hittite or Danunian deities. Thus the Weather-god and the Sun-god are prominent both in Anatolian and Syrian religion; and even אל קן ארץ, a title of the supreme Canaanite deity El in his function as 'creator' or 'owner' of the earth (cp. Gen. xiv 19, 22) was known in Hittite mythology in the story of Elkunirsa (Kramer, *Mythologies of the Ancient World*, 155). El does not figure in any Hittite pantheon, however, and in the HH version (*Aa*) he is not equated with any native deity, but with the Mesopotamian god of wisdom (Ea; Sumerian Enki), perhaps because the latter was known to have had important functions in the creation and organization of the universe (Kramer, op. cit., 98 ff., 120 ff.). My own impression is that Azitiwada (though he may not himself have worshipped them) is actively invoking the aid of the Phoen. deities Baal, El, and Shemesh to protect his building achievements; and this must imply the existence among the Danunians of a considerable number of ethnic Phoenicians or at least of people who had been deeply affected by Phoen. religion and culture as well as being proficient in the Phoen. tongue. On the other hand, it has to be admitted that we are dealing with a conventional formula, which Azitiwada may have adopted without much thought. There is, for instance, no trace of any typically Phoen. triad or any mention of a female deity.

19. This long line is written on the base on which the steles stand, beginning under *l.* 18 and continuing for the length of this and the fifth (uninscribed) stone. שמש עלם; cp. Ugar. *špš 'lm* (in a letter); Hebr. אל עולם (Gen. xxi 33). דר בן אלם; cp. דר כל קדשן (23 Arslan Tash i 12); Ugar. *dr 'il* 'the generation of El' parallel to *'ilm* 'the gods' (15 iii 19) and *dr bn 'il* parallel to *mpḥrt bn 'il* in religious texts; כל בן אלם (23 Arslan Tash i 11); Hebr. בני אלם (Ps. xxix 1 lxxxix 7); בני (ה)אלהים (Gen. vi 2, 4 Job i 6 ii 1 xxxviii 7); see further at 6 Yehimilk 4. ממלכת 'kingdom' or (abstract for concrete) 'ruler' as in 25 Yehaumilk 2, thus parallel to רזן in 12. הא = [hū(')] masc., [hī(')] fem.

A iv

1. אפס; Hebr. 'only' or with כי 'save that, howbeit, etc.' With the following phrase cp. Ps. lxxii 17, II 5 Zakir C 1–2, and less directly *Ugaritica V*, alphabetic text no. 2, rev. 11 (*CML*[2] p. 138; 'the days of sun and moon'). These final lines are written on the body of the stone lion which formed the frontispiece of the monument with the orthostats positioned in a line behind it.

C iii

14. מתם לל; notice the different word order from A ii 16–17 (q.v.).

16. האלם ז 'this god', sing.; see further at A iii 5; an additional phrase not in A (ii 18–19) and referring to the statue on which inscr. C was carved. Too much theological weight can be put on this usage; it prob. reflects no more than attempts to treat various manifestations of a deity as a single entity, and it is perhaps significant that here a number of molten images are involved (C iv 3); cp. ארץ רשפם (Bodashtart i = *KAI* no. 15 = Magnanini, *Iscrizioni,* p. 7), referring prob. to a shrine where there were a number of statues of Resheph.

17. וברך etc. precedes the instructions about sacrifices, whereas in A iii 2 ff. it follows.

19. לתתי; A iii 4. רשאת; A iii 6. Notice that there is no mention here of the other gods of the city (A iii 5).

C iv

2. ילך; Yiph. imperf. 3 masc. sing. (indefinite); cp. A ii 19. Thereafter *KAI* suggests לאלם (with syncope), though there is room for two or even three more letters in the lacuna; restore אש, or perhaps לכל אלם was written by mistake.

3. The mason then adds כל המסכת and resumes with ז, which refers back to אלם, intending presumably the sense as given in the translation. There is at any rate some evidence of confusion; this line is a very short one and the letters are slightly smaller, though it is not strictly speaking a gloss, since it is allotted the normal space for a line and was therefore an addition made as the text was being carved.

4–5. Restored after A iii 1–2.

6–12. Cp. A iii 7–11.

14. Dittography of מ. יאמר 'gives orders' or 'has it in mind'; cp. Gen. xx 11 and the similar formula in II **8** Sefire ii C 1 ff.

15. מחת; infin. costruct. ב 'from'; A iii 14. סמל; here clearly the statue on which the inscr. is carved; cp. Deut. iv 16 Ezek. viii 3, 5 2 Chron. xxxiii 7, 15. No satisfactory derivation has been proposed.

16. שם = [šmō] with vocalic suffix.

18. שמי = [šmī]. עלי; A iii 16.

20. For מלח perhaps read מלך; cp. 2 Kgs. xvi 18 (מבוא) 1 Chron. ix 18.

C v

The imprecations finish on the flank of one of the two steers which form the pedestal of the statue. Only the last two of the six to eight lines of writing can be read, containing the concluding wish that the name of Azitiwada (the name of the city, A ii 10, with י, is written by mistake) may last as long as the sun and the moon (cp. A iv 1–3).

16   Seville (Spain)   Pl. III, 1

The small bronze statuette of a seated and naked goddess (the seat itself is missing) has the inscr. incised on the pedestal (4.1 × 2.8 cm.) and was acquired by the Museo Arqueologico de Sevilla in 1963. It is a votive inscr. erected by two brothers to Astarte. The metal is badly corroded so that several portions of the writing are difficult to read with any certainty, but not so badly that the first editor's dating in the early 8 cent. BC can be seriously called in question. For a comparison of the script with that of other Old Phoen. remains witnessing to Tyro-Sidonian colonization and trade in the Mediterranean world see the introd. to **15** Karatepe.

Bibliography

J. M. Solá-Solé, 'Nueva inscripción fenicia de España (Hispania 14)'; *RSO* 41 (1966), 97–108.

Guzzo Amadasi, *Iscrizioni*, pp. 150–1.

Teixidor, 'Bulletin' for 1968, item 64; 1971, item 106.

M. Delcor, 'L'Inscription phénicienne de la statuette d'Astarté conservée à Séville', *MUSJ* 45 (1969), 321–41.

F. M. Cross, 'The Old Phoenician inscription from Spain', *HTR* 64 (1971), 189–95.

C. R. Krahmalkov, 'Observations on the Phoenician inscription Hispania 14', *Or. Ant.* 11 (1972), 209–14.

W. Herrmann, "ṭtrt- ḥr', *WO* 7 (1973), 135–6.

J. Teixidor, 'A note on the Phoenician inscription from Spain', *HTR* 68 (1975), 197–8.

E. Puech, 'L'Inscription phénicienne du trône d'Aštart à Séville', *RSF* 5 (1977), 85–92.

Illustrations

Solá-Solé, loc. cit., tav. I–II; Guzzo Amadasi, *Iscrizioni*, tav. LXI; Delcor, loc. cit.; Cross, loc. cit. (fig.); Puech, loc. cit. (fig.).

1 ‏--א אשׁ פעל בעלֿיתֿן‎

2 ‏בן דעמֿלך ועבדבעל ב‎

3 ‏ן דעמֿלך בן ישאל ל‎

4 ‏עשתרת חר רבתֿן כ‎

5 ‏שמע קֿל דבֿ]ר[נֿם‎

1. ...... which Baalyatan
2. son of Du'mmilk and Abdbaal
3. son of Du'mmilk of the family of YŠ'L made for
4. our mistress Astarte of Hor, because
5. she heard the voice of their prayers.

NOTES

1. Solá-Solé read מטנׁ׃ 'oblation', lit. 'something erected' (ṬN' Yiph.), but there is room for only two letters before א; Cross נשא 'offering'; cp. נשא לאלם in an inscr. from Constantine (Berthier and Charlier, *Le sanctuaire punique d'El-Hofra*, no. 87, 2) and the Latin transliteration *nasililim (DISO* p. 187); Puech attractively כסא 'throne', though the actual seat is missing and cannot have been anything as substantial as the throne of **30** (Tyre). אש (Cross) was transliterated by Solá-Solé as אז, but the 'z' form of his drawing only appears in Phoen. inscrs. in the 6 cent. (Peckham, *Scripts,* 143). If אז is read, we would have to assume not only a Cypriote influence (the prosthetic א; see at **17** Baal Lebanon) but a Byblian (cp. the relative ז in 4 Ahiram 1). פעל = [p'álū].

2. דעמלך for דעם מלך is already known from a fragmentary Tyrian inscr.; Benz, *Names,* p. 301; cp. דעמצלח from Athens, in the Greek version Δομσαλως (*CIS* i 115). The element is theophorous, perhaps an ephithet, 'the supporter', or the like; cp. Arab. [da'ama].

3. בן denotes as often בני in Hebr. membership of a clan or family group. The name ישאל is not otherwise attested; the verb is unsuitable with a divine name as subject, but the reading בני שאל with prospective suffix (**15** Karatepe A iii 4) is not very likely in a common phrase of this kind. Cp. שאל (**13** Kilamuwa i 4).

4. עשתרת חר is connected by Cross and Herrmann with the cult of Ishtar of Niniveh, who in the mid-2 millenn. BC was known at Ugarit as *Ištar-Ḫurri* and in Egyptian as *'Astar-Ḫuru* (Albright, *Yahweh and the Gods of Canaan,* p. 125 n. 88); and there may be some distant link; but as Teixidor points out, the epithet *Ḫuru* is common in much later Egyptian texts as a designation of Syria-Palestine in general and sometimes of Phoenicia in particular, and it may well have been current with these senses outside Egypt, too; it is thus more likely that חר simply identifies the original home of the goddess, which as of her worshippers was Phoenicia. רבתן = [rabbatōn(ū)] or the like; the form ρυβαθων in an inscr. in Greek letters from Constantine suggests that in Phoen. the connecting vowel before the 1 plur. suffix was the original nomin. [u]; see further Dotan, 'Stress position', p. 107. At this early period, however, it is possible that the appropriate case ending (here genit., i.e. [ē] from [i]) was retained; it was this case that supplied the connecting vowel in Hebr. [ēnū]. A reading רבתם 'their mistress' is not possible as נ‍ם would be required after the genit. [i]; the original case endings were kept before 3 plur. suffixes (see Note on phonology and grammar).

5. שמע = [šamá'ā]; fem. דברנם lit. 'their words'; the second half of the line is badly faded, and either this formula (cp. **21** Malta 5–6; Ps. ciii 20 Deut. i 34) or שמע קלם תברכם as on many votive inscrs. (cp. **32** 3) may be restored.

17   Baal Lebanon (Cyprus)   Fig. 6

The two very similar inscrs. (*a, b*) were pieced together from fragments of thin bronze, which formed parts of decorated bowls used for ceremonial purposes. They are now in the Bibliothèque Nationale in Paris. Exemplars of such bowls, in silver and gold as well as bronze, have been found as far apart as Nimrud in Mesopotamia and Praeneste in Italy (**19**); they date from the 8 and 7 cents. and along with a rather earlier series of ivory carvings represent Phoen. art at its best; see Harden, *Phoenicians*, 186 ff.; Moscati, *Phoenicians*, 66 ff. The present bowls seem to have been made from locally mined copper for the governor (סכן) of the colony at 'Carthage', but we cannot be sure whether the cult of the Baal of Lebanon to whom the bowls were dedicated was widely practised among the colonists or only in the governor's residence. Since the bowls were acquired by purchase (in 1877) from an inhabitant of Limassol, it is likely that 'Carthage' was situated in its vicinity, being therefore a different colony from the main centre of settlement at Kition farther east. The story that they were discovered by chance on a mountain twenty miles from Limassol is prob. a fabrication. The writing (see introd. to **15** Karatepe) shows no great development beyond that of the Kilamuwa incrs. (**13, 14**), but must be considerably later if the Hiram, king of the Sidonians, who is mentioned, is the same as the Hiram, king of Tyre, who paid tribute to the Assyrians in 738 BC (*ANET* p. 283). The annals of Tyre as cited by Josephus have a certain 'Pygmalion' reigning in 774 (see on this name at **18** Gold pendant). We do not know the length of the reigns of these two kings, or even whether their reigns were consecutive, but it seems reasonable on the evidence of this script to place the beginning of Hiram's reign and therefore the date of this inscr. as early as possible, say around 760–750 BC. See the discussion in Peckham, *Scripts,* 14 ff.; McCarter, *Antiquity,* 45 ff.

Bibliography

CIS i 5.
NSE p. 419.
NSI no. 11.
KI no. 17.
KAI no. 31.
Masson and Sznycer, *Recherches,* 77 ff.
Ginsberg, 'Ugaritico-Phoenicia', 145.
Magnanini, *Iscrizioni,* p. 133.
J. Teixidor, loc. cit. (see Bibliogr. to **12** Cyprus grave).

Illustrations

CIS i tab. IV; *NSE* Taf. II, 1; Diringer, *Alphabet,* fig. 122, 1.

[סכן קרתחדשת עבד חרֹם מלך צדנם אז יתן לבעל לבנן אדני   *a.*

בראשת נחשת ה]

[טב סכן קרתחדשת .... [לב]על לבנן אדני   *b.*

a.   [   ] governor of Carthage, servant of Hiram, king of the Sidonians, gave this to Baal of Lebanon, his lord, of the first yield of copper from H ... [

b.   [   ] ṬB, governor of Carthage [to] Baal of Lebanon, his lord.

NOTES

a. סכן; see at **4** Ahiram 2. That there was a Carthage in Cyprus is confirmed by the mention of *Qarti-ḥadasti* as one of ten kingdoms in Cyprus in the annals of Esarhaddon and Ashurbanipal (*ANET* pp. 291, 294). חרם; see at **4** Ahiram 1; he is called king of Tyre in the annals of Tiglathpileser, where there is no mention of Sidon (*ANET* p. 283); it appears that Tyre was the controlling power in Phoenicia at the time. The title Sidonians (in reduced form as in most inscrs. from that city; see at **27** Tabnit 1), however, does not specifically refer here to Tyrian overlordship of Sidon, but goes back to an earlier period when Sidon was the leading power and Sidonians became established as a name for Phoenicians in general; this usage is reflected in Biblical passages like Deut. iii 9 Judg. iii 3 1 Kgs. v 20 etc. and appears as here for Tyre in 1 Kgs. xvi 31 (Ittobaal). זא is the regular form of the demonstrative in the inscrs. from Cyprus; the prosthetic vowel may have arisen because of indigenous influence on the pronunciation of [z], which made it like Greek ζ a double sound [zd] or the like; the א thus fulfils in effect its normal function of breaking up an initial consonantal cluster. בעל לבנן is prob. a title of Baal, chief god of Tyre, associating him with Mt. Lebanon as the same god was in Ugarit associated with Mt. Zephon. אדני with suffix י, identifying the dialect as Tyro-Sidonian. ראשת = [rēšīt] 'first fruits', here prob. of the first yield of copper (Deut. viii 9) from a new mine or the first yield of a certain year from an older mine, the name of the place beginning with ה. Also possible is 'of choicest bronze'; cp. Amos vi 6 (of oils). The ב is either *Beth essentiae* 'as (a gift made of)' or with the manufacture rather than the giving in mind a usage like Hebr. עשה ב 'to make (something) of' (Exod. xxxviii 8), i.e. '(as a gift made) of'.

b. This copy preserves the final two letters of the governor's name.

18   Gold pendant (Carthage)   Fig. 7

Found in 1894 in a burial place in the cemetery of Douimes and now housed in the Musée Lavigerie, the tiny gold pendant or medallion (5 cm. in diameter) has been thought to originate from Cyprus because of the legendary association of Pygmalion with that island; but in fact all the name need suggest is that the first owner had contacts with Cyprus. The inscr. is therefore likely to have been written in Carthage. It records the owner's gratitude to two deities who had delivered him, which prob. means had cured him from a serious illness. The writing is earlier than the date of the grave itself (prob. 7 or 6 cent.), suggesting that the pendant had been handed down as a family heirloom for some generations before being deposited there.

The usual date given is around 700 BC, though I would prefer to place
it rather higher, around the middle of the 8 cent. (cp. particularly מ);
see further in the introd. to **15 Karatepe**. At this early period, when
Carthage was still a Tyrian colony, the language is more appropriately
called Phoen. than Punic.

Bibliography

First publication: Ph. Berger in *CRAIBL,* 1894, 453–8.
See further:
NSE pp. 171 f., 429.
KI no. 70.
RÉS no. 5.
J. Ferron, 'Le médaillon de Carthage', *Cahiers de Byrsa* 8 (1958–9), 45–56.
KAI no. 73.
G. Garbini, 'Sul medaglione di Cartagine', *RSO* 42 (1967), 6–8.
J. Ferron, 'Les problèmes du médaillon de Carthage', *Le Muséon* 81 (1968),
255–61.
Peckham, *Scripts,* 119–24.
CIS i 6057.
Teixidor, 'Bulletin' for 1973, item 137.

Illustrations

NSE Taf. II, 2; Ferron, *Cahiers;* Harden, *Phoenicians,* fig. 35; *KAI* Taf. III; *CIS* i
tab. CXVII.

1 לעשתר

2 ת לפגמלין

3 ידעמלך בן

4 פדי חלץ

5 אש חלץ

6 פגמלין

For Astarte (and) for Pygmalion, (gift of) Yada'milk son of Paday. She
has delivered him whom Pygmalion (also) delivered.

NOTES

1-2. Since there is no copula joining the two names, we should perhaps
render 'For Astarte-Pygmalion', i.e. a composite deity like Milkashtart at
Umm El-'Amed (see at **31** 2); the two deities seem to act separately in the
latter part of the inscr., but this would not preclude their being fused for
cultic purposes. פגמלין; it is almost impossible to unravel the traditions,

classical and mainly Latin (Virgil, Ovid), attached to this name. There seem in fact to have been two Pygmalions, both connected with the Phoen. world, one a king of Tyre whose sister (Elissa or Dido) founded Carthage around 814 BC, the other a mythical or semi-divine king of Cyprus and father of Cynaras. There is also the citation from the annals of Tyre by Josephus which mentions a certain Pygmalion reigning around 774 BC (*Contra Ap.* I, 125; see introd. to **17** Baal Lebanon), who must be the same as the first of these or a successor to him, to which we can add two later allusions in Athenaeus (*Fr. Hist. Gr.* ii 472) to a certain Πυμάτων and in Diodorus Siculus (xix 79) to a certain Πυγμαλίων, both of which must refer to Pumayyatan, a king of Kition and Idalion known from Phoen. inscrs. from Cyprus (e.g. *CIS* i 10, 1). All these references taken together create a presupposition in favour of the name being Semitic, though they do not to my mind justify the conclusion (on which there is a surprisingly large scholarly consensus) that the Greek Pygm– is the same as the two Phoen. divine elements found in proper names, פמי (as in פמיתן, or פמיתן פמי, עבדפמי) and פעם (as in נעמפעם; Latin *Namphamo*; Benz, *Names*, p. 393), it being assumed without much discussion of the phonetic difficulties that the first of these Phoen. elements is a contraction or alternative of the second. It seems to me just as plausible to argue that Pygmalion and Pumayyatan had nothing originally to do with each other and that the confusion between the two names arose in the Greek tradition and was carried over into the Latin. In other words, the king or kings of Tyre around 800 BC and the king of Kition in Cyprus in the 4 cent. were called Pumayyatan, a perfectly acceptable Phoen. proper name compounded of the divine element פמי and the verb 'to give', whereas the name Pygmalion is to be restricted to the early mythology of Cyprus. This name may also be Semitic, composed of the two divine elements Pygm– or פעם (there is no phonetic difficulty in linking these) and עלין 'Most High' or perhaps better אלין or אלאין 'mightiest' (= Ugar. *'al'iyn*, a title of Baal), though I am rather sceptical about this; for it involves us in the unlikely supposition that an originally Semitic divine or semi-divine figure פעמעלין or the like, of whom no trace exists in the Phoen. homeland (the element פעם is, apart from one personal name from Egypt, restricted to Punic names), was at an early stage in the Phoen. colonization of Cyprus so thoroughly appropriated by the non-Semitic population that his name is reproduced according to the Greek form in an 8-cent. Semitic inscription. I am at the moment more inclined to believe that the cult of Pygmalion was native to Cyprus, prob. (for the name is not obviously a Greek formation) going back to pre-Greek (and pre-Phoen.) times. We may therefore conclude that a few Phoenicians were attracted to this cult after settling in Cyprus, and that the family which is associated with the pendant moved later to Carthage, where they continued to venerate him in their own private circle. We know nothing of Pygmalion's character except for a statement by Hesychius that he was on Cyprus equated with Adonis.

3. ידעמלך; the element ידע only occurs here in Phoen. names.

4. פדי is a frequent name in Punic inscrs. (Benz, *Names*, p. 175), which is perhaps an argument that the pendant was manufactured in Carthage for a member of the family born there rather than transported from Cyprus. חלץ = [ḥillēṣā]; Piel fem. with Astarte as subject; though this verb is relatively common in proper names (Benz, op. cit., p. 311), it can hardly here be part of a fuller name פדיחלץ, since פדי is itself a verbal

element from the base 'to redeem'. The meaning is prob. deliverance from a mortal illness; cp. in Hebr. Ps. xviii 20   xci 15   cxvi 8, etc.

5. חלץ; this time masc. with Pygmalion as subject.

19 Praeneste bowl (Italy) Fig. 8

The inscr., consisting only of a proper name, is written in a space in the centre of a richly decorated silver bowl (19 cm. in diameter), found in 1876 in the Bernardini tomb at Praeneste (Palestrina) in Etruria and now in the Museo archeologico di Villa Giulia in Rome. The Egyptian motifs (including mock hieroglyphic inscriptions round the edge which make no sense) suggest that the artefact had been produced in Phoenicia and brought to Italy by traders (Moscati, *Phoenicians*, 68). On the date (*c.*700 BC) see the introd. to **15** Karatepe.

Bibliography

CIS i 164.
Guzzo Amadasi, *Iscrizioni*, Appendix, pp. 157–8.

Illustrations

Harden, *Phoenicians*, fig. 54; Moscati, *Phoenicians*, fig. 23; Guzzo Amadasi, op. cit., tav. LXVII.

אשמניעד ' בן עשתא

NOTES

The name Eshmunya'ad, son of Ashto, may be that either of the artisan or of the owner. On Eshmun, a Sidonian deity, see at **27** Tabnit 2. The verbal element in the first name is from Y'D 'to appoint (a time), designate, assign'. The second name is a hypocoristicon with the termination [a'] (as in **10** Abda) or by this time [ō], added to a shortened form of עשתרת or of עשתר (her male counterpart); cp. the Punic name עשתעזר (Benz, *Names*, p. 174) and עשת on a Phoen. seal; N. Avigad, *IEJ* 16 (1966), 247 ff.

20 Ur box (Mesopotamia)

The inscr. is carved on the lid of an ivory box or casket (11 × 5 cm.) found at Ur, to which it had prob. been carried by a trader or by a soldier in an Assyrian army campaigning in Phoenicia. It is now in the British Museum. On Phoen. ivory carving see Harden, *Phoenicians* 184 ff. and Moscati, *Phoenicians*, 59 ff. The dialect is Tyro-Sidonian; see on [ש]ן (1). On the date (early 7 cent.) see introd. to **15** Karatepe. Dots are used as word-dividers.

The inscr. was first published by Burrows in *JRAS* for 1927, 791–4. See further *KAI* no. 29; Ginsberg 'Ugaritico-Phoenicia', 141.

Illustrations in R. D. Barnett, *A Catalogue of the Nimrud Ivories in the British Museum*, 2nd edit. (1975), pl. CXXXII, and Driver, *Writing*, fig. 56.

1 ארן. [ש]ז. מגן. אמתבעל. בת. פטאס. אמת. אֿ[----]

2 מתת. לעשתרת. אדתי. תברכי. בימי. אדנן [----]א. בן. יסד

1. Ivory casket (which) Amotbaal daughter of PṬ'S, maidservant of ..... gave
2. as a gift to Astarte, her lady. May you bless her in her day(s)! Our master is ...... son of YSD.

NOTES

1. ארן; usually of a sarcophagus (**4** Ahiram 1   **27** Tabnit 2). The restoration ש 'ivory' is Ginsberg's; he points out that the lacuna is rather wide for ז, the usual restoration, i.e. ז[ז], 'this'. Moreover, that demonstrative is elsewhere restricted to the Byblian dialect (**4** Ahiram 2   **25** Yehaumilk 4 ff.), whereas the dialect of this inscr. is clearly Tyro-Sidonian, as is shown by the fem. suffix in אדתי (2); Byblian retains ה all through (**25** Yehaumilk 6). מגן; doubtless Piel (fem.) as in Hebr. (Prov. iv 9); cp. Ugar. *mgn* (G) 'importuned' and Hebr. [magēn] 'beggar' in Prov. vi 1ⅼ. Female names compounded with אמת are common in Phoen. (Benz, *Names*, p. 270). אמת apparently = ['amōt] (cp. the Latin transcriptions *Amobbal* and *Amotmicar*), i.e. a form like Hebr. אחות 'sister' rather than Hebr. אמה 'maidservant'. פטאס is an Egyp. name compounded of a verb 'to give' and the divine name Isis; Benz, op. cit., p. 193. Amotbaal's family may have at one time been in service in Egypt and become partly Egyptianized. The following name was prob. that of her mistress.

2. מתת = [mattat] as in Hebr. (Prov. xxv 14) or perhaps [mattēt] < [mantint] (cp. the Akkad. form of the name of a king of Askalon, *Mitinti; ANET* p. 282). אדתי with again assimilation of [n] of the base (אדן), but with י (= [yā]) for the suffix against Byblian ו (masc.) in אדתו (**8** Elibaal 2). תברכי prob. = [tbar(r)kī̆yā] with suffix [yā] following the 2 fem. imperf. ending [ī]; 'May she bless her' would have been תברך = [tbar(r)kā]; see further at **29** Baalshillem. ימי; the noun may be sing. or plur. (**15** Karatepe A iii 1). אדנן = ['dōnōn(ū)] or the like; see on this suffix at **16** Seville 4. 'Our lord' may have been Amotbaal's master and the husband of her mistress. יסד; a Semitic element from the base 'to found, establish'.

21, 22   Malta   Pl. VIII, 1 (**21**)

The two votive steles with their similar inscrs. were discovered in 1820 buried in a field near Rabat-Medina. The first stele (*CIS* i 123), of which a photograph and several sketches were taken last century, was thought to have been lost, but it has recently been found intact in the National Museum in Valletta; it measures 23.5 cm. in height by 8 cm. in breadth. The second stele (*CIS* i 123 *bis*), apparently in a much worse state of preservation, was jealously guarded by the local family into whose possession it came, and eventually disappeared; it was never photographed and is known now only from a single copy. The writing on both texts is Old Phoen., not greatly different from that of the inscrs. discussed in the introd. to **15** Karatepe. A date in the 7 cent., as suggested by Peckham, *Scripts,* 106 f., and by Sznycer, is indicated; I would myself think quite early in the cent. (cp. **ʾ**); McCarter, *Antiquity,* 49, argues for the late 8 cent. It is noteworthy that Carthaginian influence in Malta is not attested archaeologically befor the 6 cent. BC (Moscati, *Phoenicians,* 109). Culturally, therefore, these inscrs. are of some importance; they not only give us our earliest epigraphic trace of the widespread practice of child-sacrifice (מלך), but give us it in a Phoen. rather than a Punic context. There seems no reason to doubt that this practice, which so horrified classical writers, was (along with the cult of Baal-Hammon, the deity to whom the sacrificed infants were dedicated) transported to Malta straight from Tyre without any Carthaginian mediation. It may have been from Tyre also (or from a more immediate Canaanite source) that the practice reached Israel, where, if we are to judge from the fierceness of the condemnations in certain Biblical passages, it established itself more firmly among the ordinary people than Biblical scholars may sometimes care to admit. It must therefore be by chance that no *topheths* (Hebr. תפת '(place of) burning') have so far been excavated in Phoenicia itself.

Bibliography

The earliest notice to which I have had access is Gesenius, *Scripturae linguaeque phoeniciae monumenta quotquot supersunt* (1837), 107–11.
See further:
CIS i 123 and 123 *bis.*
NSE p. 426.
NSI no. 37.
KI no. 54.
R. Dussaud, 'Précisions épigraphiques touchant les sacrifices puniques d'enfants', *CRAIBL,* 1946, 371–87.
KAI no. 61 A, B.
Guzzo Amadasi, *Iscrizioni,* pp. 19–23.
M. Sznycer, 'Antiquités et épigraphie nord-sémitiques', *Annuaire de l'école pratique des hautes études,* IVe sect. (1974–5), 199–203.

Illustrations

NSE Taf. II 4 (**21**); Guzzo Amadasi, *Iscrizioni,* tav. II (**21**), fig. 2 (**22**); Sznycer, loc. cit., pl. II (**21**).

On the מלך sacrifice see in addition:
O. Eissfeldt, *Molk als Opferbegriff im Punischen und Hebräischen und das Ende des Gottes Moloch* (1935).

A. Alt in *WO* 1 (1947–52), 282 f. (Karatepe).

J. G. Février, 'Molchomor', *RHR* 143 (1953), 8–18.

A. Berthier and R. Charlier, *Le sanctuaire punique d'El-Hofra à Constantine* (1955), 29 ff.

J. Hoftijzer, 'Eine Notiz zum punischen Kinderopfer', *VT* 8 (1958), 288–92.

R. de Vaux, *Ancient Israel: its life and institutions*, Engl. transl. (1961), 441–6.

ANET p. 658.

M. Weinfeld, 'The worship of Molech and the Queen of Heaven and its background', *Ug.-Forsch.* 4 (1972), 133–54.

M. Smith, 'A note on burning babies', *JAOS* 95 (1975), 477–9.

Lipiński, 'North Semitic texts', 234–7.

21   1   נצב מלך

2   בעל אש ש

3   ם נחם לב

4   על חמן א

5   דן כ שמע

6   קל דברי

Stele of a (human) sacrifice of one making (it), which Nahum set up for Baal-Hammon, lord, because he heard the voice of his prayers.

NOTES

1. מלך; a noun of the structure [maktēb] formed from the base HLK/YLK but taking its meaning from the causative stem, i.e. 'a bringing, offering, sacrifice'; cp. ילך זבח (Yiph.; **15** Karatepe A ii 19 C iv 2). The Hebr. nouns עולה and קרבן are similarly formed from the Qal but take their meaning from the Hiphil. The Latin transcription *molchomor* (see at **22** 1) suggests a 'segholate' form, but there are examples of transcriptions in which a full vowel or even syllables are not indicated; e.g. *Boncar* for *Bodmilkar* (i.e. בדמלקרת; Segert, *Grammar,* p. 77); they are mostly of proper names, but *molch* as a technical term could be held to be analogous. Note also the spelling מלאך (Berthier and Charlier, op. cit., no. 54, 2). For other less plausible etymologies see *DISO* p. 154. But whatever the derivation, the syntax of *KAI* no. 99 Sousse 2, which can only mean 'his gift is a בעל מלך', sets it beyond dispute that the word is synonymous with מתנת. It would seem, therefore, that Hebrew tradition has erred, whether intentionally or through ignorance, in treating מלך in Lev. xviii 21; xx 2, 3, 4, 5; 2 Kgs. xxiii 10, and Jerem. xxxii 35 as the name of a Canaanite deity, [mōlek] as pointed in the Tiberian text or *Moloch* as transliterated in the Septuagint and Vulgate. In all of these passages except one we have the phrase למלך, and a translation 'as a sacrifice' makes excellent sense (so *NEB* margin in 2 Kgs. xxiii 10); with ל meaning 'as' cp. Deut. vi 8 Isa. xlii 6. [The exception is Lev. xx 5 where peculiarly

אחרי is used instead of ל; *NEB* margin renders '(lust) after human sacrifice'.] The value of the Biblical references lies in the fact that they all have to do with the sacrificing of children (by a process of burning) and enable us in the absence of clear statements in the inscrs. to establish that מלך was the Canaanite-Phoen. technical term for human sacrifice. It is worth adding that if מלך in these Biblical passages is not a divine name, the sacrifices recorded must have been dedicated to Yahweh, which would certainly have given a motive to the orthodox circles responsible for the transmission of the Bible to falsify the tradition. מלך בעל has usually been understood as 'a sacrifice to Baal', a rather nebulous description and one moreover that fits exceedingly ill with the fact that the deity mentioned in all inscrs. of this type is Baal-Hammon, which is a title not of Baal but of El (see below). In these inscrs. בעל is one of several expressions used in conjunction with מלך, the two chief others being אדם and (as in the next text) אמר. If אדם and אמר, as is commonly assumed, mean respectively 'sacrifice of a human (child)' and 'sacrifice of a lamb', sc. in place of a human child, it seems reasonable to argue that בעל should be given a similar specific reference. Février's proposal that it should be read as the prepos. ב with the noun ['ūl] 'infant' (Hebr. and Ugar.), i.e. '(a sacrifice) in exchange for an infant', presumably of some other animal than a lamb, has been accepted by *KAI* and a number of other authorities. In my view it is illegitimate, arising out of a misunderstanding of the so-called *Beth pretii*; as far as I can judge, this ב always signifies the means by which a transaction is accomplished (e.g. Exod. xxxiv 20 'you shall redeem the firstling of an ass with a lamb') and never describes the transaction itself, though in translation it may sometimes seem to (thus Deut. xix 21 'life for life' means properly 'you shall avenge a life by taking the life of him who took it' rather than 'you shall take a murderer's life in place of the life he took'; similarly in Phoen. **13** Kilamuwa i 8 means 'a maid he had to sell to me at the price of a sheep' and not 'he had to give me back a maid in exchange for the sheep I gave to him'). A much more straightforward solution is to take בעל in its simple sense of 'citizen' (cp. *ANET*) or perhaps better 'offerer, sacrificer' (Lipiński; cp. the Punic phrse בעל (ה)זבח, *CIS* i 167 = *KAI* no. 74 Carthage Tariff 2, 3, etc.), and to interpret אמר, with which it is closely associated in the Malta find, in the light of this, especially since there is considerable doubt about whether vocalizing אמר as the word for 'lamb' is phonetically feasible; see at **22** 1–2. These two epithets at least, therefore, should be regarded as referring not to the kind of sacrifice but to the status or the attitude of the sacrificer. I am inclined to interpret אדם along the same lines as meaning '(human) sacrifice made by an individual', as opposed to the mass public sacrifices of infants which classical authors tell us were sometimes held in Punic cites; see Moscati, *Phoenicians*, 142. On the other hand, the two difficult phrases בשרם בתם (usually in apposition to מלך אדם) and אזרם אש(ת)ת (usually the object of the verbs זבח or נשא and qualified by במלך 'as a (human) sacrifice') are more likely to describe the sacrifice. On the first see *DISO* p. 154 and Lipiński, loc. cit.; and on the second the Note to **28** Eshmunazar 3.

2–3. שם; cp. Gen. xxviii 22 2 Kgs. xxi 7 Jerem. vii 30. נחם; cp. the Hebr. names Naham and Nahum.

3–4. בעל חמן; a title of El associating him with a place Hammon near Tyre; see further at **13** Kilamuwa i 16. The title must have been transported by Tyrian traders and settlers both to the Zenjirli region and to Carthage, where the god so-called became the chief Punic divinity; and as I argue in the introd., his worship, including the savage practice attached to it, prob. reached Malta directly through similar intermediaries and not via Carthage. Notice אדן unusually without a suffix.

5–6. Cp. **16** Seville 4–5.

22 1 נצ֗ב מלך

2 אמר אש ש

3 [ם אר]שׁ֗ לֹבעל

4 [חמן] אדן

5 [כ ש]מֹ֗ע קֹלֹ

6 [דב]רי

Stele of a (human) sacrifice of one promising (it), which [Arsh] set up for Baal-[Hammon], lord, [because] he heard the voice of his [prayers].

NOTES

1–2. מלך אמר; the words are transcribed *molchomor* and qualify the phrase 'a great nocturnal sacrifice' in Latin inscrs. of offerings made to Saturn found at Ngaus (formerly Nicivibus) in Algeria. These inscrs., which belong to around AD 200, show the survival of the old Punic מלך offering in a Latin-speaking environment, Saturn being the Latin counterpart of Baal-Hammon (El); but the sacrifice is not of a child but of a lamb, apparently made on a child's behalf by his or her parents (*agnum pro vikario*). There are also carvings of a ram on the steles. For the text and photographs see Eissfeldt, op. cit., 2 ff. and Taf. I. This would appear to be powerful evidence in favour of rendering אמר as 'lamb'. But even allowing for the vagaries of classical transcribers, it is very difficult to see how –*omor* could have arisen out of ['immar], in which neither of the vowels is of the [o, u] class. Similarly, the discovery of bones of small animals among the human bones at certain Punic *topheths* makes it very likely that the substitution of an animal for a child was sometimes permitted among the Carthaginians and their subjects, as it was clearly the general practice among the Latin speakers of Nicivibus. But again this evidence is indirect and it ought not to be given precedence over phonetic considerations. As Lipiński points out, –*omor* looks much more like a partic., either active ([ʾōmēr]) or passive ([ʾamūr]), of the verb 'to say'. This verb is not common in Phoen. remains, but it is found; **15** Karatepe C iv 14   **28** Eshmunazar 2. The distinction between בעל and אמר may then be that between a parent who actually carries through the sacrifice of his child and one who merely 'promises' (perhaps in his wife's early pregnancy or at the birth) to sacrifice him or her in the future; or perhaps between a parent who is present at or takes part in the sacrifice and one who 'instructs' others to make it for him; or even (reading a passive partic.) between one who willingly undertakes the sacrifice and one who has to be 'commanded' to perform the task. These suggestions may sound naïve, but we should not forget the poignancy of the dilemma in which this distressing custom placed those whose religion commended it as a duty.

3 ff. The restorations are made on the basis of the previous text. The last letter of the personal name in 3 was previously assumed to be מ, and the name Nahum was restored as in **21** 3. But there is no trace in the copy of a downward stroke and a name ending with שׁ is preferable; the restoration ארשׁ, a common name in Phoen. and Punic texts (Benz, *Names,* p. 64), is due to Dussaud. The inscrs. were therefore drawn up by different people and should be given separate numbers. [Note that it was also Dussaud who was the first to read אמר in *1.* 2; the previous reading was אסר, and the two inscrs. were linked respectively with two otherwise unknown composite deities Milk-Baal and Milk-Osiris, though commentators were unable to give a reason why the inscrs. should also be dedicated to Baal-Hammon.]

IV

INSCRIPTIONS IN A MIXED OLD
PHOENICIAN-ARAMAIC DIALECT

23 Arslan Tash i   Fig. 15

THE two small limestone plaques treated in this chapter are inscribed
with incantations against various malevolent divinities and demons.
They were acquired by purchase in Arslan Tash (the ancient *Ḥadattu*)
in Upper Syria in 1933 and are now in the Aleppo Museum. The
holes on the top of the tablets were evidently meant for hanging them
up at the doors of private houses.

Contents (i)

The first plaque, measuring 8.2 cm. high, 6.7 cm. broad, and 2.2
cm. thick, was published in 1939. It contains in relief on the obverse
face the figures of a winged and helmeted sphinx and of a she-wolf
with scorpion's tail in the act of swallowing a human child. On the
reverse is a figure carved in the Assyrian manner of a threatening
deity pictured as a bearded warrior wielding an axe. The main inscr.
was carved around and between the three figures and continued on
the edges of the plaque; three minor inscrs. in smaller lettering were
carved on the figures themselves, though that on the figure of the
deity also uses some of the space between the lines of the main
inscription. The incantation as it is interpreted here is directed against
the evil forces or spirits which the three figures represent, viz. a
goddess named 'T' who belongs to a class of demons called 'Flying
ones' (19) and 'night creatures' (20), a male deity called SSM who is
clearly a malignant power, also associated with the night (22 ff.),
though from the appearance of his name as an element in several
Phoen. and Punic proper names we may suppose that he was not
always so regarded, and a female demon called 'Strangler (or breaker
of the neck) of the lamb'. A similar title to the last is known in the
Arabic world as that of a child-stealing demon, and this has led some
to assume that 'T' and the 'Flying ones', and the god SSM, were also
demonic enemies of mothers in labour and young children; but it is
more reasonable to conclude that the plaque is a means of guarding
its owner and his house (cp. 5–8) against a number of different
demonic attackers (see the Note to *l.* 20). Of particular interest to

students of the Bible is the owner's claim in *ll.* 9 ff. to have a 'pact' or 'covenant' with a pantheon of deities who included Ashur, Baal, and Horon. Zevit regards these lines as the first clearly attested expression of non-Israelite covenant theology from the ancient Near East; there is substance in this claim, but I doubt whether the stress he lays on it is justified. It is not apparent to me that the lines reflect a 'credo' of the religious community to which the owner belongs, which he draws upon for his own private purposes in this text, rather than being simply a form of words derived from the practice of secular covenant-making in general, which he adapts, perhaps on the model of other incantation texts unknown to us, in order to elicit divine aid. For references, usually disapproving, to incantations in the Bible see Isa. xix 3 xlvii 9, 12 Jerem. viii 17; their use is specifically forbidden in Deut. xviii 10–11; cp. 2 Kgs. xxiii 24. For parallels from Mesopotamian and other cultures see H. Ringgren, *Religions of the Ancient Near East,* 34 ff., 89 ff., and the article of Gaster (1942).

Script and orthography

The script of the two plaques is Aramaic in style and finds its nearest counterpart in the Aram. endorsements on cuneiform tablets from Niniveh; see Table of Scripts in vol. II. The plaques may therefore be placed with them in the 7 cent. BC. The orthography has also been exposed to Aram. influence. Leaving aside the names of the divine beings, there are three instances (שמנה, i 18; שדה, ii 4, 5) of ה and one instance (כי, ii 10) of י being employed as final *matres lectionis.* More significant orthographically, however, are the cases where a final vowel is not so represented in the writing; e.g. בן אלם (i 11) and עבר (i 20), both plur. forms. These spellings are quite anomalous in an Aram.-speaking area and must be due to an acquaintance with Phoen. 'consonantal' writing. I cannot think of a parallel to such a mixing of two different orthographic practices; the closest is **14** Kilamuwa ii, which uses a Phoen. orthography for an Aram. text, which is not really the same thing.

Language

The language of the plaques is at first sight equally mixed in character, and has often been described as Phoen. adulterated by some Aram. forms. This explanation, envisaging a small community of Phoenicians living as a minority among Aramaeans and being affected in their speech by their environment, does not seem to me to be entirely satisfactory, and I am attracted by Segert's definition of it (*Grammar,* p. 29) as a hitherto unknown inland Canaanite dialect. Thus the usage of the 3 masc. sing. and fem. sing. suffixes is as in

Phoen. and more precisely Tyro-Sidonian; פי (i 16), צרתי (i 17). Phoen. also is the relative אש (ii 4). But the absence of diphthongs (בת, i 5; עז, ii 11) and the fem. sing. ending ת (e.g. לחשת, i 1, ii 1; אלת, i 9; בנת, ii 10) are features of Moabite as well as Phoen. (see vol. I, 72 ff.); the masc. plur. ending ן found e.g. in קדשן (i 12) is Moabite as well as Aram.; and the lack (except in the name עפתא, i 19) of any article or emphatic state is an interesting isogloss with the semi-Aram. dialect of Zenjirli (see vol. II, 62 ff.) Such a combination of features invites, as indeed does the region from which the plaques originate, a classification as a fringe dialect comparable with the dialects of Moab and Zenjirli, one, that is, not easily placed within the Canaanite or the Aramaic subdivisions of Syrian or Northwest Semitic. On the other hand, the fact that two masc. plur. forms end in ם (אלם, i 11; שממ, i 13) is a strong argument in favour of the traditional opinion, or at least of a more careful rephrasing of it. One does not expect to find two different endings for the same grammatical form in a genuine spoken dialect, fringe or otherwise. The same holds for עפתא (i 19) and ללין (i 20), which, if I interpret them aright, are conflate Phoen.-Aram. formations. It is difficult to avoid the conclusion that the writers intentionally mix Phoen. and Aram. forms in order to impart a 'magical' flavour to their texts and thus increase the potency of the incantations, in other words, that both the language and the orthography are artificial creations specially concocted for this genre of writing. The view of Torczyner and Bange that the dialect is Israelite or northern Hebr. cannot be seriously entertained.

Difficulties of text and interpretation

The problem of identifying the language is not helped by the uncertainty of the text in not a few faded or damaged sections, especially on the first plaque, and this in its turn seriously affects the confidence that can be placed in any single interpretation, the present one included. The commentator has not only to form judgements on the basis of several sets of disappointing photographs, none of which is adequate by itself though each usefully highlights different parts of the surface, but he has to contend with substantial disagreements among a number of expert epigraphists. The text of the second plaque is rather better preserved, but is so enigmatic that differences of interpretation are if anything wider. It is apparent that considerably more research will be needed before accepted solutions of these puzzling inscrs. are reached.

Poetic structure

The texts of both inscrs. are capable of being arranged in a rough metrical order with three or four main stresses to a line of poetry, though there is no obvious concern with parallelism. This semi-poetic structure was no doubt imposed to facilitate the chanting or murmuring of the spells by members of the families concerned as they passed the plaques on entering or leaving their houses. On further surviving traces of poetic style in the Phoen. inscrs. see the introduction to **13** Kilamuwa i and **28** Eshmunazar.

Bibliography

First: Comte du Mesnil du Buisson, 'Une tablette magique de la région du Moyen Euphrate', *Mélanges syriens offerts à M. René Dussaud*, I (1939), 421–34.

W. F. Albright, 'An Aramean magical text in Hebrew from the seventh century B.C.', *BASOR* 76 (1939), 5–11.

A. Dupont-Sommer, 'L'Inscription de l'amulette d'Arslan Tash', *RHR* 120 (1939), 133–59.

T. H. Gaster, 'A Canaanite magical text', *Orientalia* 11 (1942), 41–79.

H. Torczyner, 'A Hebrew incantation against night-demons from Biblical times', *JNES* 6 (1947), 18–29; with reply by Gaster, 186–8.

A. van den Branden, 'La tavolette magica di Arslan Tash', *Bibbia e Oriente* 3 (1961), 41–7.

KAI no. 27.

ANET p. 658.

F. M. Cross, R. J. Saley, 'Phoenician incantations on a plaque of the seventh century B.C. from Arslan Tash in Upper Syria', *BASOR* 197 (1970), 42–9.

Bange, *Vowel-Letters*, pp. 137 f.

Magnanini, *Iscrizioni*, pp. 48–50.

A. Caquot, 'Observations sur la première tablette magique d'Arslan Tash', *JANES* 5 (1973), 45–51.

W. Röllig, 'Die Amulette von Arslan Taş', *NESE* 2 (1974), 17–28.

A. Zevit, 'A Phoenician inscription and biblical covenant theology', *IEJ* 27 (1977), 110–18.

Lipiński, 'North Semitic texts', 247 ff.

Illustrations

Du Mesnil du Buisson, loc. cit., pl. at p. 422; figs. 1, 5 a–d; *ANEP* no. 662; Cross and Saley, op. cit., fig. 1 (reverse); Röllig, op. cit., Taf. II–III. Note also that Caquot had access to a squeeze made at the time of discovery.

Obverse:

1 לחשת ' לעתא ' אלת > ' ל <

2 ססם ' בֿן פדרשׁ

3 שא אל}וֿ{

4 ול ' חנקת ' א

5 מר ' בת אבא '

6 בל תבאן

Reverse:

7 וחצר ' אדרך

8 בל ' תדרכן ' כ

9 רת ' לן ' אלת

10 עלם אשר ' כרת

11 לן ' וכל בן אלם '

12 ורב ' דר כל ' קדשן

13 באלת ' שממ ' וארץ ' ע

14 דֿ ' עלם ' באלת ' בעל

Bottom edge:

15 [אדן ' כ]לֿ ' ארץ ' באלֿת '

Left edge:

16 [א]שֿת חורן ' אש ' רֿתם ' פי

Top edge:

17 ושבע ' צרתי ' ושם

Right edge:

18 נה ' אשת ' בעל ק[ד]שׁ

On the sphinx:

19 לעפתא ' בחדר ' חשך

20 עבר פעם ' פעם ' ללין

On the she-wolf:

21 בבֿת ' לֿחצת ' הלך

On and near the figure of the god:

22 מֿצֿֿא ' ל

23 פתח

24 י ' וא

25 ור ' ל

26 מזזת ' יצא ' שמש

27 סֿסֿם

28 חלף ' ולדֿ

29 עף

1. Incantation against 'T', goddess, ⟨against⟩

2. SSM son of PDRŠ-

3. Š', god,

4. and against the Breaker-of-the-lamb's-neck:

5. The house I enter

6. you shall not enter,

7. and the courtyard I tread

8. you shall not tread.

9. Ashur had made an eternal pact

10. with us, he has made (it)

11. with us, and all the sons of the gods

12. and the numerous generation of all the Holy ones (have made it);

13. (it is accompanied) by oaths of the heavens and the earth,

14. the eternal witnesses; by oaths of Baal,

15. [the lord of all] the earth; by oaths

16. of the wife of Horon, whose mouth is bound,

17. and of her seven co-wives, of the eight

18. wives of the holy Master.

19. Against the Flying ones: From the dark chamber

20. pass now, now, night demons!

21. From the house begone outside!

22. It has arrived at

23. my door

24. and has

25. thrown light on the

26. doorposts; the sun has risen!

27. SSM,

28. pass on and for all time

29. fly away!

NOTES

1. לחשת; cp. Ugar. *lḥšt* 'whisper'; Akkad. *luḫḫušu* 'to whisper', used particularly of murmuring an incantation; Hebr. מלחשים 'charmers' (Ps. lviii 6); לחש 'whisper' (Isa. xxvi 16), 'charm' (Jerem. viii 17 with ל 'against'), 'amulet' (Isa. iii 20). The next word in the text is עתא, which most commentators assume to be an error for עפתא (19), which is written on the body of the sphinx. There is prob. a mistake (dittography) at the end of 3, but that does not involve so important a word as the name or title of a goddess (אלת); and it seems a wiser policy with du Mesnil to connect 'T' with the second element in the conflate name Atargatis (Aram. עתרעתא), an Aramaean goddess known in sources of the Hellenistic period and pictured with the attributes of a winged sphinx at Baalbek; see H. Seyrig, *Syria* 10 (1929), 330 ff., and cp. the (male) composite deity Milkashtart at Umm El-'Amed (**31** iv 2). Whether עתא is a form of the name Anat, sister of Baal and in the Ugar. texts (e.g. **3** B, where she slaughters her own guests), an erratic and often malevolent goddess, is more questionable. At the end of the line I am more inclined to restore ⟨ל⟩; there is room for a letter, though there is no trace of one on the photographs. On the other hand, we may regard the first ל as a 'double-duty' prepos. qualifying both עתא and ססם; this is a well-known feature of Ugar. verse and increasingly to be recognized in Hebr. poetry; see M. Dahood, *Psalms* III, 435 ff., and for another possible example in Phoen. **28** Eshmunazar 16–17. An alternative interpretation of the opening lines (assuming restoration of ל) is to take the three instances of ל (the third occurs in 4) as 'vocative *Lamedhs*', a usage well attested in Ugar. (see *CML*² p. 149) and occasionally in Hebr. (e.g. Ezek. xxxiv 2), i.e. 'Incantation: O Flyers etc.'. This interpretation is not, however, so suitable in ii 1, where if מזה is vocative, there is (on my interpretation) a very large gap before an imperative construction occurs. A third interpretation, not so convincing, is the translation (cp. *ANET*, Caquot, Lipiński), 'Incantation against the Flying ones (Lipiński: for the right moment). Pact of SSM, son of PDRŠ. Speak the following (lit. lift these) and say to the strangling demons ...' This, while it removes from the text a double meaning of אלת ('goddess' here and 'covenant, pact' in 9 ff.) and incidentally makes SSM (in spite of his axe) a beneficent deity, identifies עפתא too closely with חנקת, as if they were interchangeable names, when in fact we have two quite different creatures pictured in the figures on the plaque; it also involves a rather awkward and stilted syntax.

2. ססם; a deity known elsewhere only from proper names (Benz, *Names*, p. 368). Caquot regards the doubtful ש at the end of the line as a larger than usual dividing stroke (cp. the one at the end of ii 6), which would make the name of the god's father PDR, a deity known at Ugarit (see *CML*² p. 47, n. 1). For some speculations on the fuller name PDRŠŠ' see W. Fauth in *ZDMG* 120 (1979), 229 ff.

3. אלו. If אל 'god' qualifies ססם as אלת 'goddess' qualifies עתא, the ו must be a case of dittography. Caquot, who renders שא אלו by 'pronounce these (words)', compares Mishnaic Hebr. ['illū] and Poenulus *ily*. For the verb NŠ(Ś)' in phrases implying direct speech see Brown, Driver, Briggs, *Lexicon*, p. 670.

4. חנק 'to break the neck' like a dog shaking a rabbit rather than lit. 'strangle'; cp. Nah. ii 13 (of a lion dispatching its prey). The precise

parallel with Arab. *ḫānūq al-ḥamal* 'strangler of the lamb', a by-name of the female wolf-like demon called *Qarīnat*, who was believed to attack and carry off children during the hours of darkness (du Mesnil), suggests that only one creature is meant here, though there is an allusion in Ugar. to *'iltm ḫnqtm* 'the two strangling goddesses' (*Ugaritica* V p. 594).

5. With the omission of ב before בת construed with the verb BW' cp. Judg. xviii 18 2 Kgs. xi 19. Note also the omission of the relative, frequent in Hebr. poetry and not uncommon in prose (unless we prefer to regard the nouns in such examples as being in the construct before the following clause). The parallelism of בת and חצר (7) is found both in Hebr. (Ps. lxxxiv 11 xcii 14 cxxxv 2 etc.) and in Ugar. (e.g. **3** E 46–47 **14** 132–133).

6. בל; see at **28** Eshmunazar 3. The final ן of תבאן is not drawn in du Mesnil's sketch but is perfectly clear on his photograph. The verb is prob. masc. (indicative ending [ūn]; see at **13** Kilamuwa i 10), since ססם is included. If the address is only to the 'Stranglers', it will be fem. ([nā]).

8. A letter has been erased after כ at the end, prob. ר; Cross and Saley think it is visible enough to be another case of dittography (cp. 3).

9. In Hebr. כרת ברית is frequently followed by ל, as is אלת here, instead of the usual את or עם; cp. Josh. ix 6, 1 Sam. xi 1, 2 Sam. v 3, and particularly apposite Jerem. xxxii 40 (ברית עולם). In Hebr. אלה has the more precise meaning 'covenant oath' as distinct from 'covenant', but in a number of passages there is evidence that the distinction is breaking down; cp. Deut. xxix 11 where it and ברית are both objects of the verb כרת and ibid. 19, 20, where both words are successively qualified by the adject. כתובה. לן 'with us', i.e. with all the inhabitants of the house, or possibly 'with me' (cp. **27** Tabnit 4).

10. עלם; cp. Jerem. xxxii 40 and many other passages in Hebr. where it qualifies ברית. אשר; the god Ashur, who has apparently replaced (or been identified with) El as the head of an otherwise Canaanite pantheon; this would be an act of deference towards the Assyrian imperial power. Cross and Saley render עלם by 'the Eternal One', i.e. El (though they cite no specific parallel), and make it the subject of the first כרת, with (following some earlier commentators) אשר = Asherah, i.e. Ugar. *'aṯrt*, El's consort, as subject of the second (though the name of this goddess, or rather אשרת, which would be the expected form, does not occur in any Phoen. inscription). They assume that in this form only the Phoen. [at] has become vocalic, citing Hebr. as a parallel; it would also be possible to cite Aram. and note this as another instance of intentional mixing of dialects. Lipiński makes ססם the subject of both clauses (he translates אלת in 1 by 'treaty of SSM') and seems to render אשר by 'bond'.

11. בן אלם; **15** Karatepe A iii 19 Ps. xxix 1 lxxxix 7.

12. רב 'the multitude of' or possibly 'the chief of' (i.e. El). דר; see **15** Karatepe A iii 19 and references there; in 28 the word has its other meaning '(for) ever'. קדשן; cp. Hebr. קדשים in Ps. lxxxix 6, 8 (with קהל and סוד) Job v 1 xv 15. This and the following two lines transgress the margin; their final letters are visible on the right edge of the plaque under the word ק[ד]ש (18). See Röllig's photo. (Taf. III, 4).

13. באלת is very awkwardly rendered 'along with a pact of …', and perhaps here is plur., i.e. 'along with oaths uttered by …', a meaning that suits particularly well in 16. Zevit interestingly compares the construction

with the Hebr. *Beth instrumenti,* or more exactly that variety of it wherein a transitive verb is sometimes strangely followed by ב rather than a direct object; e.g. נתן בקולו (Ps. xlvi 7) over against יתן קולו (Amos i 2). The verb in question is כרת in 7, i.e. 'All the sons of the gods etc. have established with us a covenant of heaven and earth etc.' There is rather a large gap, however, between כרת and באלת, which tells against this solution. For the invocation of heaven and earth in association with ceremonies of covenant making see II **7** Sefire i A 11 Deut. iv 26 xxx 19 Isa. i 2. עד; this reading is due to Caquot, who points to the traces of ע on the right edge to the left of the ו of the previous line and to the right of the (ב)על of the next line. The ד (14) is just visible to the right of the deity's foot. In the context 'the eternal witnesses' is better than 'for ever'.

15. The beginning and end of this line, written on the bottom edge, are badly mutilated. In du Mesnil's photo. (fig. 5a) the last letter of the word before ארץ is partially visible. Caquot restores [אדן כ]ל, which fills the available space better than the usual [אד]ן. The same title occurs in Josh. iii 11 Ps. xcvii 5 Mic. iv 13 Zech. iv 14 vi 5, predicated of Yahweh. Cp. also Baal's frequent epithet in the Ugar. myths (e.g. **3** A 3–4) *zbl b'l 'ars* 'the prince, lord of earth'. At the end באלת can just be traced, after which there seems to be a dividing stroke. Caquot regards this as the letter י, i.e. באלתי, which he thinks finishes the sentence, though he has difficulty giving a meaningful translation (cp. also Lipiński).

16. This line is written on the left edge (left, that is, looking at the obverse). The first visible letter can hardly be other than שׁ, though it is rather large; there is space before it for a further one or two letters. There is no justification, therefore, for Cross and Saley's reading לת (16) {באל}, which would give another case of dittography. Caquot restores [לח]שׁת and argues that a new incantation starts here and occupies the two side and top edges of the tablet. He points out that the line begins on the opposite side of the tablet from the end of 15 and that the scribe must have turned the tablet over to write it, whereas if he had been continuing the same phrase he would most naturally have used the right edge. This is true, but is perhaps not so significant an observation as it seems when one considers that he prob. held the tablet in his hand and would be shifting its position all the time as he wrote. The best restoration seems to me to be אשׁת (du Mesnil); א is a broad letter and the mention of Horon's (chief) wife both explains the reference to his own mouth being bound (he himself could not utter the oaths) and supplies an antecedent to צרתי 'her co-wives'. חורן; perhaps an Aram. spelling with the diphthong marked. The god Horon appears by name in many sources of the 2 and 1 millenn. BC (in Palestine in the place-name Beth-Horon), but little is known about him. He was apparently a chthonic and therefore one assumes a dangerous deity; thus he is invoked to deliver punishment twice in the Ugar. myths (**2** i 7 ff. **16** vi 54 ff.), yet he plays as here a more positive role in the long but difficult text RS 24.244 (*CML*² pp. 138–9), prob. a charm against snake-bite, which he alone among all the gods is able to remove. רתם 'to attach, bind' (cp. Mic. i 13); the clause prob. contains a mythological allusion, whether it is Horon's own mouth that is bound (in my view the most likely interpretation) or whether he has bound his wife's mouth or, às Caquot argues, 'her mouth', meaning one of the female demons. פי =

[pīyū] (or fem. [pīyā]); the noun is nomin. (or accus.), but it ends in a 'long' vowel and therefore takes the suffix in י.

17. צרתי with the fem. suffix [yā], the noun being genit.; it means lit. 'rival (-wives)'; cp. 1 Sam. i 6.

18. אשת; in Hebr. this plur. form occurs only in Ezek. xxiii 44; there is no other certain example in Phoen., but it was prob. the regular form, since the plur. of אש is אשם (15 Karatepe A i 15). The pairing of seven and eight in this passage has been compared with the peculiar numerical idiom of Ugar. and Hebr. poetry found in, e.g. 14 Keret 8–9 ('seven brothers ... eight mother's sons'), Prov. vi 16 ('six ... seven'); but if Horon's chief wife is counted (16), the arithmetic of the two clauses is the same. בעל קדש 'holy lord' or perhaps 'lord of the sanctuary', an epithet of Horon; cp. שר קדש of Eshmun (28 Eshmunazar 17). The ק and ש of קדש can be seen on the obverse of du Mesnil's sketch, this word having been pushed almost on to the face of the tablet by the long lines 12–14.

19. Understand לחשת before ל or possibly take ל as a vocative particle (see at 1). עפתא is apparently a plur. form meaning 'the (fem.) flying ones', since it has to be related syntactically to ללין in 20; it is not, however, a pure Aram. form, since in Aram. participles from medially weak bases retain the י (or have א in its place). It seems that we have a mixed form, perhaps intentionally created for such decidedly odd texts, consisting of a Phoen. fem. plur. partic. עפת and an Aram. emphatic ending. עתא (1) may have been the leader of this class of demons. In the context ב prob. has the meaning 'from' (see at 7 Abibaal 2), though cp. Exod. xii 12 'pass through'. חדר may be plur., referring to all the rooms in the house, dark because these demons only visited them at night.

20. עבר = ['ibrū]; plur. imper.; there is no need to suppose that it is an infin. absol. (Cross and Saley). פעם פעם; cp. הפעם in Judg. xvi 18. ללין is best explained as a plur. of Aram. type, prob. fem. in [ān], formed from the Phoen. adject. ללי 'night creature', therefore another mixed form since the pure Aram. form would have been ליליּן. Cp. לילית in Isa. xxxiv 14, in the original perhaps simply a bird like 'nightjar' (NEB) and unconnected with the Akkad. demon lilītu or the Lilith of Jewish folklore; the last two names go back to Sumerian and can therefore only have to do at a secondary level with the Semitic word for 'night'. On the legends that grew up around this demon see the article Lilith in Encycl. Judaica. The present inscr. links both עתא (by association here) and ססם (in 22 ff.) specifically with nightly activity, but not necessarily חנקת אמר (though her Arab. counterpart seems to have worked at night); on the other hand, only חנקת אמר is specifically linked (in the figure of the she-wolf swallowing an infant) with child-stealing.

21. On the left the sequence חצת הלך is clear, though there is some interference from strokes representing the hair on the neck and shoulders of the she-wolf. It may be that there is similar interference on the thigh of the animal under its tail. Only a single ב in the centre of the thigh is obvious; there may be a letter before it, while between it and the ח of חצת on the wolf's body there is room for 4 to 5 further letters. Du Mesnil reads ומבזת מחצת 'And, (o) despoiler (BZZ), smiter (MHṢ)'; Cross and Saley (and Röllig) read בבת ' לפחצת 'From the house, o crusher' (PHṢ by metathesis from PṢH); Caquot, less certain, reads בב-תחצת-. I am inclined to read בבת ' לחצת; the ל, however, is very small and there is rather a large space between the second ב and ת (or is it

בית with Aram. spelling?). With לחצת cp. Hebr. לחוץ construed with יצא (Ps. xli 7) and חוצות '(in) the streets' (Lam. ii 21). הלך; prob. imper. (fem.), as occasionally in Hebr. instead of the more usual (י)לכ, or take as infin. absol. standing for the imperative.

22-29. The best photo. of the inscr. on and near (26, 28) the body of the deity is that of Cross and Saley, though their own reading does not seem to me to be so accurate as that of Caquot, which can be traced quite clearly on it with the exception of the first two letters of 22 and the faded *l*. 27 (the latter line was not read in the original edition). Cross and Saley find several more letters than Caquot, but on closer examination and comparison with the other photos. these are just as likely to be parts of the design of the god's clothing. Only in *l.* 27, where they read the deity's name ססם (though with an extra ל not visible on any of the photos.), do I prefer their text to that of Caquot, who has נסס. For מצא with ל in Hebr. see Ps. xxi 9. The subject is שמש, not actually mentioned till 26. אור; Piel against Hebr. Hiphil; prob., construed with ל, more properly 'to make light for, upon' than 'to enlighten, illumine'. מזזת; cp. Deut. vi 9 xi 20; in later Judaism the term מזוזה was applied not only to the doorpost but to the encased parchment commonly affixed to it and containing the passages Deut. vi 4–9 and xi 13–21; this 'charm', an orthodox adaptation obviously of the kind we are dealing with here, is interestingly described in the Talmud (Pal. *Peah* 15 *d*) as 'guarding you when you are asleep'. חלף; cp. Job. ix 11. לדר; cp. לדר דר(ו) (Exod. iii 15   Ps. lxxvii 9 etc.). עף; cp. Ps. xviii 11 (of Yahweh). Röllig prefers סף 'come to an end' (cp. Ps. lxxiii 19). The precise nature of the allusion in these lines to the rising sun may indicate that a short ceremony was sometimes held beside the plaque at dawn, or had been so held when it was first pinned to the doorpost.

24   Arslan Tash ii   Fig. 16

The second incantation plaque measuring 5.3 by 3.3 cm. was like the first acquired in 1933 but remained unpublished until 1971, owing no doubt to the difficulties encountered in translating and interpreting the text, which is extremely cryptic, though most of the letters are relatively clear. The reverse of the plaque has carved on it a gnome-like figure with large protruding eyes and scorpion feet, who is swallowing a man or a child. The figure prob. represents the destructive power of the evil eye, personified in the inscr. as a demon called מזה (1) or 'Spatterer (sc. of blood)' and later referred to as עין or 'Eyer' (8). For possible allusions in the Bible to the practice of the evil eye see Prov. vi 13   x 10   xvi 30, and for comparative material from elsewhere the article of Gaster. Matters of script and language are discussed in the introd. to the first text.

Bibliography

First: A. Caquot, R. du Mesnil du Buisson, 'La seconde tablette ou petite amulette d'Arslan Tash', *Syria* 48 (1971), 391–406.

T. H. Gaster, 'A hang-up for hang-ups: The second amuletic plaque from Arslan Tash', *BASOR* 209 (1973), 18–26.

F. M. Cross, 'A second Phoenician incantation text from Arslan Tash', *CBQ* 36 (1974), 486–90.

W. Röllig in *NESE* 2 (1974), 28–36 (see Bibliogr. to i).

M. Liverani, 'Proposte sul secondo incantesimo di Arslan Tash', *RSF* 2 (1974), 35–8.

Lipiński, 'Miscellanea', 50–4.

idem., 'North Semitic texts', 249 f.

Illustration

Syria 48 (1971), fig. 1 at p. 392, fig. 4 at p. 396, pl. XXI–XXII.

Obverse:	1 לחשת ' למזה ' . בעל
	2 אסר ' מרכבתי ' ורבען
	3 אתי ' אל['][שיי '] [י'צא
	4 אש ' בשדה ' וגלען
	5 בשדה ' אי ' אל[']
	6 שיי ' קדׁש ⁺
Reverse; behind the demon:	7 נעלת ' מנעל
Above the demon:	8 ברח עין
In front of the demon:	9 בדד ' בראש מגמר '
	10 בנת ' בראש ' חלם כי'
Left edge:	11 הלמֹת ען בתם ' ען ית
Top edge:	12 ם ' ענך
Bottom edge:	13 מנתי ' כמגלת

1. Incantation against the (blood) Spatterer: Baal
2. has harnessed my chariot, and the Great-eyed one
3. is with me. El ŠYY has sent forth
4. his fire on the fields, and the Open-eyed one
5. is in the fields. Where is El
6. ŠYY, the Holy one?
7. I have fastened the bolt.

8. Flee, caster of the evil eye,
9. separate youself from the head of him achieving
10. understanding, from the head of him who dreams! For
11. I have struck the eye full square, the eye of the Orphan,
12. your eye.
13. My spells are according to the scroll.

NOTES

1. לחשת with ל; i 1. מזה; Yiph. partic. with final vowel-letter, lit. 'the one who causes (blood, water) to spurt', a verb most commonly used in Hebr. in cultic contexts, but cp. Isa. lxiii 3 (Qal). Lipiński translates מזה by '(for) the man sprinkling (water)' and עו (2,4) by 'fountain', regarding the obverse as a rain-making charm and only the reverse as concerned with the evil eye. But one would in that case have expected each text to begin with לחשת. As I understand it (cp. Gaster), the references on the obverse side to Baal, also called אל שיי, and his two companions רבען and גלען, are a warning to the demon that the householder who commissioned the plaque has divine power on his side; they fulfil much the same purpose as the 'covenant' with Ashur and other deities invoked in the first plaque. Cross takes למזה as vocative (see at i 1) and regards the other epithets as referring to a second demon banished with him (יצא in 3 is construed as an infin. absol. used for the imperative).

2. מרכבתי; for אסר with this noun see Gen. xlvi 29. Cross renders 'O Blood-splatterer, lord who readies his chariot (for battle)' (i.e. partic.), but if אסר is (as here) taken as a perfect, the suffix must be 1 person; the noun is accus. and a Phoen. 3 masc. sing. suffix ([ō]) would be unwritten. Similarly אתי (3) is 'with me'. The allusion cannot therefore be to the clouds or wind as the Weather-god's chariot (cp. Ps. civ 3 of Yahweh, and the Ugar. epithet of Baal, rkb 'rpt, 2 iv 8 etc., which is prob. reflected in Ps. lxviii 5), but is metaphorically to Baal being with his worshipper in his (the worshipper's) chariot, fighting alongside him, as it were. רבען lit. 'great of eye' and גלען (4) lit. 'open of eye' I take to be epithets of two demigods accompanying Baal who have the power (thus their names) to defeat the demon of the evil eye, or perhaps better of the two messengers or scouts (and thus necessarily keen-eyed) of Baal who are mentioned under different names in the Ugar. myths (Gupn and Ugar; see CML² p. 9, n.).

3. אל שיי. There is a wide space between ל and ש, though it is hardly wider than the internal space between כ and ב in מרכבתי in the previous line; but the outline of a word-divider is just visible and there may also be one after אל in 5 (see du Mesnil's sketch). The weight of evidence is therefore against taking אלשיי as an adject. meaning 'Cypriote' (= Baal or the name of a demon; from Alašiya, the ancient name of the island) and in favour of taking it as a divine title consisting of El (or 'god') plus שיי. Cross explains שיי as שי שי 'booty' (Ps. lxviii 30) (?) with the adjectival ending [ay] found in Canaanite divine names (e.g. Ugar. 'arsy, ṭly, the daughters of Baal; Hebr. אל שדי); the phrase means, therefore, 'the god Spoiler', which he applies along with רבען and גלען to his second demon (see at 1). אל שיי יצא seems to me, however, to parallel בעל אסר (1–2), and I take both verbs as perfects and אל שיי (offering no explanation) as another name of Baal. יצא; prob. Yiph. (see on 4).

4. אש 'fire' with or without (unwritten) suffix; cp. Ezek. xxviii 18 with הוציא; another metaphor of Baal's power calculated to strike fear into the demon

being addressed. For Baal's lightning see in Ugar. **3** C 23   D 69–71 and cp. Ps. xcvii 3   civ 4   cxliv 6, etc. For Phoen. אש 'fire' see **13** Kilamuwa i 6. Alternatively, but more prosaicly, אש is the relative, i.e. 'El ŠYY has come forth, he who is, was, in, from the fields'. שדה; **28** Eshmunazar 19. גלען = [glū'ēn] or the like; cp. גלוי עינים said of Balaam in Num. xxiv 4, and the Hebr. form עשו (Job xli 25) without the final י.

5. אי etc. (cp. Lipiński) may reflect the Ugar. formula put in El's mouth in Baal's absence in the underworld: *'iy 'al'iyn b'l 'iy zbl b'l 'arṣ*, 'Where is mightiest Baal? Where is the prince lord of earth?' (**6** iv 28–29); cp. also the Hebr. names Jezebel and Ichabod. It is here used ironically to bring it home to the demon that Baal is almost upon him. Alternative suggestions are 'island' (i.e. Cyprus) and 'Woe!', addressed to 'the god Spoiler' (Cross: Hebr. אוי). Liverani suggests א(ת)י, a restoration that makes the two phrases beginning with רבען and גלען similar in structure. He takes אל as a negative and שיי as a perfect verb from ŠYY = Hebr. ŠWY, i.e. 'and the Great-eyed one (demon) is not equal with him (Baal)'; this gives good sense but is unacceptable not only because of the archaic verbal form, not found in Phoen. after the time of the Old Byblian inscrs. (see at **4** Ahiram 2), but because of the negative אל, which belongs properly with the imperf. (jussive), and is not, as far as I know, used elsewhere with a perfect.

6. קרש is the usual reading, but Cross is prob. right to prefer קדש; ר in these inscrs. generally has a longer tail than ד, but cp. אדרך (i 7) and תדרכן (i 8), where the two letters are contiguous and almost indistinguishable. For קרש Caquot suggests 'the cruncher', referring to the demon (Arab. [qaraša]); Gaster 'Freeze!', addressed to the demon, and Lipiński 'He (the Cypriote) is hardened' (the Hebr. meanings); Röllig 'his (the Cypriote's) home' (Ugar. *qrš* 'pavilion'; but see *CML*[2] p. 53). This line ends with a long stroke, dividing the part about divine assistance from that in which the demon is directly commanded to depart (or in the opinion of some, the two separate incantations).

7. In the enigmatic Ugar. text RS 24.244 (see at i 16) the god Horon is requested to bar the door against the serpent (*1.* 70). Lipiński reads *1.* 12 (on the top edge) after 7, i.e. 'I have fastened with bolts your eye'; for a similar construction see Ezek. xvi 10. But though the beginning of 12 is on the plaque not far from the end of 7, the first letter (ב) of *1.* 8, which is written above the gnome, intervenes, proving that 8 was written before 12.

8. עין; partic.; cp. 1 Sam. xviii 9 (Qere).

9. בדד; cp. Isa. xiv 31 of a straggler separated from the ranks. Lipiński 'the one who casts the evil eye on the breast'(?). Cross reads בדר '(flee)' from the (my) home'; cp. Isa. xxxviii 12. מגמר may parallel עין and describe the demon as a 'destroyer of understanding', but following בראש is best understood as referring like חלם (10) to those sleeping in the house (Lipiński, the wizard reciting the spell); cp. גמר (Qal) of God fulfilling (sc. his purpose) on behalf of the worshipper (Ps. lvii 3 cxxxviii 8); Akkad. *gummuru* (D) and Syr. [gammēr] 'to accomplish, fulfil, perfect, etc.' as well as 'to bring to an end, destroy'. The phrases thus reflect the common ancient belief that the gods communicated with men in dreams; apparently the demon of the evil eye was thought to come by night and disrupt this process.

10. בנת; Hebr. בינה. Cross reads ענת ('consumer of eyes'). At the end perhaps כל 'everything' for כי (cp. Röllig).

11. This line on the left edge (looking at the obverse; the right edge is uninscribed) is clear on the photograph and I follow the first editor's

reading, though the מ is odd and could (Röllig) be כ ligatured with ל. Röllig, beginning at the end of 10, reads כלה לכלת 'cease to consume, destroy the eye'; cp. Lev. xxvi 16 Job xxxi 16. Cross regards the final ת as a scratch or a dividing stroke as in 6 (so also Lipiński; see at 7 above) and reads עני ... חלם תען '(from the head of the dreamer when) he dreams. Let his eye see perfectly!'; but though he is confident that the first letter is ת, it does not seem to me to be greatly different from the ה of מזה in *l.* 1, and in any case עני for 'his eye' (nomin.) is unacceptable. The same objection holds against Lipiński's '(I have smitten ...) his eye' (accus.). הלם; cp. Judg. v 26 and in Ugar. myth (of Baal defeating Yam) **2** iv 14, 24. בתם; this phrase is common in Punic inscrs. of gifts or payments made 'totally' at the donor's own expense; see *DISO* p. 329. יתם 'the orphan', a peculiar expression, but apparently an epithet of the demon; perhaps he was so abhorrent that in the mythology that lies behind this text he was given no parentage.

12. On Lipiński's location of this line see at 7 above. Cross places it after 13 as the last in the inscr. and reads מענם, i.e. '(the scroll of) the enchanter' (cp. Deut. xviii 10). He regards the word-divider, which is slightly longer than usual, as a random scratch, but in addition to the divider there is a considerable gap between the מ and the ע.

13. מנת; cp. Akkad. *minûtu;* Ugar. *mnt* (in the incantation texts **24** 46, RS 24.244, 4 *et passim*). The scroll is likely to have been one owned by a local expert in magic (or lodged in a local temple) from which the inscr. on the plaque was copied, and it is mentioned no doubt to remind the demon (and for that matter the household) that the incantation had proved effective on other occasions in the past.

PHOENICIAN INSCRIPTIONS

V

INSCRIPTIONS FROM BYBLOS

25   Yehaumilk Pl. IV

THE stele (1.13 by 0.56 m.) with the inscr. on its lower register was unearthed in 1869 by a local resident planting trees on the tell. The bottom right corner was missing, but was discovered some 60 years later near the site of the two great temples of Byblos in the excavations conducted by M. Dunand, so that the text is now all but complete. The additional fragment was in a rather poor state of preservation, however, and a sizable section down the middle of the stone itself is badly faded, making the reading of certain key words very problematic. The upper register depicts the king in Persian dress offering homage to the Mistress of Byblos; a winged solar disk is carved above the two figures. The text concerns the dedication of certain additions — notably an altar, a gateway (or as some prefer, an engraved object), and a portico — made to a small shrine, traces of which were found in the vicinity by Dunand. The stele is only roughly finished on the back and was prob. set into a wall in the portico just mentioned.

There are two fragmentary inscrs. earlier than Yehaumilk, that of the son of a second (or third) Shipitbaal (*KAI* no. 9 = Magnanini, *Iscrizioni*, pp. 32–3), which is usually dated to around 500 BC. and that published by Starcky in 1969, which seems to me to be a little earlier (cp. particularly ס); see the Bibliographical Notes. The inscr. of Yehaumilk must be separated from the first of these by at least one full reign (see Note to *l.* 1), but the writing (cp. particularly מ, כ, ה) suggests that a rather longer interval should be allowed, and I would prefer to place it in the second half of the 5 cent. with the inscr. of Batnoam (**26**) following in the early or mid-4 century. See further on the writing of Byblos Peckham, *Scripts*, chapt. II and W. Röllig, *NESE* 2 (1974), 12–13.

Bibliography

CIS i 1.
NSE p. 416.
NSI no. 3.
KI no. 5.
M. Dunand in *Fouilles de Byblos* I (1939), pp. 56 f.

idem., 'Encore la stèle de Yehavmilk roi de Byblos', *BMB* 5 (1941), 57–85.
A. Dupont-Sommer in *Semitica* 3 (1950), 35–44.
KAI no. 10.
ANET p. 656.
J. Friedrich in *ZDMG* 114 (1964), 225–6.
Magnanini, *Iscrizioni*, pp. 27–8.
S. Yeivin, "Ēdūth', *IEJ* 24 (1974), 17–20.
G. Garbini, 'L'iscrizione di Yeḥawmilk', *AIUON* 37 (1977), 403–8.

1 אנך יחומלך מלך גבל בן יחרבעל בן בן ארמלך מלך

2 גבל אש פעלתן הרבת בעלת גבל ממלכת על גבל וקרא אנך

3 את רבתי בעלת גבל ושמ̊ע̊ [הא] ק̊ל ופעל אנך לרבתי בעלת

4 גבל המזבח נחשת זן אש בח[צר]ן̊ ז והפתח חרץ זן אש

5 על פן פתחי ז והעפ̊ת חרץ אש בתכת אבן אש על פתח חרץ זן

6 והערפת זא ועמדה והכ̊[ת]ר̊ם אש עלהם ומספנתה פעל אנך

7 יהומלך מלך גבל לרבתי בעלת גבל כמאש קראת את רבתי

8 בעלת גבל ושמע קל ופעל לי נעם תברך בעלת גבל אית יחומל̊ך̊

9 מלך גבל ותחוו ותארך ימו ושנתו על גבל כ̊ מלך צדק הא ותתן

10 [לו הרבת ב]עלת גבל חן לען אלנם ולען עם ארץ ז וחן עם אר

11 ץ ז [קנמי את] כל ממלכת וכל אדם אש יסף לפעל מלאכת עלת מז

12 בח זן [ועלת פת]ח חרץ זן ועלת ערפת זא שם אנך יחומלך

13 מלך גבל [תשת את]ך̊ על מלאכת הא ואם אבל תשת שם אתך ואם תס̊

14 ר̊ מ[לא]כ̊ת זא̊ [ותס]ג̊ את ה̊[–––] ז̊ דֹל יסֹדה עלת מקם ז ותג̊ל

15 מס̊תרו תסֹרח̊[ו] הרבת בעלת גבל אית האדם הא וזרעו

16 את פן כל אלן ג[בל]

Illustrations

Minus the fragment: *CIS* i tab. I; *NSE* Taf. III; *ANEP* no. 477; Moscati, *Phoenicians*, p. 23. Of the fragment: *Fouilles* I, Atlas, pl. XXIX. Of the complete stele: Dunand, *BMB* 5, pl. V and fig. 5; Dunand, *Byblos, son histoire, ses légendes, ses ruines* (1963), pl. at p. 33.

1. I am Yehaumilk king of Byblos, son of YḤRBʻL, grandson of Urimilk king of

2. Byblos, whom the lady, Mistress of Byblos, made ruler over Byblos. I called

3. upon my lady, Mistress of Byblos, and she heard my voice. And I made for my lady, Mistress of

4. Byblos, this altar of bronze which is in this court, and this gateway of gold which is

5. opposite this gateway of mine and the winged disk of gold which is (set) within the stone which is above this gateway of gold,

6. and this portico and its pillars and the capitals which are upon them and its roof. I Yehaumilk

7. king of Byblos made (them) for my lady, Mistress of Byblos, when I called upon my lady,

8. Mistress of Byblos, and she heard my voice and did kindness to me. May the Mistress of Byblos bless Yehaumilk

9. king of Byblos and give life to him and prolong his days and his years over Byblos; for he is a lawful king! And may [the lady],

10. Mistress of Byblos, give [to him] favour in the sight of the gods and favour in the sight of the people of this

11. land! [Whoever you are], be you ruler or be you commoner, who may do further work on

12. this altar, [or on] this gateway of gold, or on this portico, [you shall put] my name Yehaumilk

13. [beside] your own on that work; and if you do not put my name beside your own but

14. remove this work and [shift] this [(pillar)] along with its base from this place and uncover

15. it hiding-place, may the lady, Mistress of Byblos, destroy both that man and his seed

16. in the presence of all the gods of Byblos!

NOTES

1. יחומלך = [yḥawmilk] 'May Milk preserve alive!'; Piel jussive; cp. יחועלי (Samaria ostracon lv; I, p. 13). On Milk at Byblos see at **6** Yehimilk 1. יחרבעל; an unparalleled name; etymologies from ḤRY (Hebr. 'to be hot (anger)'; Syr. Ethpe. 'to contend') or ḤRR (N.-Hebr. Piel, Syr. Pael 'to set free a slave') give possible meanings, though it is difficult to see what form is being used. The readings יהרבעל (cp. Hebr., Aram. YHR 'to be haughty') and יחדבעל (cp. Hebr. יחדיאל 'El rejoices') are to be resisted; see Benz, *Names*, p. 322. ארמלך = ['ōr(ī)milk] 'Milk is (my) light'; cp. Akkad. *Urumilki*, of a previous ruler of Byblos (Benz, op. cit., p. 274). The fact that YHRB'L is not described as king suggests that Yehaumilk succeeded his grandfather Urimilk. If the latter is restored as the name of Shipitbaal's son in the first line of the earlier fragmentary inscr. *KAI* no. 9, the gap between that inscr. and the present one need not be much more than a single reign; see, however, the introd., where I argue on epigraphic grounds for a rather wider interval.

2. אש; the Standard (Tyro-Sidonian) relative, which has replaced ז of the older Byblian dialect (**4** Ahiram 1). פעלתן = [p'alátnī]. With the syntax of the relative clause cp. Gen. xlv 4. הרבת; the form אדת is used in the Old Byblian texts (**8** Elibaal 2). בעלת גבל; see at **6** Yehimilk 3. ממלכת 'ruler, king'; abstract for concrete; cp. Hebr. ממלכה in 1 Kgs. x 20. קרא אנך; on this construction see at **13** Kilamuwa i 7.

3. את, also used with the verb קרא in 7, is perhaps not a shortened form of the object marker אית (8, 15), but the prepos. את used with the meaning 'to'; cp. קרא with ל or אל, and (below 16) את פן, which is equivalent to לפן (**6** Yehimilk 7). However, this explanation does not seem to suit the occurrence in 14, although the text of that line is badly damaged; and a form את (also ת) for the object marker occurs elsewhere, particularly in Punic. For an attempt to link אית and את as 'accusative' and 'dative' particles, a distinction obscured in Punic, see Harris, *Grammar*, p. 63. רבתי = [rabbatí/ēyā] or the like after a genit. noun; contrast קל = [qōlī] with unwritten vocalic suffix after an accusative. After the 9 cent. (see Note on phonology and grammar) the Tyro-Sidonian dialect uses י (= [ī]) irrespective of the case. [הא] fits the traces, especially in Lidzbarski's drawing, rather better than [אית]; cp. also 8, where שמע קל occurs without the object marker.

4. המזבח נחשת; there are two possible explanations of this, of the following הפתח חרץ, and of העפת חרץ (5); the absence of a demonstrative with the last of these phrases shows that it is not a relevant feature (see Note on phonology and grammar; זא cannot be supplied since minor works associated with the three major improvements do not have 'this'; cp. הכ[ת]רם, 6): (a) the article is used anomalously as possibly in הברך בעל in **15** Karatepe A i 1 and as certainly in the Hebr. phrases cited in the Note there, though in all of these the second member is a proper name or a place-name, which is not the case here; cp. also המזבח בית אל (2 Kgs. xxiii 17); (b) נחשת and חרץ are in apposition to the preceding definite nouns; again there are parallels in Hebr., though they are not quite exact; e.g. המזבח הנחשת (2 Kgs. xvi 14), in which both nouns have the article, and מצלתים נחשת (I Chron. xv 19), in which neither has; but cp. in Phoen. הדלת הנחשת (**36** Lapethos ii 12). The second explanation is prob. preferable. As regards the demonstratives, there seems in *ll.* 4–6 to be a semantic distinction between the two words for 'this', the series זו, fem. זא, referring to the objects (altar, gateway, portico) newly constructed by the king, the

series זֹ, fem. also ז (perhaps like אש borrowed from Tyro-Sidonian), referring to things that were already there (courtyard, second gateway). Similarly in *ll.* 11–14. Contrast הא (masc. and fem.) 'that' in 13, 15. בח[צר]ון; so Dupont-Sommer; a form with the termination [ōn]; cp. Hebr. חצרון (place-name). Since the courtyard was already there, ז is used. פתח; cp. Hebr. פתח of the entrances to the Debir and the nave of Solomon's temple (1 Kgs. vi 31, 33), both with wooden doors overlaid with gold; of the entrance of the gateway in Ezekiel's temple (xl 11); of a city gate itself (1 Kgs. xvii 10); cp. also the golden gates at Hierapolis mentioned by Lucian (*Dea Syr.* 30). We are to think most probably of a gateway into the court of the shrine, opposite (על פן, 5) an already-existing one (ז) leading into the palace court, the latter being described as Yehaumilk's own (פתחי); cp. שער המלך (1 Chron. ix 18); מבוא המלך (2 Kgs. xvi 18). Less likely is פתח = [pittūḥ], either 'engraved object' (cp. 1 Kgs. vi 29). or 'inscribed object' (Exod. xxviii 11). In the first case perhaps a gold statuette of the goddess is meant, set in a niche in the shrine itself, which as at contemporary Amrit was prob. not a large building but an aedicule or small chapel (Moscati, *Phoenicians*, 46 f.). The difficulty with this interpretation is to find a similar object opposite or in front (על פן) which could be described as the king's own; would the king have a statue of himself set up in such a place? If, on the other hand, we take פתח as 'inscribed object', the reference is implausibly to some other inscription nearby, perhaps incised on a gold plaque, and פתחי (5) with ז not זז describes the present stone. Since the present stone celebrates the renovations, what could have been the purpose of the new inscription? Garbini suggests (cp. Harris, *Grammar*, p. 104) that חרץ may mean not 'gold' but 'chiselled' as in **32** Umm El-'Amed xiii 1 (cp. Lev. xxii 22), i.e. a chiselled statuette or inscription; but the way in which its use exactly parallels נחשת makes this improbable.

5. עפת; the middle letter is very uncertain; from the base 'WP 'to fly'; cp. עפתא 'flying creatures' (**23** Arslan Tash i 19); Ugar. *'pt* 'bird' or 'birds' (**22** B 11); Hebr. has only עוף, masc. collective 'birds, insects'. It is likely that a winged solar disk of gold is meant, inset in the lintel stone (אבן) of the gateway; cp. the one carved in the upper register of the inscription. If, on the other hand, [pittūḥ] is read in 4, the disk is attached to the top horizontal stone of the niche containing the goddess's statue (cp. the solar disk carved on an aedicule from Sidon; Moscati, op. cit., 53 f. and pl. 2), or to the stone wall above the gold plaque containing the other inscription. Yeivin prefers to read עדת with a similar meaning; he compares the difficult Hebr. term עדות in 2 Kgs. xi 12, which he thinks comes not from the base 'WD but from 'DY and means some kind of ornament or piece of jewelry, and which he argues from the context of this inscr. may have been carved in the shape of a solar disk. The solar disk was a motif of Egyptian origin, but was widely used as a symbol of deity throughout the whole ancient Near East. בתכת; cp. Hebr. בתוך; a plur. form of the prepos. like Hebr. בינות and Phoen. עלת (11); syncope of [h] of the article is according to Lambdin's theory to be assumed after בתכת and in the next phrase after על (where there is a demonstrative following the noun). Similarly after על in 13, after עלת in 11, 12, 14, after לען in 10 (twice), and in the construct relation עם ארץ ז in 10–11. See the Note on phonology and grammar.

6. ערפת 'portico, colonnade'; cp. **31** Umm El-'Amed iv 1 **41** Piraeus 5, and for a possible etymology Arab. [ġurfatu] 'gable, balcony, upper room'. The portico may have been an extension of the gateway, making it something like a college lodge, or may have surrounded the courtyard of

the shrine. כתרם; the reading, which is very uncertain, is suggested as much by Hebr. כתרות of the capitals of the two pillars outside the Jerusalem temple (1 Kgs. vii 16, etc.) as by the faded writing; the plur. form, fem. as in Hebr., כתערת (in which ע is a *mater lectionis*), found on a Neo-Punic stele from Leptis Magna (*KAI* no. 119, 2) makes its adoption very questionable. *CIS* restores ראשם, used also in 1 Kgs. vii 16 ff. for the 'tops' of the pillars where the capitals were set and in Exod. xxxvi 38 for the capitals of pillars themselves (in the Tabernacle). עלהם = ['lēhōm] < ['alayhumu]. מספנת; cp. Hebr. [sippūn] of the 'ceiling' of the Temple in 1 Kgs. vi 15.

7. כמאש formed of כם (cp. Hebr. כמו) and the relative אש (2), thus equivalent to Hebr. כאשר. Syntactically the beginning of this line may go with 'this portico' (6), since פעל has no object stated; in that case a new sentence begins at this point and the ו in ושמע is *Waw apodosi*, i.e. 'when I called upon ....., she heard .....' קראת = [qarŏtī]; cp. Poenulus *corathi* (an error for *carothi*). את; see at 3.

8. נעם; cp. **15** Karatepe A i 10 and the similar Hebr. phrase עשה חסד עם (or טוב). The base N'M is common in Phoen. and seems to have a similar range of meaning to Hebr. ṬWB, which Phoen. lacks. אית = ['iyyāt] or the like; see at **12** Cyrpus grave 3.

9. תחוו prob. = [thawwēw]; Piel jussive with suffix [ēw] < [ēhū]; cp. **6** Yehimilk 2 **15** Karatepe A i 3 (Yiph.) Ps. xli 3. תארך etc.; cp. **6** Yehimilk 3 ff. ימו = [yamōw] < [yamăyū] < [yamáyhū]; a similar origin is to be presupposed for Hebr. [āw], where י is retained in the orthography; the development in Tyro-Sidonian is slightly different (see at **13** Kilamuwa i 7). Note the masc. plur. form against ימי of Yehimilk; Tyro-Sidonian and Hebr. also possess both forms. צדק; **6** Yehimilk 6; Yehaumilk seems to have succeeded his grandfather directly since his father (1) is not called king; there may have been other claimants, explaining his insistence here on his legitimacy. תתן prob. = [tētēn]; jussive from YTN (**28** Eshmunazar 18).

10. לו (restored) = [law] or the like < [láhū]. חן לען; cp. Gen. xxxix 21 Exod. iii 21 with בעיני. לען; Exod. vii 20 etc. אלנם; see at **15** Karatepe A iii 5. The mason seems to have written some words twice at the end of the line; prob. the correct formula was וחן לען עם ארץ ז. ז = [zō]; fem. agreeing with ארץ (see at **15** Karatepe A ii 9).

11. [קנמי את]; for the restoration see **28** Eshmunazar 4, 20. *KAI* restores [וחן לען], i.e. '... and favour in the eyes of all rulers', but this splits ממלכת and אדם, which come together in the formula in Eshmunazar. קנמי את is the exact equivalent of מי את in **27** Tabnit 3 and is usually explained as related to Syr. [qnūm] 'person, self' with the addition of מי 'who'; Neo-Punic קנאם (*DISO* p. 260) may be connected; cp. also Aram. מן את (II **18** Nerab i 5 **19** ii 8). It is followed here first by a 3 person verb (יסף) and then by 2 peson verbs (תשת, 12, 13) with, however, a reversion to the 3 person (אית האדם הא) in the final two lines; similarly in **28** Eshmunazar 4 ff.; מי את in Tabnit is followed consistently by 2 person constructions; מן את in Nerab ii is followed first by 2 person verbs then by a 3 person construction. Cp. also the changes of person in II **34** Guzneh 2 ff. (after זי מן). יסף is prob. Yiphil; Hebr. הוסף ל. לפעל = [lip'u/ōl]; Poenulus *liful*. מלאכת prob. = [mlōkat]; Punic מלכת; Hebr. [mlākā]. עלת is prob. a plur. form like בתכת (5).

12. אז = [za'] or [zō]; fem. of זן as in the Zenjirli dialect (II, pp. 62–3); although it may have had a similar pronounciation, it is to be distinguished from the

fem. form ז (see at **15** Karatepe A ii 9). שם = [šmī] with vocalic suffix unwritten. With the strengthening use of the independent pronoun cp. בימתי אנך **(15** Karatepe A ii 5).

13. תשת אתך is restored from later in the line. With the phrase cp. **15** Karatepe A ii 10 iii 14. הא = [hi'] or [hī] (fem.), 'that' referring to the hypothetical work in the future. אבל; the general Phoen. negative is בל, but a longer form like this appears in Punic as איבל, so it is prob. a combination of the two negatives אי and בל, both found, though rare, in Hebr.; Hebr. לא, on the other hand, is not found in Phoen. (though see at **28** Eshmunazar 3).

14. The restoration, beginning with ואם (13), is Dupont-Sommer's and, though printed (with one omission) in the text, is suspect on a number of grounds; there is no article (or object marker) before מלאכת; את later in the line for the object marker goes ill with אית in the next line; and ג[תס] is restored on the basis of Hebr. Hiph. הסיג (base SWG), which is largely restricted to the stereotyped phrase 'to remove a landmark' (גבול; Deut. xix 14 etc.). Both תסר and תסג are Yiphil imperfects. The general sense, however, is as required (cp. II **5** Zakir B 16 ff.), since there is mention later of a 'foundation' or 'base' and of uncovering hidden things. The omitted restoration is אשת after את. A fem. noun is needed to go with the suffix in יסדה; ז must therefore be feminine. אשת is, however, masc.; Hebr. sing. presumably שת, so the א of the Phoen. form is prosthetic (ŠYT); cp. the plurals (fem. only in form) Hebr. שתות 'stays, pillars' (Ps. xi 3 Isa. xix 10) and Phoen. אשתת in an inscr. from Cyprus (**33** Tariff A 13). Understand therefore some other word meaning 'pillar'. Apparently we have to think of a pillar beneath which was buried at the original dedication of the shrine (ז is used) a cache of valuable objects (cp. מסתרו, 15). Such a deposit was discovered in the foundations of one of the great temples at Byblos; see Montet, *Byblos et l'Égypte,* chaps. III, IV. Yehaumilk's reference to this cache of treasure suggests that he himself had been responsible for constructing the shrine, to which he is now making improvements and additions. The pillar or support prob. formed part of the structure of the temple or aedicule in the centre of the courtyard. דל 'with'; **15** Karatepe A ii 6. יסד; Hebr. [ysōd]. מקם referring prob. to the sanctuary precinct as a whole (cp. Gen. xii 6 Deut. xii 2, 5, etc.). Note עלת with the meaning 'from'; cp. על in **4** Ahiram 2. ותגל מסתרו; cp. Jerem. xlix 10 Isa. xlv 3. The noun may be either sing. or plur., giving a suffix [aw] < [áhū] (the case is accus.) or [ōw] < [áyhū] (see at 9), referring back to מקם (masc.).

15. סרח; cp. Syr. Peal, Pael, 'multilate, destroy'; the suffix (= [ēw]) is restored, and is prospective (cp. **15** Karatepe A iii 4 **28** Eshmunazar 9–10). זרעו = [zar'aw], the noun being accus.; note that אית is not repeated.

16. את פן; see at 3. The phrase here is equivalent to לפן אל גבל in **6** Yehimilk 7.

26 Batnoam

The funerary inscr. of Batnoam is carved in tiny letters in a single long line (94 cm.) on the side of a fine white marble *theca.* Batnoam was the mother of Azbaal (or Azzibaal), a king of Byblos known already from his coins. Since his father is described as a priest and not as a king, he was prob. the founder of a new dynasty, and the beginning of his reign has been associated with a Phoenician revolt against Persia in 351 BC; but, with Peckham (*Scripts,* 48 ff.), I would prefer to place him earlier in the 4 century. The sarcophagus was discovered in 1929 near the site of a Crusader castle, which is thought not to have been its original resting-place; it is now in the Beirut Museum.

Bibliography

M. Dunand in *Kêmi* 4 (1931), 151–6 (not seen by me).
idem, *Fouilles de Byblos* I (1939), pp. 30 f.
J. Friedrich, 'Eine phönizische Inschrift späterer Zeit aus Byblos', *Orientalistische Literaturzeitung*, 1935, 348–50.
R. Dussaud, 'L'Inscription du sarcophage de Batno'am à Byblos', *Syria* 17 (1936), 98–9.
KAI no. 11.
Magnanini, *Iscrizioni*, p. 31.

Illustrations

Kêmi 4 (1931), pl. X; *Fouilles* I, pl. XXXIII; *KAI* Taf. III.

בארן זן אנך בתנעם אם מלך עזבעל מלך גבל בן פלטבעל כהן בעלת שכבת

בסות ומראש עלי ומחסם חרץ לפי כמאש למלכית אש כן לפני

In this coffin lie I Batnoam, mother of King Azbaal, king of Byblos, son of Paltibaal, priest of the Mistress, in a robe and with a tiara on my head and a gold bridle on my mouth, as was the custom with the royal ladies who were before me.

NOTES

בארן = [bāʾrōn] or the like with syncope of [h] of the article. בתנעם 'daughter of pleasantness'; cp. Hebr. Naomi, Naamah. עזבעל '(my) strength is Baal'; cp. Akkad. *Aziba'al* (a king of Arvad) and Greek *'Αζβαλος* (correction); Benz, *Names*, p. 374; the Akkad. transcription suggests a Phoen. noun [ʾazzī] against Hebr. [ʾuzzī]. פלטבעל 'my deliverance is Baal'; cp. Hebr. פלטיאל. בעלת perhaps lacks the article because it is tantamount to a proper name; for the full title see **25** Yehaumilk 2. שכבת; fem. partic.; cp. **27** Tabnit 2 Gen. xlvii 30 Isa. xiv 8 Job vii 21. סות; **13** Kilamuwa i 8. מראש; some kind of head-dress or tiara; cp. Jerem. xiii 18. מחסם לפי; cp. Ps. xxxix 2; prob. some kind of muzzle or clip closing the lips to prevent the entry of demons. לפי = [lpīyā] or the like. כמאש; **25** Yehaumilk 7; here comparative, lit. 'according to what (was) to'. מלכית = [malkiyyōt] or the like, fem. plur. of [malkī(y)] 'royal person'. כן = [kōnū].

VI

INSCRIPTIONS FROM SIDON, TYRE, AND VICINITY

27 Tabnit (Sidon)   Pl. III, 2

THE inscr. is carved on the base of a sarcophagus of black basalt found in a necropolis at Sidon in 1887. The sarcophagus is of wholly Egyptian workmanship and contains an earlier inscr. in hieroglyphics giving the name of a previous occupant who was an Egyptian general. It can hardly, therefore, have reached Sidon and been reused for the burial of one of its kings with Egyptian approval, a factor which should be taken into account when looking for a suitable date (see below). Apart from a notice of Tabnit's title and lineage, the text is mainly taken up with an imprecation against grave robbers violating the tomb. The monument is housed in the Museum of Antiquities in Istanbul.

Historical circumstances and date

The date around 300 BC once assigned to the inscrs. of Tabnit and his son Eshmunazar (which is on a similar sarcophagus; 28) is now seen to be impossible. This late dating was largely based on the belief that the title אדן מלכם (**28** Eshmunazar 18) must refer to the Ptolemaic kings, but an Aram. rendering of the same title has since turned up in an inscr. belonging to the 6 cent.; see the Note to the passage for details. The evidence of archaeology also points to a much higher date. Further study of four coffins of Greek style which were found in the same rock tomb complex as Tabnit's has led to the conclusion that they belong to the late fifth or the fourth cent. and that the coffins of the two Sidonian kings, which are purely Egyptian in style, are almost certainly still earlier (see Harden, *Phoenicians,* 112 f., 192 f.). Their inscrs., therefore, precede rather than follow the series of Phoen. coins incised with the initials of rulers of Sidon, which take us back from 322 (on the eve of Alexander the Great's occupation of the city) well into the 5 cent. (Peckham, *Scripts,* 75). It is probable, moreover, that the full names of three of the earliest of these kings are given in the recently discovered Baalshillem inscr. (**29**; q.v. introduction). It appears then that the dynasty to which Baalshillem belonged began ruling around 425 BC at the latest, which means that the dynasty of Tabnit and Eshmunazar has to be placed in the earlier part of the 5 century. We cannot go much higher than that since the Egyptian-style sarcophagi could not have been carried to Sidon until after the Persian invasion of Egypt in 525; the Phoenician cities were allies of Cambyses in that invasion and the coffins may indeed have been part of Sidon's share of the booty. The proposal by K. Galling that Dor and Joppa (see at **28** Eshmunazar 19) were ceded to Sidon by the Persians for naval assistance given at the battle of Salamis in 480 BC (Phoenician contingents in the Persian forces are mentioned by Herodotus) yields a satisfactory scheme of dates. We may assume that Eshmunazar died (aged 14) soon after this transaction, and it is likely that his father had a short reign; for Tabnit died before the 'orphan' Eshmunazar was born (**28** 3). We may therefore reconstruct the reigns as follows, beginning with Tabnit's father, who was also called Eshmunazar:

Eshmunazar I	?–500
Tabnit	500–490
Eshmunazar II	489–475

Peckham (op. cit. 85 ff.) does not accept Galling's arguments, preferring to think that the Sidonian admiral at Salamis whose name is given by Herodotus (VII, 98) as Tetramnestus and who was put to death by the victorious Greeks, was not an officer of Eshmunazar's but the last king of a previous dynasty. Eshmunazar I's dynasty assumed the throne at that point, Tabnit succeeding around 470 and Eshmunazar II perhaps five years later. For a detailed treatment of the late Tyro-Sidonian scripts see Peckham, chapt. III.

Bibliography

First publication by E. Renan in *CRAIBL,* 1887, 182 f.
See further:
NSE p. 417.
NSI no. 4.
KI no. 6.
S. R. Driver, *Notes on the Hebrew Text of the Books of Samuel,* 2nd edit. (1913), pp. xxiii ff.
RÉS no. 1202.
A. Poebel in *Assyriological Studies* 3 (1932), 15–18 (an article not seen by me).
KAI no. 13.
ANET p. 662.
Greenfield, 'Scripture', 258 f.
Magnanini, *Iscrizioni,* pp. 6–7.
Lipiński, 'Miscellanea', 55–6.
idem, 'North Semitic texts', 262.

Illustrations

NSE Taf. IV, 1; Driver, op. cit., pl. VI; *KAI* Taf. V.

1 אנך תבנת כהן עשתרת מלך צדנם בן

2 אשמנעזר כהן עשתרת מלך צדנם שכב בארן

3 ז מי את כל אדם אש תפק אית הארן ז אל אל ת

4 פתח עלתי ואל תרגזן כ אי אר לן כסף אי אר לן

5 חרץ וכל מנם משר בלת אנך שכב בארן ז אל אל תפת

6 ח עלתי ואל תרגזן כ תעבת עשתרת הדבר הא ואם פת

7 ח תפתח עלתי ורגז תרגזן אל י>כ<ן ל>ד< זרע בחים תחת שמ

8 ש ומשכב את רפאם

1. I Tabnit, priest of Astarte, king of the Sidonians, son of
2. Eshmunazar, priest of Astarte, king of the Sidonians, lie in this
3. coffin. Whoever you are, any man at all, who come upon this coffin, you must not
4. open up (what is) over me nor disturb me; for they did not gather together silver for me, they did not gather together
5. gold for me nor any riches whatsoever, but only I myself lie in this coffin. You must not open up
6. (what is) over me nor disturb me; for such an act is an abomination to Astarte. But if
7. you in fact open up (what is) over me and in fact disturb me, may you have no seed among the living under the sun
8. nor a resting-place with the shades!

NOTES

1. תבנת (with a divine name suppressed) may be connected with Hebr. [tabnīt] 'pattern, figure' (e.g. Deut. iv 16 Ps. cvi 20 Isa. xliv 13) and derive from a royal ideology which sees the king as an image of the divine; but cp. also the Hebr. name Tibni, lit. 'strawman, scarecrow' held by a rival of Omri (1 Kgs. xvi 21; Greek Θαμνει) and the place-name Kafr Tibnīt south of Sidon, which may mean something like 'straw-heap' or 'midden' (cp. Hebr. מתבן in Isa. xxv 10), an etymology that suggests quite opposite notions. It is noteworthy that this inscr. also calls Tabnit a priest, apparently highlighting the priestly functions of the king; cp. in Hebr. Gen. xiv 18 Ps. cx 4 Zech. vi 11–13. His son Eshmunazar, however, makes no such claim, though his mother, Tabnit's wife, is described as a priestess (28 14–15). Astarte (Ugar. 'ttrt) was the sister-consort of Baal, the chief god of Sidon, and with her brother-husband and Eshmun, the young god, made up the Sidonian triad of leading deities, corresponding to El, Baalat, and Adonis at Byblos (see at 6 Yehimilk 2–3) and Baal, Astarte, and Melcarth at Tyre (see introd. to 30 Throne of Astarte). She was equated by the Greeks with Aphrodite. The Biblical form (Ashtoreth) is falsified in the pointing to suggest a comparison with בשת 'shame'; cp. אשבשת for אשבעל. צדנם with reduced plur. ending [īm] < [iyyīm]; so in 28

Eshmunazar and earlier **17** Baal Lebanon *a*; contrast צדנים (**41** Piraeus 1) where the fuller ending is retained.

2. אשמנעזר 'Eshmun has saved', grandfather of the king celebrated in the next inscr.; it should not be pronounced Eshmunazor (see the Note on phonology and grammar). Eshmun, a god of healing, if the equation with Greek Asklepios has picked up his primary function, and prob. also a vegetation god (see introd. to **30** Throne of Astarte), is, unlike most other Phoen. deities, unknown outside the Phoen.-Punic area. There is no agreement about the name's etymology, whch has been variously traced to שמן 'eight' (with prosthetic [']), to שם 'name', and to שמן 'oil'; see Lipiński's full study in *AIUON* 33 (1973), 161 ff. שכב; partic.; cp. שכבת, **26** Batnoam and references there.

3. מי את כל; cp. קנמי את כל (**28** Eshmunazar 4, 20); Aram. מן את (II **18** Nerab i 5   **19** ii 8). The following verbs are consistently 2 person; see further at **25** Yehaumilk 11. תפק from the base PYQ 'to obtain, find'; in Ugar. **14** Keret 12; in Hebr. Prov. iii 13. אית; note that the following article is written; in many other cases there may be syncope of [h] (e.g. **15** Karatepe A iii 19). אל אל for emphasis; cp. אבל (**25** Yehaumilk 13).

4. עלתי prob. 'over me', a kind of ellipsis for 'open (what is) over me'; cp. Palmyrene לא יפתח עלוהי (*NSI* no. 145, 3) with a word meaning 'niche' following. On the form עלת see at **25** Yehaumilk 11. תרגזן; Yiphil; cp. Hebr. הרגיז in 1 Sam. xxviii 15   Isa. xiv 16; רגז in Job iii 17, 26. Greenfield also compares the incident in 2 Sam. xxi 10 ff. where David has the bones of Saul and his sons gathered together and properly buried so that the land may have relief from famine; cp. further Daniel's concern in the Ugar. Aqhat legend (**19** 105 ff.) to find and bury his son's remains. אי אר לן is in the context of II **19** Nerab ii 6 (לשמו עמי 'they did not lay with me') the most likely division of the words; cp. also **28** Eshmunazar 5 (אי שם בן מנם). It is noteworthy that אי is used with a verb in the Eshmunazar passage (as in Ethiopic); in Hebr., especially Mishnaic, it is always prefixed to a noun; the י is prob. still consonantal as in מי, though in אבל (**25** Yehaumilk 13) it is clearly pronounced [']ī]. אר is 3 masc. plur. indefinite perf. from 'RY 'to gather' (in Hebr. only Ps. lxxx 13   Song v 1). Since ר and ד are easily confused in Sidonian writing, a reading אד is also possible, i.e. from 'DY, 'they gave to me'; but this base is only attested for Arab. 'to transmit, pay a debt'. לן = [lanī] or the like; cp. Ugar. lnh '(those who work) against him' (**17** Aqhat i 30) and בן with 'invisible' suffix **15** Karatepe A ii 18   **28** Eshmunazar 5. Rather less likely, since it involves a form with prosthetic ['] for a word which is itself uncommon, is the reading אדלן '(there is not) with me'; cp. דל (**15** Karatepe A ii 6   **25** Yehaumilk 14); the suffix will be 'verbal' or added to the termination [an]; cp. תחתן, **13** Kilamuwa i 14, and see the discussion there. In either case note that the 1 pers. suffix with prepositional forms in still unwritten, whereas in nouns (**15** Karatepe C iv 18   **28** Eshmunazar 14) י is following the change [iyā] > [ī] after genitives extended by analogy to nominatives and accusatives.

5. מנם; cp. Ugar. *mnm;* Akkad. *minumma* 'whatever'. often with a following noun. משר is preferable to משד, since it allows a connection with Akkad. *mašru, mešru* 'riches'. Lipiński well cites the Babylonian Theodicy *l.* 282, 'He is a king; riches should be his' (*ANET* p. 604). No remotely satisfactory etymology has been proposed for משד (see *DISO*, p. 169). בלת conj. 'except that (I am lying)' after a prior negative; cp. Hebr. בלתי in Gen. xliii 3 Num. xi 6 etc.

6. תעבת; an exceptionally strong warning; cp. Deut. xvii 1 xxv 16. פתח; infin. absolute, ditto רגז (7); as in Hebr. (e.g. 1 Sam. xxiii 22), the Qal infin. can be used with a verb from a derived conjugation.

7. אל יכן לך זרע; corrected after **28** Eshmunazar 8. It is possible (Greenfield) that the mason also missed out ותאר between זרע and בחים; see at **28** Eshmunazar 12. Both חים and תחת שמש (with syncope?) are favourite expressions of Ecclesiastes (e.g. iv 15 vi 8, 12 vii 2 ix 9), perhaps an indication of Phoenician influence on Hebrew Wisdom (Dahood).

8. משכב; cp. Ezek. xxxii 25; also in Jewish grave inscrs. (*DISO* p. 170). את רפאם; cp. Ugar. *btk rp'i 'arṣ* (**15** Keret iii 14) Prov. xxi 16 etc.

28 Eshmunazar (Sidon) Pl. V

The famous sarcophagus of Eshmunazar, manufactured in Egypt of black basalt like that of his father Tabnit (**27**) but unlike it transported to Sidon new, was discovered in 1855 and is now in the Louvre. The tomb in which it was placed was cut out of rock but was much shallower than the deep shaft containing Tabnit's coffin and had, it seems, a stone-built entrance chamber above ground level. The inscr. was begun on the body of the coffin under the head but discontinued after a few lines because of mistakes and the whole incised afresh (but still with a number of errors) on the face of the lid. Eshmunazar succeeded to the throne of Sidon at birth, his father having recently died, and he himself died at the early age of fourteen. His mother acted as regent during his infancy and seems still to have been the power behind the throne at his death, since she is associated with him in the middle part of the inscr., which rehearses his achievements during his reign (the beginning and end of the text are occupied by the usual imprecations). These were chiefly concerned with the building (or rebuilding) of shrines for the leading deities of Sidon, but there is a particularly valuable reference in *ll.* 18–19 to the ceding of territory in Palestine (Dor and Joppa) to Sidon by the Persian emperor in return for services rendered, the importance of which for dating the dynasty to which Eshmunazar and his father belonged is considered in the introd. to **27** Tabnit.

Style

The inscr., which is the longest Phoen. royal inscr. after **15** Karatepe, offers an unusually high proportion of literary parallels with the Hebrew Bible, especially its poetic sections. Like that inscr. and some shorter royal texts such as **4** Ahiram, **6** Yehimilk, **13** Kilamuwa i, **25** Yehaumilk, and **27** Tabnit, it witnesses, if indirectly, to a rich tradition of Phoen. rhetoric which prob. had its origins in courtly and epic poetry; see further in the introd. to **13** Kilamuwa i.

Bibliography

CIS i 3.
NSE p. 417 f.
NSI no. 5.
KI no. 7.
RÉS no. 1506.
A. Poebel in *Assyriological Stuides* 3 (1932), 18–23 (see Bibliogr. to **27** Tabnit).
K. Galling, 'Eshmunazar und der Herr der Könige', *ZDPV* 79 (1963), 140–51.
H. L. Ginsberg, 'Roots below and fruit above', *Hebrew and Semitic Studies presented to G. R. Driver* (1963), 72–6.
KAI no. 14.
ANET p. 662.

1 בירח בל בשנת עסר וארבע 14 למלכי מלך אשמנעזר מלך צדנם

2 בן מלך תבנת מלך צדנם דבר מלך אשמנעזר מלך צדנם לאמר נגזלת

3 בל עתי בן מסך ימם אזרם יתם בן אלמת ושכב אנך בחלת ז ובקבר ז

4 במקם אש בנת קנמי את כל ממלכת וכל אדם אל יפתח אית משכב ז ו

5 אל יבקש בן מנם כ אי שם בן מנם ואל ישא אית חלת משכבי ואל יעמ

6 סן במשכב ז עלת משכב שני אף אם אדמם ידברנך אל תשמע בדנם כ
כל ממלכת ו

7 כל אדם אש יפתח עלת משכב ז אם אש ישא אית חלת משכבי אם אש
יעמסן במ

8 שכב ז אל יכן לם משכב את רפאם ואל יקבר בקבר ואל יכן לם בן וזרע

9 תחתנם ויסגרנם האלנם הקדשם את ממלכ<ת> אדר אש משל בנם לק

10 צתנם אית ממלכת אם אדם הא אש יפתח עלת משכב ז אם אש ישא אית

11 חלת ז ואית זרע ממל<כ>ת הא אם אדמם המת אל יכן לם שרש למט ו

12 פר למעל ותאר בחים תחת שמש כ אנך נחן נגזלת בל עתי בן מס

13 ך ימם אזרם יתם בן אלמת אנך כ אנך אשמנעזר מלך צדנם בן

Greenfield, 'Scripture', 259–65.

Teixidor 'Bulletin' for 1971, items 102, 103; 1973, item 114 (on suggestions of H. L. Ginsberg and M. Dahood).

Ginsberg, 'Ugaritico-Phoenicia', 138–9, 143–5.

Magnanini, *Iscrizioni*, pp. 3–5.

Lipiński, 'Miscellanea', 56–9.

Avishur, 'Stylistic features', 5–6, 11.

G. Garbini, 'L'iscrizione di Eshmun'azar', *AIUON* 37 (1977), 408–12.

Illustrations

CIS tab. II; *NSE* Taf. IV, 2; *NSI* pl. I. Of the sarcophagus: Harden, *Phoenicians*, pl. 16; Moscati, *Phoenicians*, pl. 8.

1. In the month of Bul, in the fourteenth (14) year of the reign of King Eshmunazar, king of the Sidonians,
2. son of King Tabnit, king of the Sidonians, King Eshmunazar, king of the Sidonians, spoke and said: I have been seized
3. before my time, the son of a (short) number of days, a smitten one, an orphan, the son of a widow; and I lie in this box and in this grave,
4. in the place which I built. Whoever you are, be you ruler or be you commoner, let none such open up this resting-place or
5. seek anything in it, for they did not lay anything in it; and let none such lift up the box in which I lie or carry me
6. away from this resting-place to another resting-place! Even if men speak to you, do not listen to their talk. For should any ruler or
7. any commoner open up (what is) over this resting-place, or lift up the box in which I lie or carry me away from
8. this resting-place, may they have no resting-place with the shades, and may they not be buried in a grave, and may they have no son nor seed
9. to succeed them, but may the holy gods deliver them up to a mighty ruler who shall have dominion over them, so that they
10. perish, both (that) ruler or that commoner who opens up (what is) over this resting-place or who lifts up
11. this box, and the seed of that ruler or those commoners! May they have no root below nor
12. fruit above nor renown among the living under the sun! For I am to be pitied; I have been seized before my time, the son of a (short)
13. number of days, a smitten one, an orphan I, the son of a widow. Yet I Eshmunazar, king of the Sidonians, son of

14 מלך תבנת מלך צדנם בן בן מלך אשמנעזר מלך צדנם ואמי אמעשתרת

15 כהנת עשתרת רבתן המלכת בת מלך אשמנעזר מלך צדנם אם בנן אית
בת

16 אלנם אית [בת עשתר]ת בצדן ארץ ים וישרן אית עשתרת שמם אדרם
ואנחן

17 אש בנן בת לאשמן [ש]ר קדש ען ידלל בהר וישבני שמם אדרם ואנחן
אש בנן בתם

18 לאלן צדנם בצדן ארץ ים בת לבעל צדן ובת לעשתרת שם בעל ועד יתן
לן אדן מלכם

19 אית דאר ויפי ארצת דגן האדרת אש בשד שרן למדת עצמת אש פעלת
ויספננם

20 עלת גבל ארץ לכננם לצדנם לעל[ם] קנמי את כל ממלכת וכל אדם אל
יפתח עלתי

21 ואל יער עלתי ואל יעמסן במשכב ז ואל ישא אית חלת משכבי לם
יסגרנם

22 אלנם הקדשם אל ויקצן הממלכת הא והאדמם המת וזרעם לעלם

NOTES

1. בל; 1 Kgs. vi 38. In Phoen. date formulas against the practice in Hebr., 'year', 'month', and 'day', are usually in the plur., though the sing. (שת) is also found (**31** Umm El-'Amed iv 5). The sequence of combined numerals with the higher preceding the lower is also the opposite of the normal Hebr., and has been thought to reflect Greek influence in the Levant; but the same order is found sometimes in Hebr., e.g. Gen. xlvi 15 (an early text), though only once in the case of a number between 11 and 19 (Ezek. xlv 12). On אסר 'ten' with [s] for the expected [š] see the Note on phonology and grammar. למלכי; prob. infin. constr. as in 2 Kgs. xxiv 12, though in later Biblical texts a noun מלכות is used (Esth. ii 16). The suffix is prospective as in **15** Karatepe A i 17 (?) iii 4; below לקצתנם (9–10). On the names Eshmunazar and Tabnit and the gentilic צדנם see at **27** Tabnit 1–2.

2. דבר; presumably Piel; outside this inscr. only elsewhere in Poenulus (*duber*). לאמר is only attested here in the surviving Phoen.-Punic remains; an imperf. form occurs in **15** Karatepe C iv 14; see also at **22** Malta 1–2. נגזלת; Niphal; in Hebr. only Prov. iv 16 of sleep being snatched away, but cp. the usage of the Niph. of the cognate base GZR

14. King Tabnit, king of the Sidonians, grandson of King Eshmunazar, king of the Sidonians, and my mother Amotashtart,

15. priestess of Astarte, our lady the queen, daughter of King Eshmunazar, king of the Sidonians, are we who built the houses of

16. the gods — the [house of Astarte] in Sidon-Land-by-the-Sea, and we (also) established Astarte (in) Lofty-Heavens; and we

17. (it were) who built in the Mountain a house for Eshmun, the prince of the sanctuary of the *Ydll*-Spring, and we (also) established him (in) Lofty-Heavens; and we (it were) who built houses

18. for the gods of the Sidonians in Sidon-Land-by-the-Sea, a house for Baal of Sidon and a house for Astarte-Name-of-Baal. Furthermore, the lord of kings gave us

19. Dor and Joppa, the rich lands of Dagon which are in the plain of Sharon, as a reward for the striking deeds which I performed; and we added them

20. to the borders of the land, that they might belong to the Sidonians for ever. Whoever you are, be you ruler or be you commoner, let none such open up (what is) over me

21. or uncover (what is) over me or carry me away from this resting-place; and let none such lift up the box in which I lie, lest

22. these holy gods deliver them up so that both that ruler or those commoners and their seed perish for ever!

    in Ps. lxxxviii 6 Isa. liii 8 Lam. iii 54 Ezek. xxxvii 11, all of a person cut off violently by death.

3. בל in בל עתי should prob. be vocalized [blō], lit. 'in not', as in the similar phrase in Eccles. vii 17 (cp. Job xxii 16), though [lō] has not been found elsewhere in Phoen.; the negative [bal] is otherwise only used with verbs or to negate a noun (בל אש; **15** Karatepe A i 15). Ugar. has all three usages, *bl* with a verb (e.g. **4** v 123), *bl* with a noun (e.g. *blmt* 'immortality', **16** i 15) and *bl* = *b* + *l* in e.g. *bl spr* 'without number' (**14** 90). The noun עתי is thus genit. following the prepos. בל, and the consonantal suffix is as expected. The whole passage may be further illustrated from Isa. xxxviii 10 ff. Ps. cii 24–5. בן מסך ימם אזרם; this is the traditional division, with אזרם seen as an adject. qualifying ימם (see below). מסך is prob. related to Aram. [skā] 'number, sum' from a base SKY, and to Syr. [sākā] 'end, limit, sum' from a related base SWK (cp. also Hebr. SWK/ŚWK 'to enclose'; Job i 10 iii 23). Hebr. [sak] 'mass, throng' (Ps. xlii 5) may also be connected. The Hebr. idiom ימים מספר, lit. 'days, a number', i.e. 'a few days' (Num. ix 20), may be compared; cp. for the thought also Job x 20 xiv 1. If אזרם is taken as a Niph. verb (see below), a translation 'I am to be cut off from, deprived of the due number of days' is not unattractive when we remember that

Eshmunazar is speaking, as it were, on his deathbed, i.e. מ(נ)סך; but it leaves בן unaccounted for ('a son (who) am to be cut off …'?). Lipiński's suggestion בנם סך etc. gives a better syntax, though it is rather imaginative, 'With the sleep of a deaf man (i.e. the deep sleep of death) I must break off (Qal) the days (of life)'; cp. Ps. lxxvi 6 where NWM may have the meaning 'to die' and Akkad. *sakku,* Arab. ['asakku] 'deaf'. These renderings have the merit of connecting אזרם not with Hebr. 'ZR 'to gird' ('a few restricted days') or (Greenfield citing Tur-Sinai) Akkad. *ezēru* 'to curse' ('a few accursed days'), neither of which is very convincing, but with the base ZRM, Arab. 'to cut off' and similarly in Hebr. in Ps. xc 5 (with God as subject), where the suffix 'them' refers to the 'years' of vs. 4 (NEB). This must surely be right. I am inclined (cp. G. R. Driver in *ZAW* 65 (1953), 259) to take אזרם as a technical term from this base denoting someone smitten early in life with an incurable disease; cp. the Arab. formation ['af'alu] (as in the word for 'deaf' above) denoting physical defects. Possibly the notoriously difficult Punic phrase אזרם אש(ת) in texts connected with the מלך sacrifice has a similar connotation, i.e. 'one afflicted, male (female)' as opposed to an unblemished child (in the phase בשרם בתם); see at **21, 22** Malta. אלמת = ['almat(t)] < [almant(u)] against Hebr. אלמנה < ['almanat(u)]; cp. 1 Kgs. vii 14 (of Hiram, the Tyrian craftsman); Lam. v 3. The phrase is to be taken literally, meaning that Tabnit died before his son was born, otherwise it is rather tautologous. שכב; partic.; **27** Tabnit 2. חלת; prob. referring to the sarcophagus; cp. Syr. [ḥelltā] 'sheath, bucket'; Arab. [ḥallatu] 'basket, saucepan'. On ‬ת fem. see at **15** Karatepe A ii 9.

4. קנמי את; see at **25** Yehaumilk 11 for the formula and the change of person in the following verbs (here 3 sing. changing to 2 sing. in 6 and 3 plur. in 8 ff.) Syncope of [h] of the article is perhaps to be assumed here and in 10 (cp. זי הארן את; **27** Tabnit 3); similarly after עלת (7, 10) after אם (10, 11), after תחת (12), and in the construct relation after זרע (11), בת (15), מדת (19), and גבל (20). See the Note on phonology and grammar; see also below 22. On משכב see at **27** Tabnit 8.

5. בן = [binnū] or the like < [binhū]; see at **15** Karatepe A iii 8. מנם; **27** Tabnit 5. אי שם; cp. אי אר (**27** Tabnit 4). יעמסן; prob. Piel; cp. Ugar. *'ms* 'lift up, load' (**6** i 12 with a dead body as object) but *m'ms* 'supporting, carrying' (**17** i 31); the Piel should perhaps also be read in Ps. lxviii 20. The form is jussive ending in [ū] with 1 pers. suffix [nī], over against the imperf. (ידברנך; 6) ending in [ūn]; this distinction seems by and large to be observed in older texts but is lost in Punic, where indicatives are commonly found without the ‬ן. In Hebr. the ending [un] is not uncommon, but is paragogic rather than modal, since it is found with jussives as well as indicatives; e.g. Job xxxi 10. Cp., however, Isa. xxvi 11, where when the same verb is used in different moods, the old distinction reappears. Note the parallel pair עמס and נשא, used together in Ugar. (**6** i 12, 14) and in Isa. xlvi 3 (passive participles).

6. ב 'from'; **7** Abibaal 2. עלת; **25** Yehaumilk 11; here with the meaning 'to', in 7 'over'. שני (with consonatal ending [iy]), lit. 'second', equivalent to זר in **15** Karatepe A iii 16. אף אם begins a new conditional sentence; cp. אם אף in **15** Karatepe A iii 14 introducing a new alternative protasis. Notice [dibbēr] with direct object (person), rare in Hebrew. בדנם = [baddēnōm]; Hebr. [baddīm] (Jerem. xlviii 30); from a base BDD attested in Ugar. with the meaning 'recite, chant' (of a minstrel or story-teller; **3** A 18 **17** vi 31); not, therefore, necessarily 'idle talk'. There is no need to emend

to בד\(בר\)נם, especially when דברים is always a direct object after שמע in Hebrew. Ginsberg proposes בד = Hebr. בדי, i.e. [bdē] with the sense '(listen) to'; he reads [bdē] for all occurrences of Hebr. [baddīm], possibly correctly in Job xi 3 ('keep silence before, because of') and Job xli 4 ('keep silence about') but not, I think, in Jerem. xlviii 30 and the similar passage Isa. xvi 6; moreover, none of these examples or the previously recognized ones (e.g. Jerem. li 58   Job xxxix 25) is at all comparable with the 'listen to' required here.

7. יפתח עלת with משכב, similarly 10; contrast 4, where משכב is direct object, and תפתח עלתי (**27** Tabnit 4).

8. אל יכן etc.; **27** Tabnit 7–8. לם = [lōm] < [lahumu]; contrast בנם = [binōm] (9), where the connecting vowel is [i]. יקבר; Niphal jussive plur.; cp. Jerem. viii 2   Eccles. vi 3.

9. תחתנם = [tahtēnom] with a plur. base as in Hebr.; contrast the different structure תחתן in **13** Kilamuwa i 14. סגר; jussive Piel or Yiphil (Hiph.) as in Hebr. with the sense of 'deliver up to'. את therefore has the meaning 'to' as in **25** Yehaumilk 3, 7 (קרא את). האלנם הקדשם; cp. **6** Yehimilk 5   **15** Karatepe A i 8   **25** Yehaumilk 10. ממלכת אדר; the noun though fem. in form is construed as a masc. in its derived sense of 'ruler' (**25** Yehaumilk 2); perhaps simply a wish that the grave violators be captured by a future king and punished; cp. the verb אדר in **13** Kilamuwa i 7; Ps. cxxxvi 18   Isa. xix 4. The phrase 'who will rule over them', however, does not then make much sense, so it is likely that 'a mighty ruler' is a euphemism for the god of death; cp. Ps. lxxviii 50 and Job xviii 14; cp. also the *rex tremendus* of Virgil, *Georgics* iv 469. Note that a letter is omitted from ממלכת in 11 as well. משל; surely what Hebraists would call a prophetic perf. rather than a partic.; a distinct poetic touch. לקצתנם; prob. ל with the Qal infin., i.e. [qṣōt], meaning 'to be cut off, come to an end, perish', since the object marker אית, which is consistently used in this insr. (at least with the first noun in the various sequences), is missing after יקצן (22), suggesting that הממלכת הא is there part of the subject. In that case אית ממלכת (where syncope of [h] should perhaps be assumed) is properly resumptive after the suffix in יסגרנם; see further on this construction at **15** Karatepe A i 17 iii 4. Note that the הא after אדם seems to do duty for ממלכת as well.

11. המת; **13** Kilamuwa i 13. שרש למט etc.; cp. Isa. xxxvii 31 (למטה ... למעלה), Amos ii 9 (ממעל ... מתחת), Job xviii 16 (קציר for פרי); clearly a well-known rhetorical idiom in Hebr. and Phoen., though note the slight variations in usage.

12. תאר lit. 'form, outline, appearance'; the nuance is 'imposing presence' as in 1 Sam. xvi 18 or 'dignity, renown' as in Isa. liii 2 (‖ הדר) rather than simply 'beauty, comeliness' as in Jerem. xi 16 (‖ יפה) and Isa. lii 14 (describing the Servant's ugly appearance). The word occurs in Punic texts with the meaning 'design, plan' (*DISO* p. 323). בחים etc.; see at **27** Tabnit 7. נחן; apparently Niph. partic. (with gerundive nuance as frequently in Hebr.) from ḤNN; the Niph. occurs in Hebr. only in Jerem. xxii 23, showing that it was known by the Massoretes even if the original text (cp. the Versions) had a form from 'NḤ 'to groan'. Rosenthal (in *ANET*) argues that the mason may have meant to write אנחן 'we' (cp. end of 16) and to begin at this point the sentence with כ that actually starts in the middle of 13, i.e. כ אנחן אנך etc. followed in 14 with ואמי. In his opinion the sentence 'I have been seized, etc.' is out of place here, though the inscr. is elsewhere heavily loaded with

repetitions. He may be right, but we have still to suppose that what the mason in fact put down makes sense. נגזלת etc.; see above 2–3 and notice the extra אנך, this time at both the beginning and end of the sentence.

13–14. אמי = ['immī]; nomin.; cp. שמי (**15** Karatepe C iv 18; accusative). אמעשתרת; possibly 'Astarte is my mother', a name found in Punic, though of a male; but more prob. 'handmaid of Astarte' (cp. **35** 3) with the [t] of אמת assimilated to the following consonant, or dropped altogether, as in אמאשמן and אמשמן 'handmaid of Eshmun'; references in Benz, *Names*, pp. 61, 62, 269; on the form of אמת see at **20** Ur box 1. Amo(t)ashtart (or Immī'ashtart) was a half-sister of her husband Tabnit, both having Eshmunazar I as their father. She is described as priestess of Astarte, though the kings do not in this inscr. have the title priests, as Tabnit called himself and his father in his own inscr. (**27** 1). Perhaps the titles are omitted here because Eshmunazar (II) was not old enough to have become a priest; or perhaps the Sidonian kings did not make as much of their priestly role as modern scholars do; or again, it is possible that only some kings were priests (Azbaal of Byblos is not called a priest, though his father, who was not king, was one; **26** Batnoam). During her son's infancy Amotashtart would be the effective ruler and since she is mentioned in connection with all his achievements prob. shared the rule with him till his early death; cp. the role of the *tavannana,* mother of the heir apparent, in the Hittite empire and of the [gbīrā] or 'queen mother' in Judah; that the authority of the latter was substantial is shown by the ease with which Athaliah seized power on the death of Ahaziah (2 Kgs. xi 1 ff.). See further de Vaux, *Ancient Israel,* chapt. 6, sect. 2.

15. רבתן; on the connecting vowel with the 1 plur. suffix ([u]) see at **16** Seville 4; perhaps like Hebr. [gbīrā] a title given to the queen mother. אם is clearly an error for אש 'the ones who', predicate of ואמי ..... אנך. בנן = [banīnū]; in the case of the buildings mentioned perhaps 'rebuilt', as often in royal inscrs. (e.g. **15** Karatepe A ii 9). בת; plur. construct, since at least four 'houses' built or rebuilt by Eshmunazar and his mother are mentioned in the following lines; we have prob. to think of smaller shrines like the one renovated by Yehaumilk (**25**) rather than of large temples like the one erected by Bodashtart for Eshmun at Bostan Esh-Sheikh (*KAI* nos. 15, 16 = Magnanini, *Iscrizioni,* pp. 7–9).

16. אלנם; **15** Karatepe A iii 5. Comparison with the Bodashtart i inscr. (*KAI* no. 15) suggests that צדן ארץ ים and צדן ים are alternative names for a district within the Sidonian state, prob. the central city area as distinct from צדן שד (Bodashtart), the country district a little to the north where the Eshmun temple was built, and ההר (17), a district further inland. שמם אדרם (cp. Ezek. xvii 23) like שמם רמם (the same?) and the two names following it in Bodashtart will then describe shrines or sacred precincts within צדן (ארץ) ים; in the one here a goddess's statue is set up, and the ones in Boadashtart i are 'built'. ישרן; a mason's error for ישבן (17); cp. **15** Karatepe A ii 18 II **13** Hadad 19. The prepos. ב has to be understood before שמם אדרם here and in the next line, in both cases following a ב in the previous clause; cp. Bodashtart i, where ב is used with צדן ים but not with צדן שד; are these examples in prose of the well-known 'double-duty' prepos. of Ugar. and Hebr. verse? See further at **23** Arslan Tash i 1.

17. שר קדש; also in Bodashtart; that ר should be read in preference to ד

seems certain in view of Hebr. שרי קדש (1 Chron. xxiv 5 and possibly Isa. xliii 28), a title of high officials in the Jerusalem temple and perhaps an adaptation of an older Canaanite title. It is here an epithet of Eshmum associating him with his chief sanctuary in צדן שד (a predecessor of the temple built by Bodashtart); for the Baalshillem inscr. (**29**), which was found on the site of Bodashtart's temple, makes it clear that the spring (Hebr. עין) of ידלל or (Baalshillem) ידל was in that vicinity and not in ההר, a name that can only denote a mountainous district inland from Sidon. Garbini reads ען ידל לבהר, making the name of the spring the same as in Baalshillem, but situating 'the house' 'at the pool' (cp. Hebr. באר), which could have been in Sidon itself. He cites in support a plur. form בהרם occurring in a Neo-Punic inscr.; but this reference is questionable (see *DISO* p. 32), especially as the Hebr. plur. is בארת; and the local sense given to ל is also awkward. ישבני = [yōšabnūyū] or the like with consonantal suffix after [ū].

18. בעל צדן; the chief god of Sidon (Baal) who with his consort Astarte under the title 'name-of-Baal' are in a special sense not applicable to Astarte in other roles or to Eshmun the 'gods of the Sidonians'. שם בעל; a title of Astarte as a manifestation or reflection of her husband; it occurs in Ugar. as *'ttrt šm b'l* (**16** vi 56); cp. the Biblical phrase 'the Name of Yahweh' to describe his manifested presence (Exod. xxiii 21 1 Kgs. viii 16 Isa. xviii 7, etc.); cp. also סמל בעל (Abdeshmun inscr. 3 = *KAI* no. 12; Magnanini, *Iscrizioni*, p. 30). This shrine of Astarte is different from the one mentioned in 16 and may have been contiguous to that of Baal. עד; Hebr. ['ōd], though not in this usage. יתן; perfect. לן prob. = [lu/ōn(ū)]; see at רבתן (**15**); alternatively [lanī] 'to me' in agreement with פעלת (19); see at **27** Tabnit 4. אדן מלכם; in **31** Umm El-'Amed iv 5 the title refers to the Ptolemies, but in this inscr. it must refer to the Persian emperor; cp. II **21** 1, where in the 6 cent. Aram. letter of Adon an Aram. rendering of the title (מרא מלכן) refers to the Egyptian Pharaoh. It used too readily to be assumed that the title was derived from the Greek κύριος βασιλέων of Ptolemaic inscrs. and that this and the previous inscr. therefore belonged to around 300 BC; but it is now accepted that all three titles, the Greek, the Phoen., and the Aram., are prob. connected with the late Assyrian *bēl šarrāni*, and it is not impossible that the Phoen. title is primary, signifying the imperial ruler of the day. The occurrence in Dan. ii 47, where it is applied to Yahweh, doubtless depends on the Akkad. usage. The title is to be distinguishd both from the Greek κύριος βασιλειῶν (Rosetta stone), which reflects an indigenous Egyp. epithet 'lord of the (two) kingdoms', and the Achaemenid 'king of kings' (Ezra vii 12 Dan. ii 37). See further in Galling's article and at II **21** 1.

19. דאר (Hebr. דאר, דור; Akkad. *Du'ru*) and יפי (Hebr. יפוא, יפו) on the Palestinian coast were with their hinterland the Plain of Sharon prob. ceded to Eshmunazar in return for naval assistance in the Persian wars with Greece (Galling); similar blocks of coastland were, according to Pseudo-Scylax, granted to Tyre (see M. Avi-Yonah, *The Holy Land from the Persian to the Arab Conquest*, 1966, 27 ff.). Because of their commercial rivalry with the Greeks throughout the Mediterranean, it was in the interests of the Phoen. states to remain on cordial terms with their Persian overlords, and in fact they rarely attempted rebellion. On the importance of this reference for dating the Tabnit and Eshmunazar inscrs., see the introd. to the former (**27**). The fertile lands of coastal

Palestine would serve as granaries for the Phoen. urban populations, as is hinted at in the following reference to lands of דגן, whether this is the god Dagon, long associated with the area (Judg. xvi 23) or the related(?) term [dagān] 'corn' (Deut. xxxiii 28). האדרת; plur. fem.; cp. Zech. xi 3 (NEB 'their rich pastures'). שד = [šadē]; Hebr. [śadē]. שרן; Isa. xxxv 2 lxv 10. למדת עצמת; cp. כמדת (*CIS* i 165 = = *KAI* no. 69 Marseilles Tariff 17) 'in conformity with', lit. 'according to the measure of' and Hebr. עצומות 'powerful, striking', used of words (Isa. xli 21 Ben Sira xvi 5). The allusion is most obviously to assistance given to the Persians (see above); for that reason a connection with Hebr. and Aram. מ(נ)דה 'tribute', a loan-word from Akkad. *mandattu* (e.g. Neh. v 4 Ezra iv 20 vi 8) is unlikely, i.e. 'in return for the massive tribute which I made'; moreover פעל in this sense is not easy to parallel, and one would also expect the article with עצמת as a sing. adjective. Note the change to a 1 pers. verb, perhaps because the help given to the Persians was ratified in the king's name but perhaps just a careless slip since the next verb is 1 plural. ספננם; Qal or Yiph. perfect with 'heavy' suffix after [nū]; cp. I **16** Mesha 21, 29 (Qal) II **5** Zakir B 4 (Haphel). The suffix is prob. fem. ([nēm]), referring to Dor and Joppa; this is the usual practice in Hebr., though there are exceptions; see Note on phonology and grammar.

20. עלת; 6. לכננם = [lkūninēm] or the like. קנמי את etc.; see at 4 ff. עלתי; **27** Tabnit 4.

21. יער = [y'a(r)rē]; Piel jussive; cp. 2 Chron. xxiv 11. לם 'lest'; cp. Hebr. למה (originally 'why?') in Gen. xxvii 45   xlvii 19   Exod. xxxii 12   Ps. lxxix 10 etc., recognized by the Septuagint (μήποτε, ἵνα μη) but not often by modern translators. See Ginsberg's note ('Ugaritico-Phoenicia', 138–9). יסגרנם; prob. jussive (cp. 9) expressing the potential mood 'or else they may', in contrast with יקצן (22), which is imperf. following ו expressing consequence; i.e. [yasgīrūnōm] (Yiph.) and [yiqṣūn] (Qal). On QSY (Qal) 'to perish' see at לקצתנם (9) and for further examples of the distinction between jussive and imperf. in the 3 plur. see יכבד (**13** Kilamuwa i 14) and יתלנן (ibid. 10).

22. Note that there is no article with אלנם, though there is one with the following adjective; this may be a mason's error (there are several in the inscr.), but if not, it casts considerable doubt on Lambdin's attempts to regularize the usage of the Phoen. article (see Note on phonology and grammar).

29 Baalshillem (Sidon)

The inscr. is written in small characters in a single line 50 cm. long on a plinth which had once carried the statue of a child. The fragment was discovered along with ten other such objects, mostly uninscribed, in the excavations of the temple of Eshmun at Bostan Esh-Sheikh carried out by Dunand in 1963–4; its inscr. is the only one that is well preserved. A number of fragmentary ostraca, which supply welcome information on Phoen. cursive writing, were also found in the excavations; see Bibliographical Notes. The statues, with or without inscriptions, were apparently dedicated to Eshmun or to Eshmun in company with other deities on behalf of children who were ill. In the case of the present inscr. the child in question was a prince and prob. the crown prince or heir apparent, since a full genealogy is supplied reaching back to his great-grandfather, who had the same name (Baalshillem) and was presumably the founder of the dynasty; the other two names are Ba'na and Abdamun. It seems very likely that these four kings (assuming the young Baalshillem to have recovered from his illness and succeeded in due course) are denoted by the monograms ב (Baalshillem), במ (also Baalshillem), בע (Ba'na), עב (Abdamun), and עם (also Abdamun) on some of the earliest known coins from Sidon. All four reigns must have been over by c.375 BC, when according to Peckham (*Scripts,* 74) the coins of a certain Straton I (prob. for Abdashtart) begin. Since son regularly succeeded father, at least the two middle reigns must have been upwards of 20 years, which indicates a date not later and prob. a decade or so earlier than c.425 for the start of the dynasty. Baalshillem being still a child when his inscr. was written, we may date it around 400 or a little after. With the other finds from the same excavations, it is housed in the Museum at Beirut.

Bibliography

M. Dunand. 'Nouvelles inscriptions phéniciennes du temple d'Eshmoun à Bostan esh-Chekh, près Sidon', *BMB* 18 (1965), 105–9.
Röllig, 'Beiträge', 121–4.
Teixidor, 'Bulletin' for 1972, item 115 (with photograph).
Magnanini, *Iscrizioni,* p. 12.
E. T. Mullen, 'A new royal Sidonian inscription', *BASOR* 216 (1974), 25–30.

הסמל ז אש יתן בעלשלם בן מלך בענא מלך צדנם בן מלך עבדאמן מלך

צדנם בן מלך בעלשלם מלך צדנם לאדני לאשמן בען ידל יברך

This (is the) statue which Baalshillem son of King Ba'na, king of the Sidonians, son of King Abdamun, king of the Sidonians, son of King Baalshillem, king of the Sidonians, gave to his lord Eshmun at the *Ydl*-Spring. May he bless him!

NOTES

בעלשלם 'Baal has requited' (Piel verb); Benz, *Names,* p. 417. בענא with the ending [a'] or [ō]; the same name is found in Hebr. (1 Kgs. iv 12), and is prob. an abbreviation of a fuller name like בעלחנא (Benz, op. cit., p. 90) or בעליתן (94). עבדאמן 'servant of Amun'; the name occurs again at Elephantine and in Punic (Benz, op. cit., p. 149), but it is surprising to find an Egypt. divine element in a Phoen. royal name of the Persian period, and some think

116 PHOENICIAN INSCRIPTIONS

אמן is a weakened form of חמן; cp. עבדחמן (2 Byblos cone); see further Lipiński in *Bibl. Or.* 32 (1975), 77, 79. עז ידל; the name of a spring at the site of the temple and very prob. the same as the עז ידלל of **28** Eshmunazar 17 (q.v. Note). יברך = [ybar(r)kō] (Piel) with unwritten vocalic suffix, the connecting vowel being [a], i.e. [ō] < [ahū]; in Hebr. the connecting vowel is usually [i], giving [ēhū], but cp. יאהבו (1 Sam. xviii 1, Keth.), ירדפו (Hos. viii 3) etc. That a suffix should be there is shown by forms like יברכא with א = [ō] (*KAI* no. 98 Sousse 4–5 and other Punic examples).

30 Throne of Astarte (Tyre)

The inscr., which belongs to the 2 cent. BC and is now in the Louvre, is written across the socle of an empty stone throne flanked on either side by a griffin or sphinx. The wings of these creatures support the seat and encircle the back of the throne, the latter being made up of two steles, on each of which is carved in relief a male divine figure; the figures are doubtless of Baal (Baalshamem) and Melcarth, who form with Astarte the Tyrian triad of chief deities (see *Note* below) corresponding to El, Baalat, and Adonis at Byblos (see at **6** Yehimilk 1–2) and Baal, Astarte, and Eshmun at Sidon (see at **27** Tabnit 1). On the front of the seat above the inscr. and between the two creatures is further carving that includes a large crescent and two lotus flowers. The empty throne may have been intended to take an effigy of the goddess, but it is more prob. that it and a few other (uninscribed) exemplars from the region of Tyre and Sidon fulfilled in Phoen. rituals a similar role to the Ark of the Covenant with its Cherubim on Israelite cultic occasions and represented the invisible presence of the deity; cp. Exod. xxv 10–22 for a description of the Ark, and the allusions in 1 Sam. iv 4   2 Sam. vi 2   2 Kgs. xix 15   1 Chron. xxviii 2   Ps. xcix 5   cxxxii 7   Ezek. xliii 7. See further H. Seyrig, *Syria* 36 (1959), 48 ff.; R. de Vaux, *Ancient Israel,* part II, chapt. 2, sect. 3.

[*Note*: that at Tyre the leading god was Baal and not Melcarth is indicated by the section in Esarhaddon's treaty with the king of Tyre which lists the deities of the respective partners (*ANET* p. 534). Tyre's gods are given in this order: the Weather-god under three aspects (Baalshamem, Baalmalage, and Baal-Saphon), then Melcarth and Eshmun, and lastly Astarte. It seems clear from the mention of Eshmun of Sidon alongside Melcarth, and from the curse they are invoked to bring about should the king of Tyre break the treaty ('may they make disappear food ... clothes ... oil'), that not only is Melcarth to be distinguished from Baal but that both these 'young' deities are vegetation gods like Adonis of Byblos; contrast the quite different curse to do with the destructive force of the wind which the 'Baal' deities are invited to put into operation. See further on these matters the Note to **6** Yehimilk 3; Teixidor, 'Bulletin' for 1974, item 56; and for another interpretation, which I find too subtle, of the pantheon of Tyre, R. du Mesnil du Buisson, *Nouvelles études sur les dieux et les mythes de Canaan* (1973), chapt. II.]

Bibliography

There are early studies by S. Ronzevalle in *CRAIBL,* 1907, 589–98 and in *Mélanges de la Faculté Orientale* (Beirut) 3 (1909), 755–83; and by Ch. Clermont-Ganneau in *CRAIBL,* 1907, 606 ff.
See further:
RÉS no. 800.
KAI no. 17.
J. T. Milik in *Biblica* 48 (1967), 546 ff., 572 ff.
Magnanini, *Iscrizioni,* p. 26.
Teixidor, 'Bulletin' for 1976, item 61.

Illustrations

Ronzevalle, loc. cit. (*Mélanges*), pl. IX, X; du Mesnil du Buisson, op. cit., pl. II. (*Note*: I was unable to obtain a usable photo. of this inscription.)

1   לרבתי לעשתרת אש בגו הקדש

2   אש לי אנך עבדאבסת בן בדבעל

1.   To my lady Astarte who is (enthroned) in the holy congregation,
2.   that which is my very own (gift), 'BD'BST's son of Bodbaal.

NOTES

בגו should prob. not be rendered 'in the midst, interior (of the sanctuary)', i.e. like the Ark which was lodged in the Holy of Holies in the Jerusalem temple; for this prepositional phrase is only attested for Aramaic (see *DISO* p. 48). The word is rather (with Milik) to be related to גו 'body of people, community, congregation' as in **41** Piraeus 2 ff., where it parallels τὸ κοινόν in similar Greek inscriptions; in Hebr. in Job xxx 5. The two words have of course ultimately the same etymology, but that does not mean that they have to be confused semantically; other words from the same base are Hebr. גו 'back', גויה 'body', גוי 'nation', and Syr. [gawwā] 'interior of the body' but also 'community'. The usage גו הקדש may be compared with Hebr. עם (ה)קדש in Isa. lxii 12 Dan. xii 7. אש לי may go with Astarte, i.e. 'who is (also) my (goddess)' (cp. **36** Lapethos ii 9), in which case a verbal phrase has to be understood with אנך, e.g. 'I 'BD'BST ... (vowed this gift)'. Preferably here, however, אש means 'that which' (as commonly on votive inscrs.) and describes the object being dedicated, though לי in the sense of '(given, vowed) by me' sounds rather strange; אנך will then have a strenghening function, 'yes, mine', as in **15** Karatepe A ii 5 **25** Yehaumilk 12. Not possible is to take אש לי with קדש, i.e. 'the sanctuary (or congregation) which belongs to her' (Astarte), since that would require ל = [lā] as in **15** Karatepe A iii 16. עבדאבסת 'servant of

Bastet', i.e. the Egypt. cat goddess, written with the prosthetic ['] which sometimes appears in Egyp. spellings (thus not a Phoen. feature); attested in Phoen. names from Elephantine and Abydos, but also from Cyprus and Carthage; Benz, *Names*, pp. 258–9. Names with Egyp. divine elements become relatively common in late Phoen. texts and reflect the close relations between Egypt and Phoenicia that developed during the period of Ptolemaic overlordship in the 3 cent. BC, though it is uncertain how far they should be taken as evidence of a widespread adoption of Egyp. cults. בדבעל; see on names of this structure at **2, 3** clay cones.

31 Umm El-'Amed iv (222 BC)

The inscr., which is carved on a stone plaque, is dated internally to 222 BC and is now in the Louvre. It was purchased in 1885 from inhabitants of Ma'ṣub, a village between Tyre and Acco, but its true provenance is clearly Umm El-'Amed, a ruined site a little to its north, since the temple referred to in *l.* 4 must be the same as the temple uncovered in the excavations conducted there in the 1940s. The ancient name of Umm El-'Amed, as the inscr. indicates (3, 4), was חמן, very likely to be indentified with the חמון of Josh. xix 28, which was in the same area. The inscr. describes the dedication of a portico in the temple to Astarte, though the temple itself belonged to a male divinity called Milkashtart. Several other inscrs., mostly like this one dedicatory or votive in content, were found at Umm El-'Amed, either by Renan in his expedition of 1861 or in the later excavations; they were gathered together and assigned numbers in the book by Dunand and Duru (see below), the present inscr. being no. iv.

Bibliography

First published by Ch. Clermont-Ganneau in *Revue Archéologique*, III, 5 (1885), 381–4.
See further:
NSE p. 419.
NSI no. 10.
KI no. 16.
RÉS no. 1205.
E. Meyer, 'Untersuchungen zur phönikischen Religion', *ZAW* 49 (1931), 1 ff.
KAI no. 19.
M. Dunand, R. Duru, *Oumm el 'Amed, une ville de l'époque hellénistique aux échelles de Tyr* (1962), 185–7.
J. T. Milik in H. Seyrig, 'Les grands dieux de Tyr à l'époque grecque et romaine', *Syria* 40 (1963), 26–7.
A. Caquot in *Semitica* 15 (1965), 29 ff. (on Milkashtart).
A. van den Branden, 'L'iscrizione fenicia di Ma'ṣub', *Bibbia e Oriente* 7 (1965), 69–75.
Magnanini, *Iscrizioni*, p. 17.

Illustrations

NSE Taf. V, 3; Dunand-Duru, op. cit., pl. LXXXVIII, 1.

1 ערפת כברת מצא שמש וצ

2 פלי אש בן האלם מלאך מלך

3 עשתרת ועבדי בעל חמן

4 לעשתרת באשרת אל חמן

5 בשת 26 לפתלמיס אדן

6 מלכם האדר פעל נעם בן פת

7 למיס וארסנאס אלן א[ח]

8 ים שלש חמשם שת לעם [צר]

9 כמאש בן אית כל אחרי ה[מק]

10 [דש]ֿם אש בארץ לכן לֿם לֿ[סכר]

11 [ושם נעם ל] עֿלם

1. The portico of the west quarter and
2. its ....., which the god the Angel of Milkashtart
3. and his servants the citizens of Hammon built
4. for Astarte in the shrine of the god of Hammon,
5. in the 26th year of Ptolemy, lord of
6. kings, the noble, the beneficent, son of
7. Ptolemy and Arsinoë, the divine brother and sister,
8. (being) the fifty-third year of the people of [Tyre],
9. just as they built all the other [sanctuaries]
10. which are in the land, to be to them [for a memorial]
11. [and a goodly name for] ever.

NOTES

1. ערפת; **25** Yehaumilk 6. כברת; cp. Hebr. כברה 'space, distance' (Gen. xxxv 16) and Akkad. *kibrātu*, usually plur. of the four 'quarters' of the world. Perhaps assume syncope of [h] of the article before שמש, this defining the whole phrase; or כברת is an 'accusative of place' as in Exod. xxxiii 10 Ruth iii 8 etc., though this is less likely since one would then expect the opening word to have the article. צפלי; unknown plur. noun with י indicating the suffix (fem.); if the word were sing., the suffix would be vocalic and unexpressed in the orthography; cp. עבדי (3).

2. האלם 'the god'; see at **15** Karatepe C iii 16. This is a strange statement, in which a divine being called the 'angel' or 'messenger' of the deity

Milkashtart is associated with the citizens of Hammon in building the portico. Before the latest inscrs. from Umm El-'Amed were discovered האלם was thought to be a title of human 'envoys' (מלאך) or officials of the cultus (cp. אילי מואב, lit. 'rams of Moab', Exod. xv 15; אילי הארץ, Ezek. xvii 13, etc.); but inscr. xiii (32), in which Milkashtart and the Angel of Milkashtart are together called האלנם (plur.) makes this interpretation untenable; and in fact other inscrs. are known in which deities are involved in the dedications; see the book by Milik mentioned in the Bibliogr. to 32. Milkashtart, a deity especially worshipped at Umm El-'Amed, is a fusion of two deities, El ('the king'; see at 6 Yehimilk 1; Benz, *Names,* p. 344) and Astarte, a compound deity like אשמנעשתרת (*CIS* i 245, 3 f.), עשתר כמש (I 16 Mesha 17) and the Ugar. gods Kothar-and-Khasis, Qodesh-and-Amrur, etc. The phrase *mlk 'ttrth* of the Ugar. text RS 24.244, *l.* 41 (*CML²* p. 139) is prob. unconnected, since the goddess's name there has *h-locale* and is thus a shortened form of a place-name. The suggestion that the name means 'Melc(arth) (husband of) Astarte' wrongly equates Melcarth with Baal (see in the introd. to 30 Throne of Astarte).

3. בעל חמן; cp. xiii (32) 2, where בעל is sing. following a proper name; בעלי כתר (II 7 Sefire i A 4) etc. חמן is prob. the same as חמון in Josh. xix 28, claimed as belonging to Asher; this Canaanite area was, however, only briefly conquered by David and was ceded to Tyre during Solomon's reign (2 Sam. xxiv 6–7   1 Kgs. ix 11). The name may survive in that of the Wadi Ḥamūl, which runs by the site of Umm El-'Amed, though this does not have the double [m] of the Biblical name. It prob. also occurs in the title of the Carthaginian deity Baal-Hammon, who as the reference to him in 13 Kilamuwa i 16 (q.v.) shows, cannot have been Punic in origin; his cult was prob. carried to both areas by Tyrian colonists or traders; see also at 21 Malta 3–4. In other words Baal-Hammon is the predecessor of the god (אל) of Hammon in *l.* 4, which is here a title of Milkashtart but may earlier have been a title of El (as is Baal-Hammon itself) associating him with this holy place. The divine name Baal-Hammon cannot of course be read here in conjunction with עבדי.

4. אשרת is to be connected with Hebr. אשרה '(sacred) place, grove, shrine' and Akkad. *aširtu* 'sanctuary'; it has nothing to do with the goddess Athirat or with sacred trees or poles as her symbol. See the discussion by Lipiński in *Orientalia Lovaniensia Periodica* 3 (1972), 111 ff. A masc. form occurs in אשר קדש, 42 Pyrgi 1; cp. Akkad. *ašru* with the meaning 'shrine' and the Hebr. plurs. אשרים and אשרות. אל prob. 'god', referring back to Milkashtart, rather than the divine name El.

5. בשת; prob. construct as Hebr. שנת in 1 Kgs. xxii 41. The numeral is formed of the sign for 20 followed by two sets of 3 strokes. In 8 where the numeral is written out שת follows; this is the commonest order in Hebr. (e.g. 2 Kgs. xviii 13); in 28 Eshmunazar 1 the plur. שנת is used, the usual construction in Phoenician. אדן מלכם; 28 Eshmunazar 18; here referring to Ptolemy III (247–221 BC). Phoenicia along with Palestine passed to Seleucid overlordship not long after this.

6. האדר prob. reflects the Greek title μεγαλοδόξος used by the Ptolemies, as does פעל נעם Ptolemy III's epithet εὐεργέτης, though both have Phoen. antecedents; 13 Kilamuwa i 5   15 Karatepe A iii 4   25 Yehaumilk 8. His father was Ptolemy II Philadelphos (285–247 BC).

7. ארסנאס, i.e. 'Αρσινόη (the Phoen. transliterates the Greek genit.), wife

and sister of Ptolemy II. אלן א[ח]ים means lit. '(the) gods, (the) two brothers', and is intended to render the Greek θεῶν ἀδελφῶν, 'the divine brother and sister' (genit.), as in a bilingual inscr. of Canopus (238 BC), where the pair are so styled. Note that the dual of אח retains the [y] of the base, i.e. ['ḥayēm] or the like; the dual is rare in Phoen. as in Hebr. (apart from nouns for parts of the body which go in pairs) and is prob. used here artificially because it translates a Greek title referring to two people. It is unlikely that the use of such titles indicates any more than an appropriation of Ptolemaic dating procedures, though there is some evidence from Cyprus that the cult of the deified Ptolemy was practised, at least in official circles, after that island passed into Egypt. possession; see at **36** 5.

8. לעם צר; as in i 6 (*KAI* no. 18 = Magnanini, *Iscrizioni*, p. 16); the first era of Tyre, which according to the synchronisms of these two inscrs. was calculated from 274 BC, when she must have become a republic.

9. כמאש; **25** Yehaumilk 7 **26** Batnoam. אחרי; cp. אחרי השאר, 'the rest of the flesh' (*CIS* i 65 = *KAI* no. 69 Marseilles tariff 4, 8); the ' is apparently a consonantal ending, not a *mater lectionis* for [ē] (?).

10–11. המקדשם is a conjecture but the remaining lacunas are filled after i 6–8. לכן followed by the prepos. ל twice; cp. in Hebr. Gen. xxviii 21 Exod. xxix 28 xl 15 etc. לם = [lōm] < [lahumu]. סכר; so (with a few exceptions) the base ZKR in Phoen., perhaps because of the following [k]; cp. in Hebr. Exod. iii 15 Prov. x 7 Isa. xxvi 8 (all parallel to שם) Hos. xiv 8 Eccles. ix 5. שם נעם; cp. II **19** Nerab ii 3 Ps. cxxxv 3.

32 Umm El-'Amed xiii

The inscr. is written on the socle (45 cm. broad) of a statue of a sphinx, of which only the front feet survive. The monument, now in the Beirut Museum, was found in the later excavations and first published in the book by Dunand and Duru, pp. 192–3; pl. XXXI with a sketch on p. 192.

See further the articles by Milik and Caquot mentioned in the Bibliogr. to **31** (iv); Milik's book, *Recherches d'épigraphie proche-orientale*, I, *Dédicaces faites par des dieux (Palmyre, Hatra, Tyr)*, 1972, 424–5; C. R. Krahmalkov in *RSO* 47 (1971), 33 ff.; Teixidor 'Bulletin' for 1973, item 118; Magnanini, *Iscrizioni*, p. 22.

1 לאדני למלכעשתרת אל חמן כפרת חרץ מתם אש יתן עבדך

2 עבדאדני בן עֿבדאלנם בן[ן] עשת[ר]תעזר ב[–?]על חמן כמאשי

3 להאלנֿםֿ מלכעשתרת ומלאך מלכעשתרת כ שמע קל יברך

1. To my lord Milkashtart, god of Hammon, a propitiatory offering of an entire sculpture which your servant
2. Abdadoni son of Abdelonim son of Ashtartazara, citizen of Hammon, has given as his donation
3. to the gods Milkashtart and the Angel of Milkashtart, because he heard his voice. May he bless him!

NOTES

1. On the deity and the title אל חמן see at **31** iv 2 ff. כפרת; so Caquot. This reading is preferable to Dunand's כשרת 'skilled work, sculpture' (base KŠR) and Krahmalkov's ככרת 'talent'. It invites comparison with Hebr. [kappōret], lit. 'something propiatory' (hardly simply 'cover') referring to the gold slab or plate placed on top of the Ark of the Covenant (Exod. xxv 17–22), which along with the Ark was regarded as the seat of the deity. This brings us into the same realm of ideas as the 'Throne of Astarte' inscr. from Tyre (**30**), and one is tempted to translate 'mercy seat of gold', though that would demand that some other object than the stone sphinx is meant and that the sphinx's purpose was to act as guardian alongside it. It is prob. safer, therefore, to conclude that Abdadoni gifted the sphinx itself to be used as the priests thought fit, and that he hoped his offering would serve as an atonement for his sins. Two other stone sphinxes found in the excavations are assumed by Dunand and Duru (p. 167) to have been placed outside the temple building to guard the entrance. חרץ can thus hardly be 'gold' as in **25** Yehaumilk 4, 5, but must be a passive participle from the base 'to cut in, incise' (cp. Lev. xxii 22) meaning 'sculpted object' or the like (it cannot be an adj. as כפרת is feminine). מתם is clearly not the adv. 'always' (**15** Karatepe A ii 16), but must be connected with the base TMM, perhaps Yuphal partic. [mūtam] 'completed, finished', added to emphasize that the object was an entire sculpture as opposed to a bas-relief (Milik).

2. עבדאלנם 'servant of the gods'. עשתרתעזר 'Astarte has helped' with fem. verb ['azārā]. בעל חמן; see at **31** iv 3; there is a space with some scratches after ב, and the correct text may be בבעל (Milik), 'from the citizens of'; see at **7** Abibaal 2. כמאשי 'as his gift', i.e. a noun [ma'ōš] or the like from the base 'WŠ; cp. Arab. ['awsu], Ugar. 'ušn (*CML*[2] p. 143), both 'gift'; it is prob. not to be confused with מ(א)ש, which seems generally to mean 'statue' or 'image'; see the discussion at **36** Lapethos ii 1.

3. להאלנם; the retention of the article after the prepos. is unusual, but not without parallel; see Friedrich, *Grammatik*, p. 53. On the 'angel' of Milkashtart see at **31** iv 2. Notice the vocalic suffix [ō] with קל and יברך (see at **29** Baalshillem).

VII

INSCRIPTIONS FROM FURTHER AFIELD

33   Temple tariff A, B (Cyprus)   Pl. VI

THE many Phoen. inscrs. from Cyprus, of which two of the earlier
(nos. **12** and **17**) were included in chapt. III and a further selection
belonging to the second half of the 1 millenn. BC is now given, are
written in the Standard, i.e. Tyro-Sidonian dialect, with the possible
exception of those from Lapethos (e.g. no. **36**), which offer some
meagre but telling evidence that they should be assigned to the
Byblian dialect. In addition, there are occasional indications of a
phonetic kind, e.g. the frequent use of forms with prosthetic א and
the treatment, particularly in transliterated names and, as it happens,
particularly in the Lapethos inscrs., of certain consonants, which
suggest that the indigenous Cypriote language had an effect on the
way Phoen. was pronounced on the island. On the writing see
Peckham, *Scripts,* chapt. I.

   The tariff inscrs., which are painted in black ink on both sides of a
limestone tablet, were found in 1879 north of Kition, the main centre
of Phoen. settlement on Cyprus and today called Larnaca, apparently
quite near the site of a large Phoen. temple excavated by V.
Karageorghis from 1967 to 1970, which must then be the temple
mentioned several times in the text. The tablet, which is incomplete,
measures about 11 cm. broad and from 12 to 15 cm. long. Inscr. A
uses it lengthwise and thus contains more lines than inscr. B which
uses it breadthwise. The two texts are by different scribes and though
new and improved photographs are now available, they are not easy
to read, especially text A where the lettering is very small. The cursive
writing seems in general closer to the 6 cent. Saqqarah papyrus from
Egypt than to the 5 and 4 cent. ostraca from Sidon (see Bibliogr.
Notes and Table of Scripts), although it should be noted when
making such comparisons that all three surfaces are different. I am
inclined to favour Peckham's date in the mid-5 cent. over the
traditional dating in the early 4 cent., which is followed (though not
without reservations) by A. Vanel in his detailed study of the ostraca;
Healey's 6-cent. date prior to the Saqqarah text is much too high.
Where the letter forms of the two texts differ significantly, those of B
are usually the more archaic, but the contents being so similar, it
seems wiser to put this down to different scribal styles than to separate

the texts by date. Both texts give lists of expenses incurred by the temple administration in two different months and though we do not know whether the months were consecutive, they seem to be parts of a continuing series which are therefore better designated under a single heading than given distinct numbers of their own. The number of officials and the sums of money involved are not large, which suggest that the lists concern normal monthly expenditure, in particular that associated with the new-moon festival (cp. the reference to 'this day' in A 6, 14, 16); a similar festival was known in Israel (cp. Amos viii 5 Hos. ii 13 Isa. i 13, prophetic passages which do not look upon it with much favour). However, at least the building operations mentioned in A 4 and 13 and possibly alluded to in B 5–7 were longer term, so we ought not to restrict all the references to the one ceremonial, though the payments seem to have been disembursed on that day. The tablet is now in the British Museum.

A 1 תבֿלת ירח אתנם

2 בחדש ירח אתנם

3 לאלן חדש קפא 2

4 לבנם 4 אש בן אית בת עשתרת כת קר 2

5 לפרכם. ולאדמם אש על דל קֹצֹר 20]

6 לשרם בער אש שכנֹ למלכת קדשת בים ז ק]

7 לנערם 2 קפא 2

8 לזבחם 2 קר 1

9 לאפם 2 אש אף אית תֹנֹא חלת למלכת [קדשת]

10 את פרמן קר 3ֿ

11 לנערם 3 קפא 3

12 לגלבם פעלם על מלאכת קפא 2

13 לחרשם 20 אש פעל אשתת אבן בבת מכ]ל

14 לעבדאשמן רב ספרם שלח בים ז קר 3 וק]פא

15 [לכלבם] ולגרם קר 3 ופא 3

16 [ ] א שלח בים ז קר 2 וֹקֹ]פא

17 [ ] עֹמֹכ ------[

Bibliography

CIS i 86 A, B.
NSI no. 20.
KI no. 29.
KAI no. 37.
A. van den Branden, 'Elenco della spese del tempio di Cition', *Bibbia e Oriente* 8 (1966), 245–62 (with postscript in *RSF* 2 (1974), 141–2).
J. B. Peckham, 'Notes on a fifth century Phoenician inscription from Kition', *Orientalia* 37 (1968), 304–24.
Masson and Sznycer, *Recherches*, 21–68.
Magnanini, *Iscrizioni*, pp. 109–11.
A. Dupont-Sommer, 'Les Phéniciens à Chypre', *Report of the Dept. of Antiquities, Cyprus*, 1974, 92 f.
J. P. Healey, 'The Kition Tariffs and the Phoenician Cursive Series', *BASOR* 216 (1974), 53–60.
J. Teixidor in *American J. Arch.* 78 (1974), 189 f.

Illustrations

CIS i tab. XII; Peckham, loc. cit., tab. XLIX, L (reproduced by Healey); Masson and Sznycer, op. cit., pls. IV, V.

A   1. Expenses for the month of Etanim.
     2. (Paid) on the day of the new-moon in the month of Etanim.
     3. To the leader(s) of the new-moon festival, 2 QP'.
     4. To the 4 masons who repaired the temple of Astarte at Kition, 2 QR.
     5. To the 20 janitors and men who (were stationed) at the door of the sanctuary [
     6. To the singers from the city who were in attendance on the Holy Queen this day, ... [
     7. To the 2 pages, 2 QP'.
     8. To the 2 sacrificers, 1 QR.
     9. To the 2 bakers who baked the basket of cakes for the [Holy] Queen
   10. along with ......, 3 QR.
   11. To the 3 pages, 3 QP'.
   12. To the barbers working at the service, 2 QP'.
   13. To the 20 craftsmen who made the pillars of stone in the temple of MKL [
   14. To Abdeshmun, chief of the scribes, on duty this day, 3 QR and .. QP'.
   15. [To the 'dogs'] and to the 'lion's whelps', 3 QR and 3 P'.
   16. [   ] on duty this day 2 QR and .. QP'.
   17. ......

B 1 [---] עקב

2 — בחדש ירח פעלת

3 — לאלן חדש קפא 2

4 — לבעל יֹםֹ בסבב אלםֹ]

5 — לנפש בת אש לאשתת מכל וש]ן

6 — לעבדאבסת הקרתחדשתי]

7 — לאדם . אש לקח מכנבם קפא]ן

8 — לרעם . אש בד–פלכד קר 2 אש בכֹ]ת

9 — לעלמת ולעלמת 22 בזבח]ן

10 — לכלבם ולגרם קר 3 ופא 3

11 — לנערם 3 קפא 3

12]— קפ[א 2

NOTES

A   1. תכלת 'expenses' from the base KLY; the כ is only partially visible. אתנם; the month in which only the 'permanent' (Hebr. איתן) water-courses still flow, thus Sept.-Oct., the seventh month, just before the rains came; 1 Kgs. viii 2.

2. חדש; the original meaning '(day of the) new-moon' is retained in Phoen.; in Hebr. Amos viii 5 Hos. ii 13 Isa. i 13 of the festival held on that day (the meaning here in *1*.3); the usual meaning in Hebr. is 'month', for which Phoen. uses ירח, found, but much rarer, in Hebrew.

3. אלן can hardly here mean 'gods', as it is a question all through not of offerings but of payments made to officials; whether it is the same word with the sense 'leader, ruler' (in which case it is plur.) or an independent formation from the same base ('WL) like the Hebr. ['ēlōn] 'terebinth' (in which case it could be sing.) cannot be determined, nor is it clear what the duties of the office were. Contrast האלם in **31** Umm El-'Amed iv 2, where the meaning 'god' is to be preferred over 'envoys' or 'officials'. On אלנם 'gods' see at **15** Karatepe A iii 5 and on האלם 'the god' (sing.), ibid. C iii 16. קפא and the parallel terms קר (4) and פא (15) prob. denote coins or weights; their values are unknown, but קר seems to be a larger denomination than the other two (14, 15). The payment in this line is therefore not a great sum, which favours a single official rather than a number of them. Possible etymologies for the three denominations are QP' 'to congeal', QWR 'to bore', and P'Y 'to cleave, split'; cp. the Hebr. weight בקע from a base 'to break open'.

4. בן = [banū], here doubtless in the sense of 'rebuild, repair'. The

B

1. ... audit.

2. – (Paid) on the day of the new-moon in the month of P'LT.

3. – To the leader(s) of the new-moon festival, 2 QP'.

4. – To the master(s) of the days at the procession round the deity [

5. – To the temple personnel who were (responsible) for the pillars of MKL and ... [

6. – To 'BD'BST the Carthaginian [

7. – To the man who removed their .... QP'.

8. – To the shepherds who (live) in D-PLKD, 2 QR; (to those) who (live) in Ki[tion

9. – To the (temple) girls and to the 22 girls (employed) at the sacrifice [

10. – To the 'dogs' and to the 'lion's whelps', 3 QR and 3 P'.

11. – To the 3 pages, 3 QP'.

12. – [   ], 2 QP'.

numeral 'four', written above the line, prob. goes with בנם, which has a space after it, the scribe being at first unsure how many workmen were involved; cp. the 'two' following נערם in 7, etc. There is a wider gap than usual between *ll.* 3 and 4, which may have been left for the same reason. כת; a short form of the usual כתי (e.g. **34** 1), found elsewhere only on coins from Sidon. כתי is reflected in Hebr. כתיים, which refers to inhabitants of Cyprus in general (Isa. xxiii 12) or in an extended sense to the coasts of Asia Minor or of the Aegean islands (Jerem. ii 10); it is applied in a Hebr. ostracon from Arad to Greek-speaking mercenaries serving in the Judaean army (I, pp. 51–52).

5. The older readings פרכם and דל are to be preferred to Peckham's דרכם 'marshals' (sc. of a procession; lit. 'marchers') and סל '(processional) route' (cp. Hebr. מסלה). פרכם is usually compared with Hebr. פרכת describing the 'curtain' or 'veil' before the Holy of Holies (Exod. xxvi 31 ff.), which is in its turn connected with Akkad. *parāku* 'to lock (a door), enclose', meaning, therefore, that which shuts off or is shut off; the traditional interpretation (*CIS*) compares Lat. *velarii*, the slaves who drew the curtains, but it is easier with Masson and Sznycer to think of a participial or professional form from the verb, i.e. those who have charge of the sanctuary locks, janitors, or the like. דל; a masc. sing. form found once in Hebr. (Ps. cxli 3); a plur. דלהת occurs in Umm El-'Amed i 3 (*CIS* i 7 = *KAI* no. 18) and a sing. fem. דלת in **36** Lapethos ii 12. The final word (before the sign for 20) is badly faded; *CIS* וקר (with the otiose ו unexplained); van den Branden קפא; Peckham and Healey רצד 'the men who watched' (cp. Ps. lxviii 17, though there in its only

occurrence in Hebr. the verb has a nuance of envy or malice); Masson and Sznycer קצר 'the men who (were stationed) at the door of the shrine' (cp. Nabat. קצרא 'small room, cell'). Of these readings, the last is preferable both on grounds of epigraphy and of syntax. On the recent photographs the second letter cannot be either ק (*CIS*) or פ (van den Branden), but could well be צ with the downward stroke almost invisible; similarly, if one looks hard enough the shape of a loop can be traced to the right of the first letter, thus giving ק and neatly closing the space after the ל of דל. Syntactically, too, this interpretation has a noun following דל, whereas Peckham has a verb placed awkwardly at the end of a relative clause. The numeral 20, then, must refer back to both פרכם and אדמם; doubtless the sum paid to these functionaries was contained on the piece of stone broken off at this edge.

6. לשרם is relatively clear on the new photographs; the older reading was לאדם; a meaning 'singers' (1 Kgs. x 12 1 Chron. xxv 7) suits better in the context than 'princes'. ער occurs only once elsewhere in Phoen. (*CIS* i 113, 1, 2) and may have had a more precise meaning than קרת, the usual term for 'city'; there is prob. a survival of such a meaning in Hebr. in phrases like עיר בית הבעל (2 Kgs. x 25), which seems to refer to a part of a temple (*NEB* 'keep') or perhaps as Fisher argues (*JSS* 8 (1963), 34 ff.) to the central quarter of a city around the temple. Apparently the singers lived in the vicinity of the temple and the reference here is to those who were on duty for the new-moon festival (בים ז). שכנם; the מ is uncertain and could be י, but the parallel with 1 Kgs. i 2 (ותהי לו סכנת) suggests that we have here an irregular spelling of סכנם 'stewards, servants, attendants' brought about by the instability of the 'sibilant' sounds in the Cyprus dialect. For the masc. sing. סכן in the technical sense of 'minister, ambassador' see **17** Baal Lebanon; see further at **4** Ahiram 2. מלכת קדשת; a title of Astarte to whom the temple was dedicated, presumably lacking the article because it is almost a proper name. Less satisfactory is to take מלכת as equivalent to מלאכת (12), i.e. 'who are in residence (ŠKN) for the holy service'. בים ז; note that the prosthetic א characteristic of the demonstrative in the Cyprian inscrs. (see at **17** Baal Lebanon *a*) is absent; this is not necessarily significant, since the א represents a sub-phonemic 'helping vowel', and scripts are not always regular in catching such features.

7. נערם; presumably a class of temple functionaries; cp. 1 Sam. ii 13, 15, where the title possibly refers to Eli's sons. The two in this line are obviously to be distinguished from the three of *l*. 11, their number identifying their role. On the נער in Israelite society, where it is chiefly but not exclusively a military office and is always held by people of some rank, not necessarily young, see J. Macdonald, *JNES* 35 (1976), 147 ff.

8. Cp. the Punic בעל הזבח (*CIS* i 165 = *KAI* no. 69 Marseilles tariff 4; *CIS* i 167 = *KAI* no. 74 Carthage tariff 2).

9. The reading אף (formerly אם) for the verb is clear on the new photographs, and though the פ in אפם is more dubious, the formula in 4 confirms it; אית follows, again as in 4. The next word finishes with א, though the two previous letters are too faded to be read with any certainty; Peckham טנא 'basket' (Deut. xxvi 2, 4 xxviii 5, 17); Healey ספא 'portion of food'. חלת; Exod. xxix 2–3 Lev. viii 26 etc.

CIS i 165 = *KAI* no. 69 Marseilles tariff 14; syncope of [h] of the article should perhaps be assumed with this word, making the whole phrase definite. Since the next line seems to be a continuation of this line, קדשת should be restored as in 6 rather than a sum of money; there is a trace of a letter after ת and the space following shows signs of damage.

10. את 'with'; **27** Tabnit 8   **28** Eshmunazar 8, 9. Unless פרמן is a proper name (Peckham), syncope of [h] of the article should again perhaps be assumed; if it is a noun, it may be construed either with אפם or with טנא חלת, describing, therefore, a related profession or another baked article. There are only two strokes visible at the end, though there is room between them for a third, which may have faded.

12. גלבם; cp. גלב אלם 'barber of the divinity' (*CIS* i 257, 4). Barbers were required to cut the hair of those making sacrifices and perhaps also to make ritual incisions, practices forbidden in Israel (Lev. xix 27–8), particularly in mourning rites (Lev. xxi 5   Deut. xiv 1). Actual offerings of hair (perhaps thought to attach the worshipper to his god and, at a more primitive level, to contain and thus represent a man's vital force) are alluded to in Lucian and, according to its editor, in a recently discovered fragmentary inscr. from Kition dating to about 800 BC (Dupont-Sommer, *Mem. AIBL* 44 (1970), 9–28; see also his article in the Bibliogr.) Healey translates 'the tonsured'; cp. the Hebr. Nazirites, although these do not seem to have been particularly associated with the cult. מלאכת with perhaps syncope of [h] of the article; Exod. xxxvi 1–3   2 Chron. xxix 34   Ezra iii 9, etc.; prob. here referring to the cultic observances at the new-moon festival.

13. Peckham followed by Masson and Sznycer reads the numeral 20 in the space after חרשם. On אשתת (sing. אשת = Hebr. שת; masc.) see at **25** Yehaumilk 14. The temple of מכל (cp. B 5) was prob. a smaller shrine within the temple of Astarte, dedicated to a deity of that name. In other inscrs. from Cyprus (e.g. **34** 2) there is mention of a god רשף מכל and once (in a fragment cited in Teixidor, 'Bulletin' for 1969, p. 338) רשף המכל. The use of the article in the latter quotation suggests that we may be dealing not with a composite deity like Milkashtart at Umm El-'Amed (see at **31** 2), but with an epithet of Resheph, the epithet being used here for the fuller name. Perhaps it means 'the finisher, destroyer' (Piel partic. from KLY), a not unsuitable description of the god of plague; cp. רשף חץ (*KAI* no. 32, 3 = Magnanini, *Iscrizioni*, p. 95). There is thus no need to bring in a connection with an ancient Canaanite deity Mekal known from 2 millenn. Egyp. sources; see H. O. Thompson, *Mekal: The god of Beth-Shan* (1970). Resheph was equated by the Greeks with Apollo; cp. the bilingual *CIS* i 89, 3, where לרשף מכל is rendered in Cypriote *to A-po-lo-ni to A-mu-ko-lo-i*, i.e. in Greek τῷ 'Απόλλωνι τῷ 'Αμυκλοι, which must, if what is said here is correct, be a secondary identification with the Apollo revered at Amyclae in Lacedaemon. The line is perhaps to be completed with another divine name or epithet as in B 5 as well as with the sum payed in this case.

14. שלח is to be read for *CIS* ולח. It may (Masson and Sznycer) be a passive Qal perf. 'there has been sent', indicating that the scribal community lived outside the temple precincts and that the payment due was despatched to their chief (cp. 1 Chron. ii 55). In 6, however, בים ז refers to duties performed at the festival, and it is better to

regard שלח as a passive partic., 'deputed, commisssioned, on duty', or the like (cp. Healey), Abdeshmun being the leader of the group on call that particular day. Two denominations are mentioned in the sum of money; QR, coming first, was prob., therefore, a larger sum than QP' (and than P'; 15).

15. כלבם is restored from B 10; in Deut. xxiii 18–19 כלב is clearly an alternative of קדש, so the word describes a class of sacred male prostitutes like the Biblical קדשים, who had a role in worship, though their employment was condemned as of Canaanite inspiration (cp. 1 Kgs. xiv 24, xv 12, and 2 Kgs. xxiii 7, which mentions their 'houses' within the Jerusalem temple area). גרם prob. = [gūrīm] (Gen. xlix 9) or [gōrīm] (Jerem. li 38) 'lion's whelps' rather than [gērīm] 'sojourners, clients'; it must describe a similar profession. Peckham and Healey prefer to think in this line of cultic actors who wore animal masks, a practice attested in ancient Egypt.

B 1. The base 'QB has a wide range of meanings in the various Semitic languages; possibilities here are 'result', 'continuation', 'repayment' (cp. Ps. xix 12), or 'investigation' (Arab. and especially Syriac). The writing is smaller than in ll. 2 ff., suggesting that the word is not a heading like תכלת in A 1 but was added later by a different scribe as an identification note for the tablet or an indication that the entries had been checked. There are two or three marks to the right of עקב which do not look like letters and may be faded numerical signs, giving the filing number of the tablet or perhaps the total number of entries. If the first is the case it would prove conclusively that side B is the top one and was written before side A; but I am inclined to the second alternative as ll. 2 ff. (on this side only) all begin with a dash or tick which could have been added by the second scribe as he went over the contents line by line. Healey takes עקב as a proper name.

2. פעלת; the month of 'work', perhaps that of the fruit harvest, i.e. the 6th month (Aug.-Sept.) (that preceding אתנם, A 1) or of ploughing and sowing, i.e. one of the winter months (Nov.-Jan.).

3. See at A 3.

4. Ll. 3–5 are rather crushed and the letters in this line particularly are sometimes widely spaced to avoid the feet of the letters in the line above; it was perhaps inserted between 3 and 5 after these had been written. Peckham and Masson and Sznycer read the second word as מים instead of ימם (CIS), i.e. 'master(s) of the waters', presumably an office to do with ritual ablutions or other ceremonies involving water; but the retained diphthong in the orthography would be surprising in Phoen. (the word is not found elsewhere in extant remains), and I prefer the older reading 'days'. In either case syncope of [h] of the article is perhaps to be assumed. בסבב; the second ב is just visible on the new photographs (CIS ברב); the base meaning is 'to go around, surround', suggesting, therefore, a procession in which either the worshippers circumambulated a statue of Astarte or such a statue was carried round the temple. אלם (with syncope of [h]?); 15 Karatepe C iii 16. The 'master' or 'masters of the days', i.e. of festival days like the feast of the new-moon with which these inscrs. are particularly concerned, may have had, as the allusion here suggests, the oversight of the processions which were a prominent feature of the activities on such occasions.

5. נפש 'personnel', prob. a collective usage as in Gen. xii 5 xlvi 15 ff. Jerem. xliii 6, etc. In passages like Lev. xxii 11 (sing.) and Ezek. xxvii 13 (coll.) נפש clearly means 'slave'; but it is unlikely that slaves would figure in a list like this of recipients of fees or wages. The 'personnel' concerned are, it should be noted, associated with the pillars of MKL and may, therefore, be the same as the craftsmen mentioned in A 13, suggesting that at the time side B was written the pillars were still in process of construction and making side B prior to side A; or alternatively, if side A is prior and the pillars had just been finished, they are temple employees who were appointed to take care of them or to supervise some cult conducted beside them. Syntactically the final word, of which only one letter survives, is more likely to be the name of another god or another divine title than refer to other officials, when on the model of A 5, B 9 the prepos. ל would have been repeated.

6. אבדאבסת; compounded with the name of the Egyp. cat goddess Bastet; see at **30** Throne of Astarte. It is not known whether the 'Carthage' is the Cyprian one mentioned in **17** Baal Lebanon (q.v.) or the more famous one in North Africa. The person named may have been a merchant who supplied stores to the temple, perhaps in connection with the pillars of MKL, since these are still being spoken of in 7.

7. אשם (*CIS*) is to be corrected to אדם, thus dispensing with the use of two different words for 'men' in the same series of inscrs. (cp. אדמם, A 5). מכנבם cannot be split מכן בם, thus 'who took away the (old) pedestal from them', sc. the pillars (see *DISO* p. 150 and cp. Hebr. מכונה), since 'in, from them' is בנם (**28** Eshmunazar 9). Interpret therefore as a sing. noun, the suffix ם = [ōm] referring back to the pillars (אשתת; only the form is fem.). The base KNB in Arab. means 'to be course, rough'.

8. 'Shepherds' who supplied animals for the sacrifices and who are here identified by the places where they lived, ד-פלכד (or with Healey רשפלכד. lit. 'Resheph has captured') and the area of Kition itself (if correctly restored; cp. A 4).

9. עלמת; maidservants or dancing girls (Ps. lxviii 26) or perhaps sacred prostitutes, since male prostitutes are referred to in the next line; the first mentioned may have been those permanently on the staff and the second a group employed for the purpose of a particular sacrifice (זבח), doubtless that of the new-moon festival.

10–11. Cp. A 15, 7, 11.

12. Perhaps restore as in A 7.

34 Dated dedication (Cyprus)

The dozen or so dedicatory or votive inscrs. dated by the years of the kings of Kition and Idalion or of the Ptolemaic monarchs in which they were written supply valuable fixed points of reference for the study of Phoen. epigraphy during the late 5 and most of the following two cents. BC. The one given here is dated to 390 BC. It was discovered at Idalion (the present Dali) in 1869 and is now in the British Museum.

Bibliography

CIS i 90; tab. XIII.
NSE p. 421; Taf. VII, 1.
NSI no. 24.
KI no. 31.
KAI no. 38.
D. Kellerman in *ZDPV* 86 (1970), 24 ff.
Magnanini, *Iscrizioni,* p. 119.

1   מרקע . חרץ אז אש יתן מלך מלכיתן מלך כתי ואדיל בן בעלרם לאלי

2   לרשף מכל באדיל בריח . בל בשנת 2 למלכי על כתי ואדיל כ שמע קל

יברך

1.   This mace of gold (is that) which King Milkyatan, king of Kition and Idalion, son of Baalrom, gave to his god
2.   Resheph MKL in Idalion, in the month Bul in the 2nd year of his reign over Kition and Idalion, because he heard his voice. May he bless him!

NOTES

1. מרקע; the base means 'to spread out, stamp, patch' (Arab. etc.) and particularly in Hebr. (Piel) 'to beat out, overlay with metal' (cp. Jerem. x 9). The older interpretation (*CIS*), 'bowl, vessel of beaten gold' is well criticized by Cooke, who argues that the inscr. would then most naturally have been written on the object itself (cp. **17** Baal Lebanon) and not on a stone tablet. He suggests the 'plating' on the god's image and compares Isa. xl 19 and the gilded statue of Athene of Herodotus II 183 (ἄγαλμα ἐπίχρυσον); but it seems strange that only the overlay is mentioned and not the actual statue (even if it was not being presented). I prefer to follow Kellerman, who thinks of the form [maqtēl] of instruments and translates 'hammer'; if we interpret in the sense of 'mace', this would make a most suitable gift for the warlike Resheph, deity of fire and plague, and being of precious metal would justify an accompanying inscription. אז; the regular form of the demonstrative in the Phoen. of Cyprus; see at **17** Baal Lebanon; contrast אז (**12** Cyprus grave 2) and ז (**33** Tariff A 6). מלכיתן, בעלרם; in accordance with the Note on phonology and grammar, the first should be transliterated Milkyatan not Milkyaton, and the second Baalrom not Baairam. Milkyatan's dates are 392–362 BC. Baalrom is not given the title of king and is therefore prob. not the same as the Baalrom who is known from his coins to have reigned, though only for a short period, prior to Milkyatan; presumably King Baalrom died young and childless and the succession passed to another branch of the royal family, or a new dynasty began at this point. See on the names Benz, *Names,* pp. 98, 139. כתי; see at **33** Tariff A 4. אדיל; Akkad. (*uru*) Edi'il (*ANET* pp. 291, 294); in the middle of the island, NW of Kition.

2. רשף מכל; **33** Tariff A 13. בשנת lit. 'in years 2'; a few Phoen. ordinals (e.g.

שני; **28** Eshmunazar 6) are attested, but they are not found in date formulas, where the word 'year' or 'day' is given in the plur. followed by a numerical sign (as here) or sometimes by both a cardinal number and a numerical sign (as in e.g. *KAI* no. 41, 4–5); see further at **28** Eshmunazar 1; a sing. form שת, however, is used in **31** Umm El-'Amed iv 5. למלכי; **28** Eshmunazar 1. קל = [qōlō] with the vocalic suffix unrepresented in writing; similarly יברך = [ybar(r)kō]; see at **29** Baalshillem.

35 Funerary inscription (Cyprus)

The only one of a large number of inscrs. discovered and copied by R. Pococke at Kition in 1738 to have survived, the inscr. was taken to England and is now in the Bodleian Library, Oxford. With *CIS* i 122 from Malta it played a significant role in l'Abbé Barthélemy's decipherment of the Phoenician language. The text is inscribed on a white marble tablet (30 × 10 cm.). Unusually for a text in this period the words are separated by dots. Note also that the tops of the letters ע, ב, and ר are open, a sporadic feature of stone inscrs. from Cyprus which is due to the influence of the cursive style and suggests a later (3 cent.) date rather than an earlier one.

Bibliography

J. J. Barthélemy, 'Réflexions sur quelques monuments phéniciens', *Mémoires de l'Académie des inscriptions* 30 (1758), 405–427.
CIS i 46; tab. VIII.
NSE p. 420; Taf. VI, 3.
NSI no. 16.
KI no. 23.
KAI no. 35.
Magnanini, *Iscrizioni*, p. 85.

1   אנך . עבדאסר. בן עבדססם . בן חר. מצבת.

2   למבחיי . יטנאת . על משכב . נחתי . לעלם . ולא

3   שתי . לאמתעשתרת . בת . תאם . בן עבדמלך

1.   I Abdosir, son of 'BDSSM, son of Hor, set up
2.   a pillar while I was still alive (to be) over my resting-place for ever; also for
3.   my wife Amotashtart, daughter of Toam, son of Abdmilk.

NOTES

1.   אנך; the dead speaks in his own name. In other inscrs. of this character we find the donor (*CIS* i 57) and once both the donor and the dead (*CIS* i 115 from Athens) using the 1 person. עבדאסר; a name compounded with that of

the Egyp. deity Osiris. The grandfather's name חר seems to be a hypocoristicon containing only the divine element, again Egyp., 'Horus'. עבדססם; the deity is mentioned in **23** Arslan Tash i 2, 27. מצבת; the usual word in Phoen. for a gravestone or pillar erected over a tomb to commemorate the dead and perpetuate his memory among the living; similarly in Hebr., e.g. Gen. xxxv 20.

2. למבחיי; the compound prepos. ל+מן+ב is not uncommon in Phoen. and Punic (*DISO* p. 132); cp. ל+מן in the same sense in **13** Kilamuwa i 12. As a rule the pillar or obelisk was erected by a son or other relative or acquaintance; here we have an exceptional instance of its being set up by the person commemorated during his own lifetime. This was done by couples who had no children to perform this pious duty, as can be seen from 2 Sam. xviii 18. Note that the inscr., which is on a tablet, says 'a pillar', not 'this pillar', suggesting that the monument itself may have been erected elsewhere; or perhaps a tablet was used because it was not thought proper to inscribe a pillar before the person concerned was dead. משכב; **27** Tabnit 8.

3. אמתעשתרת; **28** Eshmunazar 14. תאם 'twin'; Hebr. [tō'ām] = Greek Θωμᾶς, Δίδυμος (John xx 24). On the element מלך see at **6** Yehimilk 1 **31** Umm El-'Amed iv 2.

36   Lapethos ii (Cyprus)   Pl. VII

The inscr., discovered in 1893 at Lapethos on the north coast of the island and now in the Louvre, is incised on a semicircular pedestal, on the top of which are two holes which prob. served to hold the feet of the votive statue mentioned in the opening lines. This statue was set up by a high official of Lapethos in the 11th year of one of the Ptolemies, doubtless Ptolemy II Philadelphos, who began his reign (as co-regent with his father Ptolemy I Soter) in 285/4. This would indicate 275/4 BC as the date of the inscr., though Honeyman (who has given the most thorough treatment) prefers the slightly later date 273/2, the 11th year of Ptolemy II's accession as sole ruler after his father's death (see on 11). A later Ptolemy cannot be meant, since the writing is not greatly different from that of the fragmentary inscr. iii (Magnanini, *Iscrizioni*, pp. 125–7), which belongs to the latter part of the 4 cent. when Lapethos was still an independent kingdom. The official who commissioned the text, having mentioned the erection of his own statue, then goes on (6 ff.) to rehearse some former acts of

מש לנעם 1

2 הסמל ז מש אנך יתנבעל רב ארץ בן גרעשתרת רב ארץ בן
עבד[עשתרת רב ארץ בן עבדא[סר

3 בן גרעשתרת בן שלם פﭏ כרמל אש יטנאת לי אבמקדש מלקרת סכ]ר
נעם בחי[ם לשמי

piety for which he had been responsible, and closes with a prayer to Melcarth that he be blessed with a stock to succeed him, which suggests that he may have been childless at the time the inscr. was written.

There is nothing in the small first inscr. from Lapethos (*CIS* i 95) to help us identify the dialect, but the usage of the 1 sing. suffix in the other two, and particularly the form (ו) of the 3 masc. sing. suffix in the present text (11), suggest a Byblian rather than a Tyro-Sidonian origin. It is not certain, however, that the 3 fem. sing. suffix (see at 13) has the Byblian form. We cannot, therefore, confidently argue with Lane (in *BASOR* 194, 1969, 39 ff.) that the colony at Lapethos was of Byblian foundation, though we can conclude that there was a large element of Phoenicians from Byblos in the population and that this had its effect on the language. A similar mixed situation is apparent in the religious sphere, worship being accorded both to Melcarth of Tyre (ii) and to the gods of Byblos (iii 8).

Bibliography

Ph. Berger in *RA* 3 (1895), 69–88.
Ch. Clermont-Ganneau in *Études d'arch. or.* 2 (1896), 157–81.
NSE p. 422.
NSI no. 29.
KI no. 36.
RÉS no. 1211.
A. M. Honeyman, 'Observations on a Phoenician inscription of Ptolemaic date', *J. Egyp. Arch.* 26 (1940), 57–67.
G. R. Driver in *J. Egyp. Arch.* 36 (1950), 82.
A. van den Branden, 'L'Inscription phénicienene de Larnax Lapethos II', *Or. Ant.* 3 (1964), 245–61.
Teixidor, 'Bulletin' for 1967, item 43.
KAI no. 43.
Magnanini, *Iscrizioni,* pp. 124–5.
Lipiński, 'North Semitic texts', 232 ff.

Illustration

Honeyman, loc. cit., pl. XI.

1. Effigy for good fortune.

2. This statue is my effigy, Yatanbaal's, chief magistrate, son of Gerashtart, chief magistrate, son of Abd[ashtart, chief magistrate, son of Abd]osir,

3. son of Gerashtart, son of ŠLM, 'fruit of Carmel', which I set up for myself in the sanctuary of Melcarth [as a memorial among the living to bring good fortune] to my name,

4 בחדש זבח ששם אש בשנת 11 לאדן מלכם פתלמיש בן אדן מלכם
פתלמיש

5 אש המת לעם לפֹט שנת 33 וכהן לאדן מלכם עבדעשתרת בן גרעשתרת

6 רב ארץ פר כרמל וביךח מפע אש בשנת 4̊ לאדן מלכם פתלמיש בן אדן
מלכם

7 פתלמיש אבחי אבי ישת במקדש מלקרת אית מש פן אבי בנחשת ובירח

8 פעלת אש בשנת 5 לאדן מלכם פתלמיש בן אדן מלכם פתלמיש בחי

9 אבי יתת ויקדשת חית שגית בגבל שד נרנך לאדן אש לי למלקרת

10 וֹשֹב –––– הֹח––יֹם פֹּעלת קמת עם ומזבחת לאדן אש לי למלקרת

11 על חיי ועל חי זרעי ים מד ים ולצמח צדק ולאשתו ולאדמי

12 [בחד]שֹם ובכסאם ירח מד ירח עד עלם כקדם כם הדלת הנחשת

13 [אש כ]תבת וסמרת בקר אש בן מנחת חני ופעלת אנך עלת

14 [–––] –––– אפבת בכסֹף משקל כר 100(?) ו 2 ויקדשת לאדן

15 [אש לי למ]לקרת פקת ונעם יכן לי ולזרעי ויסכרן מלקרת

16 [–––––] נֹעם שרש

NOTES

1. In view of מש in 2 this is the best division of the words. Others read משל נעם, supposedly for למזל נעם. 'for good luck', as in i 5, though the prepos. ל is missing. The substitution of ש for ז is taken as further evidence of the uncertain nature of the 'sibilant' sounds in the Lapethos region; cp. ש for ס in the name פתלמיש (4); but it is difficult to believe that ז could have been affected when we know that elsewhere in Cyprus it was a 'double' sound like Greek ζ, i.e. [zd] or the like; see at **17** Baal Lebanon (אז).

2. מש (nomin.) has prob. the suffix [ī], unwritten, followed by a strengthening אנך as in **25** Yehaumilk 12 (שם אנך; accus.), though this interpretation and its implication that the dialect is Byblian can be avoided by translating 'This statue is a מש. I am Yatanbaal ... who set (it) up'. מש must be the same word as appears as מאש in **42** Pyrgi 9 and in a number of Neo-Punic inscrs., notably in two bilinguals where in the Latin text it is rendered

4. in the new-moon of the sacrifice of ŠŠM in the 11th year of lord of kings Ptolemy, son of lord of kings Ptolemy,

5. which is the 33rd year of the people of Lapethos; and the priest to lord of kings was Abdashtart, son of Gerashtart,

6. chief magistrate, 'fruit of Carmel'. — And in the month MP' in the 4th year of lord of kings Ptolemy, son of lord of kings

7. Ptolemy, in the lifetime of my father, I placed in the sanctuary of Melcarth the effigy of the face of my father in bronze. — And in the month

8. P'LT in the 5th year of lord of kings Ptolemy, son of lord of kings Ptolemy, in the lifetime

9. of my father, I gave and consecrated roaming beasts in the borders of the plain of Narnaka to the lord who is mine, Melcarth,

10. .... I made .... and altars for the lord who is mine, Melcarth,

11. (to be serviced) on behalf of my life and on behalf of the life of my seed, day by day, and (altars) for the legitimate shoot and for his wife and for my folk

12. [(to be serviced) on the new-]moons and on the full-moons, month by month, for ever as aforetime, in accordance with the tablet of bronze

13. [which] I wrote and nailed to the wall which is there as my gift of supplication. — And I made above

14 .... of silver weighing 102 KR, and I dedicated (it) to the lord

15. [who is mine], Melcarth. May I and my seed have profit and good fortune, and may Melcarth remember me

16. [(and grant me)] the good fortune of a stock!

respectively *sacrum* 'sacred object' (Levi Della Vida, *BASOR* 87 (1942), 29 ff. = *KAI* no. 127) and *statua* 'statue' (*CIS* i 149 = *KAI* no. 172). The shorter form מש prob. also occurs in the Old Byblian inscr. of Abibaal (8 1), though it is by no means clear on the photograph. For futher discussion of the word see G. Garbini in *AIUON* 18 (1968), 231 ff., B. Rocco in *AIUON* 20 (1970), 396 ff., and P. Bordreuil in *Syria* 52 (1975), 113 ff. The lat two commentators derive it from 'WŠ 'to give' (Arab. ['āsa]), a base reflected in Ugar. 'ušn 'gift' (*CML*² p. 143), in a number of Hebr. proper names (e.g. יאוש 'Yahweh has given'; and מאוש 'gift of ...' on a seal discussed by Bordreuil), and in Phoen. in the phrase כמאשי 'as his gift' (**32** Umm El-'Amed xiii 2). In their view originally simply 'gift', the word came to mean 'gift made to a god' or 'votive offering' and then particularly, as here, 'gift, offering of a statue' (though they note that as the Latin *sacrum* shows, it was not invariably restricted to this). I believe that this etymology should be resisted, though it means that Phoen. possesses two words spelled מאש; I cannot see how a form like [ma'ōš] with a vowel both before and after the ['] could possibly contract to מש ([mōš]?). The older derivation (Lidzbarski, *Orientalistische Literaturzeitung* 30 (1927), 456) from Egyp. *mś* 'to give' did not have this difficulty, and it seemed nicely to account both for the Phoen. form מש as in 8 Abibaal and the present text, and for the א in the Neo-Punic מאש as a *mater lectionis*, i.e. [mēš] or the like; but the recently discovered example from Pyrgi, a 5 cent. text, where the א cannot be a vowel-letter, has shown this etymology to be impossible. It would seem the wisest course at present to leave the etymology open and render according to the context, which here demands 'effigy' or 'image'; cp. *l.* 7 where מש precedes פן 'face'. גרעשתרת 'client of Astarte'; Benz, *Names*, p. 298. רב ארץ (with syncope of [h] of the article?), lit. 'chief of the land'; cp. Greek χωράρχος; prob. an office in the republican government rather than in the Ptolemaic administration, which was not normally recruited locally (Honeyman). עבדעשתרת; the name both of Yatanbaal's grandfather and of his brother (5). The restoration עבדאסר is less certain, but it is a name attested on Cyprus (**35** 1).

3. שלם; cp. Hebr. Shillem, Shallum, Solomon, unless a hypocoristiocon of a longer name beginning with the divine element Shalim. פר כרמל; also in 6; the second ר here is almost an exact replica of the first ר in 6, and it seems unnecessarily cautious to cast doubt on the reading. In the light of the frequent metaphorical uses of כרמל in the Hebrew Bible (e.g. 2 Kgs. xix 23 Song vii 5 Isa. xxix 17 Jerem. ii 7) it is not fanciful to imagine Yatanbaal, after supplying so long a family tree, describing himself and his brother (6) in this extravagant way. Like Lebanon or Sharon, Carmel was proverbial in ancient Israel for beauty and fertility and could well have fulfilled a similar role in Phoen. rhetoric wherever that language was spoken. With פר in the sense of 'descendant' cp. **28** Eshmunazar 11–12; cp. also the similar figurative uses of צמח (11) and שרש (16). אבמקדש with prosthetic [']; it is omitted in 7; cp. אבחי (7) but בחי (8); being strictly speaking a sub-phonemic aid to pronunciation, it was not invariably marked. With the restoration at the end cp. Umm El-'Amed i 6 (*CIS* i 7), **27** Tabnit 7, and the third Lapethos inscr. (לסכרן בחים, 3; Magnanini, *Iscrizioni*, p. 126).

4. זבח ששם. ששם is possibly a god's name and may be the same as ססם (the spelling elsewhere, including the Lapethos i inscr.); on this deity see **23** Arslan Tash i. An alternative etymology, prob. preferable, is 'the sacrifice of sixty', referring to a month in which there were sixty sacrifices; cp. the Greek ἑκατομβαιών 'pertaining to an offering of a hundred oxen'. Or is ששם simply a mistake for שמש as in *CIS* i 13, 1 (from Kition) and **42** Pyrgi 4–5, i.e. the month of the sacrifice to the sun(-god)? שנת; plur.; see at **28** Eshmunazar 1. אדן מלכם; ibid., 18. פתלמיש with ש against ס on other inscrs. from Cyprus, an indication that these two letters were similarly pronounced in the area of Lapethos, prob. owing to local Cypriote influence.

5. המת prob. = [hēm(m)at]; fem. plur. pronoun rather than masc. [hōmat] used for both genders. לפט; the final letter is unclear, and may be ט as on coins from the city (*NSI* no. 149 B 7) or ש as in iii 1, 3, etc. In Greek it is written Λάπηθος, Λάπαθος, Λάπιθος, Λάπηθις. The differences in the Phoen. forms prob. arise from difficulty in representing Greek θ, which in the classical period was an aspirated plosive and not a fricative as in modern Greek. The numeral is made up of the signs for 20 and 10 plus three strokes for 3. According to this inscr. the era of Lapethos began in

307/6 (Honeyman 305/4), a few years after the abolition of the monarchy in 312. וכהן possibly with syncope of [h] of the article following ו; clearly an official in the cult of the deified Ptolemy; cp. *CIS* i 93 from Kition, where the years were marked by the name of the girl who was Kanephoros or 'basket-bearer'. For the date reckoned by universal, local, and ecclesiastical systems cp. Luke iii 1 ff. Abdashtart was the brother of Yatanbaal.

6. The title רב ארץ applies to Gerashtart, the epithet פר כרמל to Abdashtart. מפע; the meaning of the month name and the position in the calendar are obscure. מש פן אבי; it is obvious from this phrase that מש cannot, in this inscr. at least, mean 'gift'; see the discussion in 2 above.

7. אבחי; cp. אבמקדש (3). ישת; apparently Yiph. from ŠYT. אית; **12** Cyprus grave 3.

8. פעלת; **33** Tariff B 2.

9. שגית is usually taken as an Aramaism, i.e. for שגאת 'many'; but Phoen. is almost entirely free of Aramaic influence, and the derivation by Clermont-Ganneau and Honeyman from ŠGY 'to stray, wander' (cp. Ezek. xxxiv 6) is preferable. The form (fem. plur. in [iyyōt]) may be compared with פריה (Ps. cxxviii 3), אתיות (Isa. xli 23), etc.; cp. also קצית (**15** Karatepe A i 14), plur. of קצת (ibid., 21). Honeyman illumines the passage by alluding to the practice at a sanctuary of Astarte in Sicily, where animals, having been dedicated to the deity, were turned loose in the sanctuary estate and culled from time to time as needed for sacrifices. שד; **28** Eshmunazar 19. נרנך; the present-day Larnaka near Lapethos; the confusion of the [n] and [l] sounds is due to indigenous influence; cp. Nicosia = Leucosia. אש לי; a solemn circumlocution rather than an Aramaism; it is not uncommon in Hebr. (see Brown, Driver, Briggs, *Lexicon,* p. 83, sect. 7 b); cp. also **30** Throne of Astarte, where the same construction may be found (though another interpretation is preferred there).

10. Owing to the condition of the stone, the text and meaning of the first half of the line are quite uncertain. For a discussion of earlier readings, some of which reappear in the later ones cited here, see *NSI* p. 85. Honeyman's text is as follows:

אש בתבאת החית ימן על תקמת עם

He renders, 'that by the coming of the beasts allocation might be made for the establishment of the people and of the altars of ....' ימן is Niph. impersonal; with the meaning cp. Isa. liii 12. 'The coming' he illustrates nicely by citing the pious fiction in antiquity that sacred animals voluntarily presented themselves for sacrifice. תקמת; cp. Lev. xxvi 37. Against this interpretation (as Honeyman is himself aware) are the fact that in Hebr. תבואה does not have the simple sense 'coming' (it usually means 'produce' or 'income') and the convoluted syntax, especially the sense 'in order that' given to אש. Lipiński reads (see his note to the passage);

[ו]שבת באת (ב)(!)חית שמן על תקמת עם

i.e. '[And] I came back, I came with [fa]t beasts to the place of refuge of the people and to the altars of ...' The damaged first letter could well be ו rather than א (Honeyman) and שמן is possible for ימן; but as Lipiński clearly realizes, the letter before חית can hardly be ב, and שמן (note his brackets) ought to be שמנת. His rendering 'place of refuge' for תקמת, however, though it is based on an idiosyncratic interpretation of Lev. xxvi 37 (where the word is a *hapax legomenon*) has the not inconsiderable merit of supplying a referent for בן 'in it' in 13. An entirely different reading is proposed by van den Branden (cp. Magnanini):

[ו]זבחת החי[ת] לאלנ[ם] פעלת קרת עז

i.e. 'and I sacrificed the animals [to the god]s. I made the reservoir of the fountain and altars for ....' With קרת cp. Hebr. מקור (base QWR 'to bore, dig'). The second letter which is very faint could just as well be ז as שׁ, but I cannot see ח after it, and there does not seem to me to be nearly enough room for לאלנ[ם]; moreover, the final five letters are almost certainly קמת עם. However, I find פעלת a convincing reading, though it involves putting down a mark above the פ as resulting from damage to the surface; cp. פעלת אנך in 13. The following phrase and מזבחת then become its direct objects; both Honeyman and Lipiński have to connect ל מזבחת with a previous prepositional construction and render ל 'of'. קמת, which rather than תקמת now becomes the referent for בן (13), must describe some sort of sacred building; does it mean simply 'place (of the people)'? מזבחת; a fem. plur. form as in Hebrew.

11. על חיי etc.; cp. Palmyrene על חיוהי וחיי בנוהי (*NSI* no. 137, 2). מד; Hebr. מדי, lit. 'out of the abundance of' and hence 'as often as'; cp. particularly מדי שׁנה בשׁנה 'every year' (1 Sam. vii 16); מדי חדשׁ בחדשׁו 'month by month at new-moon' (Isa. lxvi 23). צמח צדק; cp. Jerem. xxiii 5 xxxiii 15 and further for צדק 'legitimate' **6** Yehimilk 6 **25** Yehaumilk 9. The reference here is to the reigning Ptolemy II, who as Honeyman points out was the youngest son of his father and whose claim to the throne cannot, therefore, have been undisputed. אשׁתו; according to Honeyman the reading is not in doubt, though the שׁ is not very clear. The final ו is clear, however, and can only signify the 3 sing. masc. suffix as in the Byblian dialect, i.e. [ēw] (the noun is genit.) or perhaps by this time [aw] whatever the case. The wife is doubtless Arsinoë, Ptolemy II's full sister and his second wife, who shared divine honours with him (see at **31** Umm El-'Amed iv 7). His first wife had also been called Arsinoë. Honeyman thinks both may be being referred to and renders 'his wives', arguing that the fifth year of Ptolemy, the year in which the altars were built, was likely to have been that in which he banished the first Arsinoë and married the second, namely 279/8 (i.e. the inscr. calculates from 283/2; see introd.), and that the writer is, as it were, hedging his bets by mentioning both; his case would have been stronger had the line been written in Ptolemy's fifth year instead of being a reference back to it from a time when the first wife was no longer a problem. אדמי; hardly 'his (Ptolemy's) people' or 'his blood', i.e. 'his relatives' (דם with prosthetic (?) [']) or (by an error) אדני 'his lord', all proposals which have been made. The suffix must be 1 person written י after a genit. as in the Byblian dialect. It is surely not conceivable that the Lapethos dialect should have possessed two different 3 masc. sing. suffixes and have used them side by side as here with nominal forms (a fem. sing. and a masc. sing.) that elsewhere add suffixes in the same manner. The syntax of *ll.* 10–12 is not felicitous, but as I understand them there seem to be three altars or sets of altars: one dedicated to Melcarth, where daily sacrifices were to be made on behalf of the chief magistrate and his family; one dedicated to Ptolemy and his wife and one reserved for the people of Lapethos (cp. עם in 10), at both of which sacrifices were to be made twice monthly.

12. כסא; Ps. lxxxi 4. כקדם; Jerem. xxx 20 Lam. v 21. כם; Hebr. כמו. דלת; prob. lit. 'door', here used for a double or hinged tablet, as possibly in **I 12** Lachish iv 3 (with כתבתי על); cp. Jerem. xxxvi 23 where the plur. דלתות is used of the columns of a scroll. This is more satisfactory than deriving the word from Greek δέλτος 'writing tablet' (from the shape of the letter). Phoen. also possesses a masc. form דל; **33** Tariff A 5. הנחשׁת is prob. in apposition to הדלת; see at **25** Yehaumilk 4.

13. סמרת lit. 'nailed into (ב)'; see at **14** Kilamuwa ii 1. קר; **9** Shipitbaal 1. בן =
[binnā] 'in it' (fem.) referring back to קמת in 10; cp. **15** Karatepe A ii 18;
apparently, therefore, the Tyro-Sidonian rather than the Byblian form,
since Byblian retains ה for the 3 sing. fem. suffix (**25** Yehaumilk 6). It is
not impossible, however, that in this particular case, in which the suffix is
added to an 'energic' [n] (< [binhā]), syncope of [h] could have occurred
independently either in the Byblian dialect or in the variety spoken in
Lapethos. In order to be certain that the dialect of Lapethos had always
followed the Tyro-Sidonian dialect in forming the 3 fem. sing. suffix rather
than the Byblian we would need to have an example after a genit. sing. or
a plur. masc. noun (where [h] is retained in Byblian but is replaced by [y]
in Tyro-Sidonian). There may be such an example in **42** Pyrgi בתי 'her
temple'; q.v. introduction for possible links between Pyrgi and Lapethos.
For other explanations of בן, all resulting in very peculiar constructions (e.g.
'which they rebuilt for the safety of my offering', 'which is part of, lit. from
…') see Honeyman's commentary. מנחת חני; 'my offering to obtain grace' is
in the context of a votive inscr. preferable to 'my gracious offering', though
I can find no exact parallel in Hebr. usage; cp., however, Gen. iv 4 xxxii
21 Num. v 15. עלת 'above'; cp. **25** Yehaumilk 11; not so likely in view of
כסף in 14 'burnt offerings' (Lipiński).

14. The beginning of the line is lost, the first visible sequence being אפבת;
hardly אפדת, though it is interesting that Hebr. ['puddā] is used in Isa. xxx
22 of the gold 'sheathing' of a molten image. משקל; perhaps with fem.
suffix [ā]; cp. Num. vii 13. כר; unknown, unless (Lidzbarski) it be an
abbreviation of כרש, a weight mentioned several times in the Aram. papyri
from Egypt (*DISO* p. 127). Cooke's suggestion that it is an abbreviation of ככר
'talent' gives an impossibly large weight of metal, though it should be noted that
the sign for 100 is not too clear and may be that for a smaller number.

15. פקת perhaps 'profit', 'possessions', or the like from PYQ 'to obtain' (Ugar.
pq); cp. Prov. iii 13 (Qal). Lipiński renders 'authority', a loan-word from
Akkad. *piqittu* (base PQD). ויסכרן; see at 3 above (סכר); cp. also 1 Sam. i 11
in Hannah's prayer for a son.

16. נעם; cp. Ps. xc 17. שרש; cp. Isa. xi 1, 10 and see on פר 'fruit' (3).

37, 38   Harpocrates statue i, ii (Egypt)   Fig. 17 (ii)

The two small (27–28 cm. high) bronze statues of the infant Horus,
naked with the fingers of one hand raised to his mouth, have the
similar inscrs. incised round their bases. The first, apparently
presented as a gift to the Spanish King Charles III in 1770, is now in
the Museo arqueologico nacional in Madrid; it dates to the 4 or 3
cent. BC. The second was acquired much more recently by the British
Museum; its script, which has some unusual shapes (א, י, פ, ש), points
to a rather higher date in the early 5 cent. around the same time as
27 Tabnit. The provenance of the statues is unknown, but from their
purely Egyp. style of execution and the fact that the second has an
Egyp. version of the inscr. written on one of the four panels, it can
only have been Egypt. The families who commissioned them must,
therefore, have belonged to the large Semitic-speaking population of

Egypt in the Persian and Greek periods. Ferron has some interesting but not entirely convincing arguments linking them with Carthage rather than Phoenicia. For other Phoen. inscrs. from Egypt, mostly small graffiti and ostraca or ill-presented papyri, see the Bibliogr. Notes.

Bibliography

i.

P. Schröder, *Die phönizische Sprache* (1869), 253 ff.

NSE p. 424.

KI no. 44.

RÉS no. 1507.

KAI no. 52.

J. Ferron, 'La inscripción cartaginesa en el Arpocrates madrileño', *Trabajos de Prehistoria*, N.S. 28 (1971), 359–79.

Magnanini, *Iscrizioni*, p. 82.

ii.

R. D. Barnett, 'A review of acquisitions 1955–62 of Western Asiatic antiquities', *Brit. Mus. Qu.* 27 (1963–4), 85.

Röllig, 'Beiträge', 118–20.

Magnanini, *Iscrizioni*, p. 84.

J. Ferron, 'La statuette d'Harpocrate du British Museum', *RSF* 2 (1974), 77–95.

Illustrations

i.   *NSE* Taf. X, 5; Ferron, loc. cit., pls. I–IV (the first photographs).

ii.   Barnett, loc. cit., pl. XLI a; Röllig, loc. cit., fig. on p. 119; Ferron, loc. cit., pls. XXII–XXVII.

37 i 1   חרפכרט יתן חים ל

2   עבדי לעבדאשמן בן עשתרתיתן בן מגן בן חנתס בן

3   פט בן טט בן פשמ--י

4   בשת -----

1.   May Harpocrates give life to
2.   his servant Abdeshmun son of Ashtartyatana son of MGN son of ḤNTS son
3.   of PṬ son of ṬṬ son of PŠM [..] Y!
4.   In the year ....

NOTES

1. חרפכרט meaning 'Horus the infant'; the Phoen. form seems to have been derived from the original Egyp. rather than from the Greek 'Αρποκράτης, since it lacks the final [s]. See R. Degen, *WO* 5 (1970), 218 ff. The child Horus was a frequent motif in Egyp. art, being pictured not only as in the present statues with his fingers to his mouth but as sitting on a lotus flower or being suckled by his mother Isis. These motifs also appear in borrowed form in early Phoen. art, as on the Samaria, Nimrud, and Arslan Tash ivories. Originating no doubt in the figure of Horus, son of Osiris and Isis and avenger of his dead father, Harpocrates seems to have emerged as an independent deity only in the later period of Egyp. mythology, where he is associated particularly with the rising sun, though he is also known as a dispenser of fruitfulness. He became very popular among the Greeks as a god of silence and secrecy, perhaps as a result of a misinterpretation of the motif of the raised fingers. It is impossible to know which of his various aspects was in the minds of the Phoenicians who commissioned these figures. חים 'life' may thus mean simply the recovery of health or, as Ferron suggests, it may signify new life in the afterworld for a relative who had died. The statues could, therefore, have been made either to serve as a kind of visible prayer in time of illness (cp. **29** Baalshillem) or to be a more permanent memorial for someone deceased. יתן can be understood either as a jussive or as a precative perf.; the Egyp. text of ii confirms that a wish is being expressed (see Barnett, loc. cit.).

2-3. It may be significant that the names of the more remote ancestors are Egyp., suggesting perhaps that Semitic blood entered the family through ḤNTS marrying a Phoen. woman. It should be noted, however, that in the Egyp. version of ii the Semitic names are given Egyp. counterparts, so the last names here may only be the Egyp. names of men who were Phoenicians by race. In Greek-speaking environments, too, double names were not uncommon; cp. the bilinguals *CIS* i 122 (Malta), *CIS* i 95 (Lapethos i), and below **40** (Athens). Ferron thinks that since the immediate ancestors' names are not given in Egyp. and are all common in Punic (see Benz, *Names,* for references), the family concerned may by the time the inscr. was put on the statue have left Egypt and been living for a generation or two in Carthage. With מגן cp. also **20** Ur box 1.

4. Apparently the beginning of a date formula.

38 ii 1 חרפכרט יתן

2 חים לעמס בן אשמניתן בן ע

3 זרמלך וחק נן בֹּעל בנֹא

1. May Harpocrates give
2. life to 'MS son of Eshmunyatan son of
3. 'ZRMLK! And NN, master of ...., engraved (the inscription).

NOTES

1-2. עמס; cp. the Biblical Amos. Ferron uses the fact that names with this element are otherwise attested only in Punic as evidence that the family was of Carthaginian origin. The same is true of עזרמלך; and except for one occurrence in Cyprus אשמניתן is found only in Punic or in Phoen. inscrs. from Egypt. See Benz, *Names*, for references, and see above for a slightly different argument connecting i with Carthage. It is questionable, however, whether such statistics can bear the weight Ferron places on them in view of the huge number of western inscrs. compared with eastern and the consequent preponderance of Punic names in Phoen. onomastica in general.

3. וחק etc.; these final words are written in two short lines on the left side of the panel and in a slightly smaller script than the rest of the inscr.; they apparently give the name of the engraver. Röllig reads this as נפר, a good Egyp. formation, followed by על בנא (or בלא), which he does not attempt to translate. Ferron reads the name as נג, which he claims is also Egyp., followed by בעל בנא, which he renders 'architect'; presumably this craftsman was responsible not only for making the statue and engraving its inscr. but for constructing the building (shrine or tomb) in which it was placed. Ferron's readings of ג and ב seem to me to accord better with the photographs than Röllig's פ and ר, but בנא for '(master of) building' with a *mater lectionis* is hardly acceptable at so early a date (5 cent.), even in Punic, unless we are to assume influence from Aramaic orthography (as occasionally in the graffiti from Abydos; e.g. אנכי for אנך; *KAI* no. 49 = Magnanini, *Iscrizioni*, pp. 66 ff.).

39 Rhodes

The inscr., carved on a fragment of white marble and dating, it is thought, from the 2 cent. BC, was discovered in the ruins of a temple. Of a Greek version written above it only a few letters survive. It is, because of the titles of the person named on it, the most important of three small inscrs. from the island witnessing to the presence of Phoenicians in the Hellenistic period. For evidence of earlier settlement see Harden, *Phoenicians*, 61; Moscati, *Phoenicians*, 98.

Bibliography

A. Maiuri and I. Guidi in *Annuario della scuola archeologica di Atene* 2 (1916), 267 ff.

KAI no. 44.

P. M. Fraser, 'Greek-Phoenician bilingual inscriptions from Rhodes', *Ann. Brit. Sch. at Athens* 65 (1970), 31–6; pl. 12 b–c.

Magnanini, *Iscrizioni*, p. 140.

On the titles see further:

A. M. Honeyman in *Le Muséon* 51 (1938), 288 f.

idem, 'The Phoenician title מתרח עשתרני', *RHR* 121 (1940), 5–17.

R. de Vaux, 'Les prophètes de Baal sur le mont Carmel', *BMB* 5 (1941), 7–20.

Guzzo Amadasi, *Iscrizioni*, pp. 183–4.

J.-G. Février, 'Astronoé', *JA* 256 (1968), 1–9.

Teixidor, 'Bulletin' for 1969, item 13; for 1975, item 127.

E. Lipiński, 'La fête de l'ensevelissement et de la résurrection de Melqart', *Actes de la XVIIe Rencontre Assyriologique Internationale* (1970), 30–58.

M. Delcor, 'Le *hieros gamos* d'Astarté', *RSF* 2 (1974), 63–76.

1 בעלמלך בן מלכיתן

2 מקם אלם מתרח עשתרני בֹן חֹן]

NOTES

The chief interest of the inscr. lies in the two titles מקם אלם and מתרח עשתרני. The first of these titles occurs elsewhere in the east only in the third Phoen. inscr. from Lapethos (Magnanini, *Iscrizioni*, p. 126, *I.* 1), but it is found frequently in Punic texts; the second title accompanies it in the present text and in several of the Punic texts, but has not so far been attested on its own. References in *DISO*, pp. 172, 156. There is nothing in the context of any of these occurrences to help us in determining the meaning of the phrases or even in deciding whether the second title goes with מקם or with אלם, and whether therefore we are dealing with two offices or with a single one. The titles nevertheless have given rise to considerable speculation based partly on etymology and partly on scattered allusions in classical writers, to which of late have been added certain enigmatic references in the Pyrgi inscr. (**42**). Use has also been made of the pictures on a decorated marble vase of the 4 cent. BC from Sidon published and discussed by R. D. Barnett in *Eretz Israel* 9 (1969), 6–13. On the basis of these sources Lipiński and Delcor have attempted to reconstruct the complicated ritual of a Phoen. festival which they believe originated in Tyre and took place in the spring. During this festival the tomb of the god Melcarth was burnt on a funeral pyre and thereafter the king (or a substitute figure) had intercourse in a sacred marriage with a temple prostitute representing Astarte, thus bringing about the resurrection of the god. The present titles identify the king's role in this ritual and mean 'the one who raises up the deity (and is) the Astartean bridegroom'. The festival spread from Tyre throughout the Mediterranean world, appearing in an Etruscan variant at Pyrgi, while in republican Rhodes and Carthage the king was replaced by high officials, including in Carthage a number who were *suffetes*. Language derived from such a ceremony is perhaps being used in Hos. vi 2 and Ezek. xxviii 16, 18.

The reconstruction is a seductive one which will repay more attention than space allows here, but on a number of grounds it seems to me to go well beyond the available evidence.

(a) We can accept that there was a spring festival of Melcarth's resurrection going back to ancient Tyre and that this lies behind the first title מקם אלם. This would seem to be confirmed by the occurrence of the phrase 'raiser of Herakles' (i.e. Melcarth) (ἐγερσε[ίτην τοῦ] ʻΗρακλέου[ς]) in a Greek inscr. of the Roman period from Philadelphia (Amman; see F. Abel, *RB* 5 (1908), 570 ff.), and by the statement of Josephus, citing an ealier author (*Ant. Jud.* VIII, 5, 3 § 181) that Hiram, the contemporary of Solomon, 'brought about the resurrection of Herakles' (τοῦ Ἡρακλέους ἔγερσιν ἐποιήσατο) in the spring month of Peritios; cp. for this meaning of the noun also Matt. xxvii 53. מקם is therefore Yiph. partic. from the base QWM (not otherwise attested in Phoen.) and אלם is the usual late Phoen. sing. usage (see at **15** Karatepe A iii 5 C iii 16).

(b)   Melcarth is not, however, as the reconstruction assumes, the consort of Astarte, a view which is based on a false interpretation of the divine name Milkashtart at Umm el-'Amed; nor, though his name means 'king of the city', is he the head of the Tyrian pantheon; Baal (Baalshamem) was Astarte's husband and he held that position. See further at **31** 2 and in the introd. to **30** Throne of Astarte. This mistaken identification had previously been made by de Vaux, who rendered the title 'awakener of the god (who is) husband of Astarte' and found it echoed in the language of 1 Kgs. xviii 27. The god whose worship was introduced into Israel by Jezebel was, however, clearly a weather-god (cp. 1 Kgs. xviii 24 xix 11–12), i.e. Baal, whereas if we are to trust the words used of him in Esarhaddon's treaty with the king of Tyre, Melcarth was a young vegetation deity like Adonis and Eshmun and like the Mesopotamian Tammuz. His relationship to Astarte ought, therefore, like Adonis's at Byblos, to be that of acolyte or lover rather than husband.

(c)   As far as our evidence goes the well-known ceremonies of mourning for Tammuz (cp. Ezek. viii 14) and for Adonis took place in high summer, when the vegetation 'died'. It would seem on the face of it to be to a ceremony of this kind that Ezek. xxviii 18 and **42** Pyrgi 8–9 ('the day of the god's burial') refer, from which it follows that the present title and the Pyrgi inscr. cannot be brought into connection with each other. The classical sources cited by Lipiński, which allude to a cremation or burning of Herakles-Melcarth, likewise make no reference to his resurrection at the same time. It looks as if, therefore, we may have to reckon with two different rites, one commemorating Melcarth's death in summer and one celebrating his coming to life in spring. The 'weeping' and 'laughter' involving the god Baal, on the other hand, were associated respectively with the beginning and end of the summer when the rains ceased and reappeared.

(d)   On the most obvious interpretation **42** Pyrgi 8–9 does not concern a marriage between the king and Astarte but a simple request from the goddess to the king (q.v. Note). The *hieros gamos* is therefore not to be fond at Pyrgi, and the allusion to the burial of the deity (whether Adonis or Melcarth) becomes merely part of a date formula. Is the sacred marriage to be presupposed, however, in the second title מתרח עשתרני? Since Honeyman and de Vaux related מתרח to Ugar. *mtrḫt* 'betrothed one, wife' (**14** Keret 13), most commentators have assumed that it is. I admit to being sceptical. Ugar. *mtrḫt* is usually explained as a passive partic. fem. of a derived theme meaning 'woman purchased by the marriage-price' (cp. Akkad. *terḫatu*) and מתרח as the active partic. masc. of the same theme meaning 'man who pays the marriage-price'. But in Ugar. it is the basic verbal theme (G or Qal) which has the meaning 'to pay the marriage-price' and the masc. partic. of this which is used with the sense 'husband' (**14** Keret 100); *mtrḫt* is therefore more suitably explained as a nominal form with [m] prefix and not as a fem. partic. with a masc. counterpart. I am tempted to follow the logic of (b) above and render מתרח by 'acolyte', and to take it (cp. de Vaux) along with אלם, i.e. 'the resuscitator of the deity (who is) the acolyte of Astarte'. I have, however, no etymology to suggest (unless Akkad. *tarū* 'to protect, support'?).

(e) With the removal of the Pyrgi inscr. from the argument, the only reference associating the king with the 'resurrection' of Melcarth is that in Josephus to Hiram. However, ἐποιήσατο there could mean 'celebrated' as easily as 'took part in'. In addition, there is the fact (overlooked by Lipiński and Delcor) that in the Lapethos iii inscr. a king of the city is mentioned (*1*. 3), and he is not the מקם אלם. I would therefore resist any recourse to this title as evidence for Phoen. sacral kingship.

(f) Lipiński follows Röllig (*KAI*) in explaining עשתרני as an adject. formed from the element עשתר with the addition of the two endings [ōn] and [iy], thus meaning 'having to do with Astarte', 'Astartean', or the like. But why omit the ת? Honeyman's suggestion that the name is a shortened form of the Mesopotamian 'Ishtar of Nineveh' accounts for the omission of the ת, but is otherwise no more immediately obvious than Février's that it is a late Phoen., prob. Carthaginian, combination of the names Astarte and Juno (see further at **42** Pyrgi 1). I have myself no proposal to offer. I agree, however, with most commentators that the name must be connected somehow with the Greek divine name Ἀστρονόη, though the latter has apparently been Hellenized to suggest a compound of ἀστήρ 'star' and νοῦς 'mind'. The significant point about the goddess Astronoë is that in the few references to her she is related both to Herakles of Tyre and to Eshmun of Berytus; for the passages see the studies of Honeyman and Février. There is thus a strong presupposition in favour not only of the Phoen. origin of the name but of its being a special epithet of Astarte in her capacity as patron of these young deities.

40, 41 Athens

The inscrs. are two of a number from Athens or its port Piraeus which date from the 4–2 cents. BC and witness to a considerable presence of Phoenician merchants in the Aegean world. These are chiefly on gravestones, most of the people commemorated originating from Sidon, but others from Askelon (*CIS* i 115), Cyprus (*CIS* i 117), and in one case (of a Greek woman who had presumably married a Phoenician) from Byzantium (*CIS* i 120). The community of Sidonians who had settled in Piraeus was clearly one of long standing. They seem in the land of their adoption to have maintained the organization of their native city (cp. the *suffete* mentioned in *CIS* i 118) and, by and large, their religion (though a priest to the Mesopotamian deity Nergal appears in *CIS* i 119); but there is evidence that in other ways they had adapted themselves to Greek civilization, notably in the long inscr. **41**, which records in similar terms to many Greek inscrs. of the period the typically Greek custom of voting a crown and monument to a deserving officer. There is a palaeographical study of the scripts, whch are of the Tyro-Sidonian type, by Lidzbarski, *Ephemeris* II (1908), 157 ff.

40 Athens. Marble stele found in 1795, now in the British Museum. See *CIS* i 116; *NSE* p. 424 a 2 (Taf. VIII, 1); *KI* no. 45; *KAI* no. 53; Magnanini, *Iscrizioni*, p. 135.

'Αρτεμίδωρος

'Ηλιοδώρου

Σιδώνιος

1 מצבת סכר בחים לעבדתנת בן

2 עבדשמש הצדני

Pillar of remembrance among the living for Abdtannit son of Abdshemesh, a Sidonian.

NOTES

מצבת; **35** 1. סכר בחים; see the references at **36** Lapethos ii 3. The occurrence of תנת in an eastern Phoen. inscr. is unparalleled; perhaps the man's father had had close trading contacts with Carthage. There is, however, increasing evidence that the goddess's name may have originated in the east; see most recently Teixidor, 'Bulletin' for 1976, item 138 (the first publication of a lamp from the Beirut Museum inscribed לתנת). Both her identity (Anat? Athirat? Astarte?) and the correct pronunciation of the name are as yet unagreed. For a recent study see F. M. Cross, *Canaanite Myth and Hebrew Epic* (1973), 28 ff. Note that the names on the Greek version of this inscr. ('gift of ...') are in effect translations of the Phoen.; they show Tannit to have been identified with Artemis; in the west her usual opposite was Juno (Hera).

41 Piraeus. The longest and most interesting of the Phoen. inscrs. from Greece. It clearly follows a Greek model; see *Corpus Inscriptionum Atticarum* ii 16, 589, 603, 621, etc. The only era of Sidon known to us began in 111 BC, which would date this inscr. to 96 BC. However, the Greek writing (the inscr. is given in Corpus Inscr. Att. ii Suppl. 1335b) is thought to be 3 cent., and the Phoen. writing does not seem greatly different from the others from the area; there must, therefore,, have been an earlier Sidonian era now lost to us. The stone of white marble was found in 1871 and is now in the Louvre. See E. Renan, *CRAIBL*, 1888, 12 f.; *NSE* p. 425 b4 (Taf. VIII, 6); *NSI* no. 33; *KI* no. 52; *RÉS* no. 1215; *KAI* no. 60; Magnanini, *Iscrizioni*, p. 138.

1 בים 4 למרזח בשת 14 לעם צדן תם בד צדנים בן אספת לעטר

2 ית שמעבעל בן מגן אש נשא הגו על בת אלם ועל מבנת חצר בת אלם

3 עטרת חרץ בדרכנם 20 למחת כ בן ית חצר בת אלם ופעל ית כל

4 אש עלתי משרת ית רעת ז לכתב האדמם אש נשאם לן על בת

5 אלם עלת מצבת חרץ ויטנאי בערפת בת אלם ען אש לכנת גו

6 ערב עלת מצבת ז ישאן בכסף אלם בעל צדן דרכמנם 20 למחת

7 לכן ידע הצדנים כ ידע הגו לשלם חלפת אית אדמם אש פעל

8 משרת את פן גו

Τὸ κοινὸν τῶν Σιδωνίων Διοπείθ(η)ν Σιδώνιον

1. On the 4th day of the feast, in the 14th year of the people of Sidon, it was resolved by the Sidonians in assembly: — to crown
2. Shama'baal son of MGN, who (had been) a superintendent of the community in charge of the temple and in charge of the buildings in the temple court,
3. with a golden crown worth 20 darics sterling, because he (re-)built the temple court and did all
4. that was required of him by way of service; — that the men who are our superintendents in charge of the temple should write this decision
5. on a chiselled stele, and should set it up in the portico of the temple before the eyes of men; — (and) that the community should be named
6. as guarantor. For this stele the citizens of Sidon shall draw 20 drachmae sterling from the temple treasury.
7. So may the Sidonians know that the community knows how to requite the men who have rendered
8. service before the community.

NOTES

1. ים and שת are sing. against the usual practice in Phoen. date-formulas; **28** Eshmunazar 1 **31** Umm El-'Amed iv 5. מרזח is prob. a collective noun like Hebr. משפחה 'family', meaning, therefore, a feasting community or association; so in Palmyrene (*DISO*, p. 167), in Punic in the Tariff text *CIS* i 165 = *KAI* no. 69, 16, where it is paralleled by שפח, and possibly in one Ugar. text where it is paralleled by *bn 'trt* (see *CML*[2] p. 152). Here, however, it refers more loosely to the feasting occasion, as in Biblical Hebr. (Amos vi 7 Jerem. xvi 5), in the Talmud, where it means specifically a mourning banquet, and in another Ugar. text (Gordon, *Ugaritic Texbook* no. 2032). It prob. denotes an annual period of common meals like the Greek συσσιτία rather than a festival of Semitic origin. לעם צדן; of an unknown era of Sidon; see introduction. תם בד; a peculiar phrase, lit. 'it was complete in, by the hand of', or the like; on the prepos. בד see at **2, 3** Byblos cones and **42** Pyrgi 6. צדנים; **27** Tabnit 1. בנאספת is usually read, i.e. the prepos. ב plus a noun formed from the Niph. partic., or better perhaps נאספת for מאספת (*CIS* i 6000) through dissimilation of [m] to [n] before the labial [p], though this is not the next letter; cp. Latin *Mitthumbal* for מתנבעל (Segert, *Grammar*, p. 69). An easier division, however, is בן אספת, i.e. the longer form בן as in **12** Old Cyprus 4 with a fem. noun אספת; cp. Eccles. xii 11; also 'Ασεππ in a transliterated name; Benz, *Names*, p. 272. Alternatively, בן = [bnē ...], '(being) members of the assembly'

(Dahood, *Biblica* 33, 1952, 217 f.). לעטר followed by a double accus. as in Ps. viii 6 ciii 4.

2. שמעבעל 'Baal has heard'; the Greek Διοπείθης, i.e. 'obeying Zeus' is an equivalent, not an attempt at translation. מגן; **37** Harpocrates statue i 2. נשא (Hebr. 'chief, prince, lay-head') here denotes one of several (cp. 4) officers of the Sidonian community who were responsible for the maintenance of its place of worship. Shama'baal's term of office had elapsed, and he now receives this expression of gratitude from the assembly. The latter body (אספת or מאספה) represented and made decisions on behalf of the whole community, which is described by the term גו; Greek τὸ κοινόν; see further at **30** Throne of Astarte. אלם (sing.) with perhaps syncope of [h] of the article; so also before צדנים in 1 (cp. 7), רעת (4), גו (5, 8; cp. 2), מצבת (6), and אדמם (7). The chief god of Sidon (Baal) is prob. meant; cp. **28** Eshmunazar 18, where he is called בעל צדן; so possibly in 6, though there בעל צדן is more easily rendered 'citizens of Sidon', i.e. the property owners among the Sidonians of Piraeus, who apparently made up the membership of the assembly. מבנת; perhaps plur. of מבן = [mibnē]; cp. Ezek. xl 2.

3. The ב is the so-called *Beth pretii*, 'at the cost of'. דרכנם can hardly be an error for דרכמנם 'drachmae' as in 6. It is true that in Greek inscrs. of this class the sums voted are given in δραχμαί, a larger sum for the crown and a smaller one for the stele. But δραχμαί in these denotes silver drachmae, which was the basic unit of currency in the Greek states, and 20 silver drachmae is much too small an amount for a gold crown, though sufficient for a normal stele. Those who argue for a mistake by the mason have to assume, therefore, not only that the drachmae in this inscr. denote the rarely struck gold drachmae of Greece (worth 10–12 silver drachmae) but that the stele in the present case was a gold, i.e. gilded, one, though there is not the slightest trace of gilding on the monument. It is simpler to translate חרץ in 5 not as 'gold' but as 'something sculpted, chiselled' (in apposition) as in **32** Umm El-'Amed xiii 1 (see also the note to **25** Yehaumilk 4), making the sum in (silver) drachmae there acceptable, and to regard דרכנם here as the Phoen. for Greek δαρεικόι or 'darics', a gold coin of Persian origin well known in Greece down to the Macedonian age and equivalent in value to 20 silver drachmae. Twenty darics would make a more appropriate sum for a gold crown. The fact that the daric had disappeared from circulation by 96 BC could then be taken as additional support for a higher dating of the inscr. and for the existence of an earlier Sidonian era. The Hebr. forms of the coin names are דרכמנים 'drachmae' (Ezra ii 69) and אדרכנים 'darics' (1 Chron. xxix 7); they are suspected of having been confused with each other in the scribal tradition of Chron.-Ezra-Neh., but that is no reason for assuming that they were in the present context of an inscr. written only once. למחת cp. Aram. Ithpe. 'to be approved', Syr. [tamḥī] 'to test' (weights or measures); here perhaps ל with the Qal infin. 'by the full, tested, approved weighing', or the like; the base is dubiously linked with MHY 'to wipe, wipe out' (4 Ahiram 2).

4. עלת; **25** Yehaumilk 11; here 'incumbent upon', in the next line simply 'on' of place, in 6 'on behalf of, for'; contrast על 'over' (2, 4), though there is prob. no significance in this spread of meanings between the two prepositions. משרת; a noun (perhaps formed from the Piel partic.) meaning 'service', in apposition to אש. רעת; cp. Hebr. רעי 'my thoughts' (Ps. cxxxix 2); Syr. [re'yānā] 'mind, opinion, doctrine, vote, etc.'; the base is prob. not to be confused with Aram. R'Y, Hebr. RṢY 'to take pleasure in'.

רעת ז is the object of לכתב, placed first for emphasis, and האדמם is its subject. נשאם לן, i.e. the present curators of the temple.

5. חרץ; see the discussion at 3. יטנאי; Yiph. imperf. plur. with suffix (fem.). ערפת; **25** Yehaumilk 6. עש עז; lit. '(in) the eyes of (any) man'. לכנת; Piel infin. dependent on תם בד (1); cp. Isa. xlv 4.

6. ערב; prob. partic. Qal; this verb in Hebr. is usually followed by a direct object (Gen. xliii 9 Ps. cxix 122), once by ל (Prov. vi 1); so it is better to take עלת מזבח ז as dependent, not on ערב, but on the verb which folllows; and this is in accordance with the frequent formula in the Greek inscrs., Εἰς δὲ τὴν ἀναγραφὴν τῆς στήλης δοῦναι .... The verb נשא is used in the sense 'count, count out'; cp. Exod. xxx 12, Num. i 2, iii 40, etc., and espec. xxxi 26; the tense is imperf. indicative (ending in [n]). ב means 'from' (the Greek inscrs. have here ἀπό or ἐκ); **7** Abibaal 2. בעל צדן; see at 2.

7. The first ידע following לכן is modal (without [n]); the sense is almost 'so that the Sidonians may know' (Greek ὅπως). The second ידע following כ is indicative, i.e. perf. (stative). With the two objects after שלם cp. 1 Sam. xxiv 20 Prov. xiii 21. חלפת 'equivalent, return'; cp. Hebr. חלף, Num. xviii 21, 31. There is some uncertainty about the writing of אש at the end of the line, as if the mason had begun to repeat א but quickly changed to ש.

8. את פן; **25** Yehaumilk 16.

42 Pyrgi (Italy)   Pl. VIII, 2

The gold lamina (19.3 by 9.2 cm.) inscribed with Phoen. characters is one of three discovered in 1964 at Santa Severa (the ancient Pyrgi), the port of Caere (Cerveteri) in southern Etruria, during excavations conducted by the Istituto di Etruscologia of the University of Rome. The other two (A, B) are in Etruscan, a language at present only imperfectly deciphered. From the partial renderings of those that have been attempted, it appears that we are dealing not with a bilingual text in the strict sense but with separately composed texts prepared on the same occasion, two intended for the indigenous inhabitants and one for a Phoen.-speaking community resident in the area. The gold plates are now housed in the Museo archeologico di Villa Giulia in Rome. Their date, decided from the Etruscan writing as well as the Phoen., is around 500 BC. For evidence of earlier Phoenician connections with Italy see **19** Praeneste bowl.

Interpretation

Though in the short period since its discovery the Phoen. inscr. has attracted a host of commentators, there is as yet little agreement on its detailed interpretation. The reading is not in doubt except for the last letter in 5 (which may be מ but is prob. נ), but both there and in several other places the text is so cryptic that, ironically, a solution of the difficulties may have to await a better understanding of the Etruscan versions to which it was hoped that it would supply the key. As interpreted here, the inscr. celebrates the dedication by King Thefarie Velianas or Veliiunas of a 'holy place', i.e. a small shrine, to

the Phoen. goddess Astarte. This shrine was prob. situated within the
temple at Pyrgi called B by the archaeologists, which seems to have
belonged to the Etruscan goddess Uni (the Latin Juno). The
dedication took place in the month of the sacrifice to the sun-god, but
the construction of the shrine was begun earlier in the same year (the
third of the king's reign) in the month of KRR. At this point a specific
day is named, that of the 'burial' of some unknown deity, apparently
because it was on that day that Astarte had commissioned him to
undertake the task. The inscr. closes with a wish that a statue of the
goddess placed within the shrine should stand for countless years.
Other interpretations involving a *cella* or 'inner room' as well as a
'holy place' and an allusion to a *hieros gamos* or sacred marriage are
discussed in the Notes. The most plausible explanation of the
composition of the inscr. seems to me to be that the king of Caere
allowed himself, for obvious reasons of state, to be associated with the
establishment of a place of worship within an Etruscan temple at
Pyrgi for the use of a community of Phoen. traders who had settled in
the port. The fulsome language which he uses may be compared with
the decrees of Cyrus and Darius in Ezra i 2 ff., vi 2 ff.; he need no
more have been a regular devotee of Astarte than were the Persian
emperors worshippers of Yahweh.

The dialect

In view of its date and provenance the natural assumption is that
the dialect of the inscr. ought to be Punic and the Phoenicians for
whom it was written to be Carthaginians. This assumption would seem
to be supported both by the finds of Etruscan material at Carthage
and the classical accounts of close political relations between the
Carthaginians and the Etruscans during most of the 6 cent. BC when
the two powers made common cause to counteract Greek expansion
towards the west (see Moscati, *Phoenicians*, 118 f.). In spite of this a
number of scholars have followed Levi della Vida in regarding the
dialect as eastern Phoen. and in particular as Cyprian Phoenician. In
favour of this opinion are the use of prosthetic א in the demonstrative
pronoun אז (2) and the phrase אבבת (5), and the substitution of ש for
the expected ס in the names of the Etruscan monarch and his
kingdom. The second of these features points more precisely to the
area of Lapethos, as even more strongly does the Byblian suffix ו in
בנתו (or במתו) in 5–6, though this disappears if the reading בן תו is
adopted (see the Note). Even the fem. suffix, which has the
Tyro-Sidonian י (בבתי, 10), may be as in the Lapethos dialect. For
cross-references see the Notes below. This cluster of isoglosses seems
to me to present a strong case for the conclusion that the Phoenicians
for whom the inscr. was intended came originally from northern

Cyprus. The case is weakened if the suffix ן is removed in 5–6, but it is not in my view seriously affected by the existence of a few sporadic parallels to the other features in Punic sources. These (if they did not develop independently within Punic) may show no more than that there was a similar if rather more diffused Cyprian influence in Carthage and other areas of the western Mediterranean, an influence of which we have already had a hint in the links established between Cyprus and the Carthage pendant (18).

Bibliography

G. Garbini, 'Scavi nel santuario etrusco di Pyrgi .... L'iscrizione punica', *Archeologia classica* 16 (1964), 66–76.

There is a useful series of preliminary studies by J. Ferron, J.-G. Février, G. Garbini, G. Levi della Vida, and A. J. Pfiffig in *Or. Ant.* 4 (1965) and 5 (1966).

The most comprehensive discussion to date is 'Le lamine di Pyrgi: Tavola rotonda internazionale sulla interpretazione dei testi fenicio ed etrusco (Roma, 19 aprile, 1968)' in *Acc. Nazionale dei Lincei, Problemi attuali di scienza e di cultura,* Quaderno N. 147 (Rome, 1970) (with full early bibliography).

See further:

A. Dupont-Sommer, 'L'Inscription punique récemment découverte à Pyrgi', *JA* 252 (1964), 282–302.

S. Moscati, 'Sull' iscrizione fenicio-punica di Pyrgi', *RSO* 39 (1964), 257–60.

M. Dahood, 'Punic *hkkbm 'l* and Isa. 14.13', *Orientalia* 34 (1965), 170–2.

J.-G. Février, 'A propos du hieros gamos de Pyrgi', *JA* 253 (1965), 11–13.

A. J. Pfiffig, *Uni-Hera-Astarte. Studien zu den Goldblechen von S. Severa/Pyrgi mit etruskisches und punisches Inschrift,* Osterreichische Akad. der Wissensch., Phil.-Hist. Klasse, Denkschriften 88, 2 (Vienna, 1965).

J. A. Fitzmyer, 'The Phoenician inscription from Pyrgi', *JAOS* 86 (1966), 287–97.

Guzzo Amadasi, *Iscrizioni,* pp. 158 ff.

Teixidor, 'Bulletin' for 1967, item 52.

M. Delcor, 'Une inscription bilingue étrusco-punique récemment découverte à Pyrgi, son importance religieuse', *Le Muséon* 81 (1968), 241–54.

W. Fischer, H. Rix, 'Die phönizische-etruskischen Texte der Goldplättchen von Pyrgi', *Göttingische Gelehrte Anzeigen* 220 (1968), 64–94.

G. Garbini, 'Riconsiderando l'iscrizione di Pyrgi', *AIUON* 18 (1968), 229–46.

KAI (2nd edit.) no. 277.

Röllig, 'Beiträge', 108 ff.

M. Pallottino, 'Pyrgi: Nota sui documenti epigrafici rinvenuti nel santuari', *Atti della Acc. Naz. dei Lincei,* ser. VIII, *Notizie degli scavi* 24 (1970), Suppl. 2 (Rome, 1972), 730–43.

Teixidor, 'Bulletin' for 1971, item 109; for 1975, item 127.

Lipiński, 'Miscellanea', 59 ff.; 'North Semitic texts', 243 f.

See also the articles by Delcor, Février, and Lipiński in the Bibliogr. to **39** Rhodes.

Illustrations

Archeologia classica 16 (1964), tav. XXXIV, XXXVII; *Or. Ant.* 4 (1965), tav. XXIV; Guzzo Amadasi, *Iscrizioni,* tav. LXVI; Fitzmyer, loc. cit., sketch on p. 286; 'Le lamine di Pyrgi', loc. cit., sketch following p. 67.

1 לרבת לעשתרת אשר קדש

2 אז אש פעל ואש יתן

3 תבריא ולנש מלך על

4 כישריא בירח זבח

5 שמש במתן אבבת ובֹן

6 תו כ עשתרת ארש בדי

7 למלכי שנת שלש 3 בי

8 רח כרר בים קבר

9 אלם ושנת למאש אלם

10 בבתי שנת כם הככבם

11 אל

1. To the lady Astarte. This holy place
2. (is that) which was made and which was given by
3. TBRY' WLNŠ, king over
4. KYŠRY', in the month of the sacrifice
5. to the sun-god, as a gift (and) as a temple. I built
6. it, because Astarte requested (it) of me
7. in the third year of my reign, in
8. the month of KRR, on the day of the burial
9. of the deity. So (may) the years (granted) to the statue of the deity
10. in her temple (be) years like the stars
11. above!

NOTES

1. לרבת לעשתרת; cp. **30** Throne of Astarte. For עשתרת the Etruscan text A has *Unialastres*, clearly equating her with the Etruscan Uni, i.e. the Latin Juno and Greek Hera, rather than Aphrodite/Venus, her usual counterpart in the classical world (the *al* in the Etruscan name is a grammatical ending). This identification is occasionally found elsewhere and was known to St. Augustine of Hippo as late as AD 5 cent. (*Quaestiones in heptateuchum,* vii, 16). The second part of the Etruscan

name prob. indeed represents the name Astarte. This does not necessarily mean, however, that a goddess Uni-Astarte combining attributes of both was actually worshipped in Caere. The form *Unialastres* is not attested elsewhere in Etruscan; and the name may, therefore, simply be a means of identifying for the indigenous population which particular foreign goddess was being accorded a place of worship in Uni's temple. According to Février, the name appears later in a Phoen. dress, though with its elements reversed, in the form עשתרני, i.e. Astarte-Juno; see further at **39** Rhodes, (f); but this is no more than a guess which is rather too obviously motivated by a desire to bring the Pyrgi inscr. into connection with the enigmatic title מקם אלם מתרח עשתרני. The fact that the chief goddess of the Phoenicians at Pyrgi was Astarte and not Tannit is thought by some to indicate that the community originated from the east; for outside proper names Astarte is rarely mentioned in Punic texts. We cannot, however, make too much of this, since there is evidence that Astarte may still have been prominent in Carthage at the time of this inscr. and that it was only during the 5 cent. BC that she was superseded there by Tannit (who incidentally was regularly equated with Hera/Juno). For a useful short discussion of the vexed problem whether Astarte and Tannit are to be equated with each other see the book by Cross mentioned in the Notes to **40** Athens. אשר 'place'; also in the Punic inscr. CIS i 3779, 6 (אשר הקדש); Ugar. *aṭr* (**17** i 29); Aram. אתרא. A fem. form אשרת occurs in **31** Umm El-'Amed iv 4 (q.v. Note). Syncope of [h] of the article (cp. the Punic form) is perhaps to be assumed in אשר קדש; this would regularize the construction with the following אז, though not in accordance with Lambdin's theory (see Note on phonology and grammar).

2. אז; see at **17** Baal Lebanon; a form characteristic of Cyprian Phoen., but occasionally found in the west (see CIS i 147, 2, from Sardinia = Guzzo Amadasi, *Iscrizioni*, p. 98; and for Punic instances DISO, p. 70). אש פעל (lit. 'which he made') and אש יתן occur frequently in votive texts but so far have only been found together here.

3. תבריא corresponds to Etruscan *Thefarie*, which is prob. the same name as appears in Latin as Tiberius. ת for *th* is not unexpected (it frequently renders Greek θ; contrast טברי for Tiberius on a Neo-Punic inscr., where ט reflects the Latin *t*; KAI no. 122, 2); but ב instead of פ for *f* is surprising. Prob. the explanation is to be sought in the pre-history of the name Tiberius, which seems to be neither Latin nor Etruscan, but to derive from a language stratum pre-dating both; the consonantal sound in question was reflected by an allophone of [f] in Etruscan and of [b] in both Latin and Phoenician. The אי of the Phoen. form represents the double vocalic *ie* of Etruscan, י being doubtless consonantal, though א is apparently an early example of a *mater lectionis*, used as in most examples of vowel-letters in late Phoen. and early Punic texts to express a final vowel in a name of foreign origin. ולנש represents only one of the middle vowel sounds in Etruscan *Velianas* (A) or *Veliiunas* (B); it appears from these alternative spellings that none of them was pronounced with any prominence. More interesting is ש for Etruscan *s*. There is no evidence that *s* was palatalized in Etruscan, so ש cannot represent an Etruscan allophone [š]. In later Punic the letters ש and ס were frequently confused, showing that there was in that dialect at that time little distinction between the two sounds in speech; but at this early period it is much more pertinent to compare the Lapethos inscrs.,

where ש occurs in the spelling of the name Ptolemy in place of ס elsewhere on Cyprus; see at **36** 4. מלך על 'king over' is unparalleled in a title in Phoen., though similar usages occur in more discursive contexts; e.g. **25** Yehaumilk 2 *CIS* i 90 (מלכי על כתי); cp. also 1 **16** Mesha 2, Eccles. i 12, etc. Possibly, therefore, we should construe מלך as a partic., 'ruling over', and see the phrase as an attempt to render an Etruscan office comparable to the Greek ἄρχων or the Latin *praetor,* though it cannot have been a yearly office, as a third year of his 'reign' is mentioned in 7. Or Thefarie Velianas may have been a 'tyrant' or aristocratic usurper who had seized power by force like the τύραννοι of archaic Greece. The absence of a genealogy could be used to support either of these interpretations.

4. כישריא; the first י prob. marks the diphthong in Caere (Greek Καίρη, Καιρέα) and ש (not ס; see above) the *s* in the alternative form *Cisra,* known from a scholion on Virgil's *Aeneid* (Fitzmyer); the second Greek form contains the necessary double vocalic sound to explain יא at the end. זבח שמש; a month name found in *CIS* i 13 (Magnanini, *Iscrizioni,* p. 107) and perhaps to be read as a correction of זבח ששם in **36** Lapethos ii 4, both interestingly from Cyprus. It was prob. a winter month at the time of the solstice (Dec. 21) when sacrifices to the sun were made.

5. במתן אבבת was previously read as במתנא בבת; the א was explained either as the suffix [ō], i.e. 'as his gift' (the Tyro-Sidonian form; but this is only found with nouns in the nomin. or accus., and in both Phoen. and Punic would at this early period be unmarked in the orthography; see the Note on phonology and grammar), or as a fem. ending [ō] < [at] (but there is no real evidence that this ending without [t], which in any case only develops in late Punic, was pronounced other than [ā], like the 3 fem. perf. ending in verbs; see Dotan, 'Stress position', 81 ff.). The א must, therefore, go with בבת and be the prosthetic vowel characteristic of Cyprian Phoen.; being a sub-phonemic helping vowel, it was not always written, and therefore there is nothing odd about its absence in בבתי (10); cp. אבמקדש, **36** Lapethos ii 3, but במקדש ibid., *l.* 7. אבבת should be vocalized ['ab(ᵉ)bēt] or the like, which seems to show that the noun is indefinite and to demand a translation not 'in the temple' but 'as a temple' with a second *Beth essentiae.* The shrine to Astarte was, as far as we can ascertain, situated inside the precincts of the larger temple of Uni, but seemingly neither here nor in 10 does the inscr. draw attention to that fact. The masc. form מתן is rare outside proper names (Benz, *Names,* p. 356) in Phoen., the usual form being fem. (מתנת or מתת); but cp. Hebr. [mattān], [mattanā], [mattat]; see also at **20** Ur box 2. בנתו is the *crux interpretum* of the inscription. It was at first read as במתו 'and (in) its high-place' (cp. I **16** Mesha 3) with a Byblian form of the suffix (though a late Punic form א immediately preceded it!). The reading נ is now usually preferred; it is impossible to be absolutely certain, since a rivet-hole on the edge of the plaque has spread to blot out part of the letter; but the leftwards stance of the shaft is more frequent with נ than with מ elsewhere in the inscription. בנתו is understood here as the 1 sing. perf. from BNY with the Byblian suffix ו as in the Lapethos dialect (cp. אשתו 'his wife'; **36** ii 11), i.e. [bnītīw] or the like; cp. תחוו (**25** Yehaumilk 9). It is the only 3 masc. sing. suffix in the inscr.; for with the change of person which this verb marks, the suffixes with י in 6 and 7 become 1 person. Such a change from 'he' to

'I' within an inscr. is not unparalleled; cp. **15** Karatepe at A iii 2 ff. and *CIS* i 7 (Umm El-'Amed) at *ll.* 3–4. Another interpretation which has found favour is to split בנתו into two words תו בן, i.e. 'and he built the niche, cella, inner-room'; cp. Hebr. תא in Ezek. xl 7 ff.; Aram. [tawwā]. This keeps the same person in the verbs, does away with the awkward suffix ו, and makes the 3 masc. sing. suffix י (6, 7) as in Tyro-Sidonian; but it does seem rather to complicate the sense by introducing another building operation, and surprisingly it and not the whole shrine is what is specially asked for by the goddess. This תו (if it was not the chamber where the sacred marriage took place; see the next Note) was presumably to house the מאש or 'statue' of 9.

6. ארש = ['arášā]; 3 fem. perf.; a verb not attested elsewhere in Phoen., though nominal forms ארש and ארשת occur in personal names (Benz, *Names,* p. 276); in Hebr. a noun ארשת occurs once in Ps. xxi 3, but verbal forms are found in Ugar. (**3** E 36 **14** 42 **17** vi 26); Akkad. *erēšu.* With the sentiment cp. **15** Karatepe A ii 11 **II 13** Hadad 13–14 2 Sam. vii 1–5. See also the later parallels from the Hatra inscrs. cited in Teixidor, 'Bulletin' for 1971, item 109. The syntax is awkward, since the verb does not have an object and בד (see at **2, 3** Byblos cones) is not the obvious prepos. to use; but it is not so awkward as the final sentence, and should prob., like it, be put down to lack of expertise on the part of the Phoen. carver, who belonged to a community that had been living perhaps for several generations in a foreign environment. בד, lit. 'from the hand of'; does this element in proper names like Bodashtart mean '(requested) from'? For a comparable usage cp. **41** Piraeus 1 ('resolved by'). בד is equivalent to Hebr. ביד, which often has the nuance 'by means of, through'; Exod. ix 35 xvi 3 Judg. vi 36 2 Sam. iii 18, etc.; cp. I **12** Lachish ix 7 II **5** Zakir A 12. Delcor and Lipiński, in their attempt to reconstruct an annual festival of the dying and rising of Melcarth (see at **39** Rhodes), find this meaning here, and, following Février, connect ארש not with Hebr. 'RŠ but with Hebr. 'RŚ, Piel 'to betroth', Pual 'to be betrothed' (they also derive the names with ארש and ארשת from this base, i.e. 'fiancé(e)' of such and such a god). They render along the following lines 'and he built a chamber because Astarte had been married through his mediation'. It is a peculiar statement, but they would argue intentionally so, since the king is not of course actually 'betrothed to' nor does he 'marry' the goddess but a temple prostitute who takes her place in the *hieros gamos.* Their argument would have been strengthened had the text read, 'and he built a chamber where (or, in order that) Astarte might be married ...', the תו being in their view the apartment within the shrine where in future years the sacred union would take place that would bring about the cultic resurrection of the 'dead' deity (Melcarth) mentioned in 8–9. I have already listed a number of criticisms of their reconstruction in the Notes to **39** Rhodes (including the crucial one that Melcarth was not the consort of Astarte but like Adonis her acolyte or young companion), and I find their case for a *hieros gamos* either at Pyrgi or in connection with the title מתרח עשתרני unproved. The king is merely in this line indicating that he had been instructed by Astarte herself to build the shrine. He goes on to name the day of a religious ceremony as that on which he received the instruction (i.e. when presumably a Phoen. priest or prophet had put the community's request to him in the form of an oracle); the ceremony (like the month names) was therefore prob. a Phoen. one, but there is

nothing to suggest that he himself took part in it or that it had anything
to do with the as yet unbuilt shrine.

7-9. למלכי etc.; the order of the date formula is the reverse of the usual,
beginning with the phrase 'in the reign of' and following with the year,
then the month, finishing with the day; cp. and contrast **28** Eshmunazar
1   **34** (Cyrpus) 2   *CIS* i 11 (also Cyprus). The implication is that the
third year encompasses פעל and יתן in 2 as well as בנתו in 5–6, i.e. the
building was begun in the month KRR and completed in the month זבח
שמש (4–5). KRR is mentioned a number of times in Phoen. and Punic
sources but its position in the year is as yet unidentified, though several
rather forced etymologies have been advanced. If, however, זבח שמש
was in the winter, KRR may well have been in the preceding summer.
This would accord with the point made in **39** Rhodes, Note (c), that the
ceremonies of mourning for Tammuz and his Phoen. counterparts
Adonis and Melcarth, who were all young vegetation deities, took place
in that season. The day of the god's burial concerns then not Astarte
herself but one or other of Adonis or Melcarth, who originated
respectively from Byblos and Tyre. It is interesting that there was an
influence from Byblos on the beliefs as well as the language of Lapethos
(see introd. to **36**); so if the Phoenicians of Pyrgi came from there, the
first of these cannot be ruled out. On אלם, sing., see at **25** Karatepe C iii
16.

9-11. The Etruscan word *avil* 'year(s)', known from other inscrs. in that
language, occurs in A in the position occupied by the second שנת in
Phoenician. This does not exclude the possiblility that the first שנת
has another meaning (e.g. 'shining things' from a base related to Arab.
[sanā] 'to be brilliant'; cp. Dan. xii 3), but it makes it unlikely. Etruscan
A also helps with the interpretation of מאש אלם, since it mentions two
objects (*tamia* and *heramašva*) at the beginning where the Phoen. has
only אשר קדש, and repeats the second of these (*heramve*) at the end
where the Phoen. has only מאש אלם. This makes it prob. that מאש אלם
denotes a 'statue' of Astarte placed in the shrine, and enables us to take
בת here (cp. 5) as referring to the shrine and not to the larger temple B
of which it was only a part and which can hardly have belonged to
Astarte. The notion of '(votive) gift' should prob. not be read into מאש,
nor at this early date should the א be regarded as an internal *mater
lectionis*; see the discussion at **36** Lapethos ii 2, which makes a distinction
between (a) מאש 'gift' and (b) מש or מאש 'sacred object, statue, etc.'. The
י in בבתי is the 3 fem. suffix ([yā] after a genit. noun) and is the
Tyro-Sidonian form as against the Byblian ו of the masc. in בנתו; this
mixing of forms seems significantly to occur also in the Lapethos
dialect; see on בן at **36** 13. There remains the problem of הככבם אל.
Grammatically this is most easily explained as 'these stars' ([éllē] or the
like; Poenulus *ily*); but what does the 'these' describe? Some think of
decorations in the shape of stars in the shrine, or of a form of the *clavi
annales* (these were nails by which the Romans, following it seems an
Etruscan custom, designated the number of the years; they were driven
into the wall of Jupiter's temple by the highest magistrate on the Ides of
September each year). The second of these suggestions has at least a
reference to 'years', though it does not make us think of a large number
of them, which is the sense that is surely required. My own feeling is
that the actual stars in heaven must be meant (cp. the numerical simile
in Gen. xv 5) and that we should therefore understand 'these' in a loose

rhetorical sense, 'these stars up there', or as in the English idiom 'the stars above'. The final sentence thus contains an implied wish (the syntax is not felicitous and a verb has to be understood) that the goddess's statue should last as many years as there are stars in the sky. I am also attracted, however, to Dahood's proposal that the phrase means not 'these stars' but 'the stars of El'. He cites in support Isa. xiv 13 (כוכבי אל) and Ugar. *phr kkbm* 'the assembly of the stars', which in one broken context (**10** i 4) is paralleled by *bn 'il* 'the sons of El'. We have in that case a stereotyped idiom surviving from the old mythology of Canaan which wishes upon the statue numberless years like those of the immortal gods in heaven. Grammatically the construction may be compared with הנחלים ארנון 'the torrents of Arnon' (Num. xxi 14), which in the Massoretic pointing has to be treated as a case of apposition as in המזבח נחשת (**25** Yehaumilk 4), but which Dahood prefers to explain as an instance of the anomalous use of the article before a construct relation as in הברך בעל (**15** Karatepe A 1), i.e. [hannaḥlē-m 'arnōn] or the like with the enclitic *Mem* well known from Ugaritic. See the Notes to these passages for further examples and discussion of the respective structures, and see for the enclitic *Mem CML*² p. 150. It is *a priori* not outwith the bounds of possibility that an old Canaanite idiom should carry an archaic grammatical feature with it into Phoen. (the most convincing Hebr. examples are of this kind), but if we accept Dahood's proposal, it may be safer until a more certain example of enclitic *Mem* turns up in Phoen. to adopt the first of the above explanations of the phrase.

BIBLIOGRAPHICAL NOTES

1. Eastern Phoenician texts not included in the present volume may be studied as follows:

Cyprus (*c.* 800); a new inscr. on a bowl; in A. Dupont-Sommer, *Mémoires AIBL* 44 (1970), 9–28; *Report of Dept. of Antiquities, Cyprus,* 1974, 75–94 (includes remarks on **11** Nora and **17** Baal Lebanon); Teixidor, 'Bulletin' for 1972, item 118; Magnanini, *Iscrizioni,* p. 115; E. Puech, *RSF* 4 (1976), 11–21; A. van den Branden, *Bibbia e Oriente* 19 (1977), 21 ff.

Amrit (6 cent.) in Magnanini, *Iscrizioni,* p. 40; Segert, *Grammar,* p. 269; G. Garbini, *AIUON* 37 (1977), 290 ff. (the word אז argues for a connection with Cyprus).

Byblos
  new inscr. (6 cent.) in J. Starcky, *MUSJ* 45 (1969), 257–73; Teixidor, 'Bulletin' for 1972, item 118; W. Röllig, *NESE* 2 (1974), 1–15; I. Schiffmann, *RSF* 4 (1976), 171–7.

  son of Shipitbaal (*c.* 500) in *KAI* no. 9; Magnanini, *Iscrizioni,* p. 32.

  Abdeshmun (3 cent.) in *KAI* no. 12; Magnanini, *Iscrizioni,* p. 30.

Sidon
  Bodashtart i (ten exemplars) and ii (nine exemplars) (5 cent.) in *KAI* nos. 15, 16; J. T. Milik, *Biblica* 48 (1967), 597 f.; Magnanini *Iscrizioni,* pp. 7, 9.

  Ostraca (5 and 4 cents.) in A. Vanel, *BMB* 20 (1967), 45–95; *MUSJ* 45 (1969), 345–64; Magnanini, *Iscrizioni,* pp. 12–15; J. W. Betlyon, *BMB* 26 (1973), 31 ff.

Waṣṭa (Lebanon; 3 cent.); inscr. in Greek characters; in *KAI* no. 174; Magnanini, *Iscrizioni,* p. 24; Segert, *Grammar,* p. 265 (for similar western texts in both Greek and Latin transcription see *KAI* nos. 175–80; Segert, *Grammar,* pp. 265–6; F. Vattioni, *Augustinianum* 16 (1976), 505–55).

Tyre (2 cent.); an inscr. from Malta in Tyrian script; in *KAI* no. 47; Guzzo Amadasi, *Iscrizioni,* pp. 15–17; M. Sznycer, *Annuaire de l'école pratique des hautes études,* IV e sect. (1974–5), 191–9 (this inscr. was used in the decipherment of Phoenician).

Umm El-ʿAmed (3 and 2 cents.); all the inscrs. from this site are studied in the book by Dunand and Duru mentioned in Bibliogr. to **31, 32;** Magnanini, *Iscrizioni,* pp. 16–23.

Palestine; all the known texts, mostly tiny but one apparently a מלך dedication, are gathered in B. Delevault, A. Lemaire, *RSF* 7 (1979), 1–37; a few belong to the Old Phoen. period.

Cyprus (later inscriptions) in *CIS* i 10–96; *KAI* nos. 32–43; Masson and Sznycer, *Recherches*; Magnanini, *Iscrizioni,* pp. 84–134; M. G. Guzzo Amadasi and V. Karageorghis, *Fouilles de Kition, III, Inscriptions pheniciennes* (1977).

Saqqarah (6 cent.); papyrus letter; in *KAI* no. 50; A. van den Branden, *Bibbia e Oriente* 12 (1970), 212 ff.; L. Delekat, *Orientalia* 40 (1971), 410 ff.; Magnanini, *Iscrizioni,* p. 81; Lipiński, 'North Semitic texts', 253 f.

Ostraca from Elephantine (5 cent.) in M Lidzbarski *Phön. und Aram. Krugaufschriften aus Elephantine* (1912); Magnanini *Iscrizioni,* pp. 71–80.

Graffiti from Abydos (5–3 cents.) in *KAI* no. 49; Magnanini, *Iscrizioni,* pp. 66–8.

Memphis (2–1 cents.); stone inscr.; in *KAI* no. 48; Magnanini, *Iscrizioni,* p. 63.

Greece and the Aegean (4–3 cents.) in *CIS* i 114–121; *KAI* nos. 53–60; Magnanini, *Iscrizioni,* pp. 135–42; W. Röllig, *NESE* 1 (1972), 1–8.

On the forged Old Phoenician inscr. from Brazil see most recently G. I. Joffily, *ZDMG* 122 (1972), 22–36.

Students wishing to gain some knowledge of Punic epigraphy may begin with the short selection in Segert, *Grammar,* pp. 275–81 (25 texts). There is a larger selection in *KAI* nos. 61–173, and an up-to-date list of known texts ibid. Band III, pp. 67–76.

2. Writing. The most useful handbooks are McCarter, *Antiquity* (10–8 cents.) and Peckham, *Scripts* (8 cent. onwards). On problems connected with the origin of the alphabet see Bibliogr. to chapt. I. On Phoenician cursive writing see the articles by Vanel mentioned above (Sidon).

3. Dictionaries. In addition to *DISO* we now have R. S. Tomback, *A Comparative Semitic Lexicon of the Phoenician and Punic Languages* (Missoula, Montana, 1978). This excellent reference book, which quotes passages and gives bibliographies, unfortunately reached me too late to be used in the preparation of the present volume.

4. Language. In addition to the *Grammars* of Harris, Friedrich and Segert, see the elementary *Grammaire Phénicienne* by A. van den Branden (Beirut, 1969), which uses Phoenician characters. On some problems which are not fully treated in the Grammars see the Note on Phonology at the beginning of this volume, and more recently G. Garbini, 'I dialetti del fenicio', *AIUON* 37 (1977), 283–94.

5. On the history and civilization of the Phoenicians consult:

D. Ap-Thomas, 'The Phoenicians' in D. J. Wiseman (ed.), *Peoples of Old Testament Times* (Oxford, 1973), 259–86.

F. Barreca and others, *L'espansione fenicia nel Mediterraneo* (Rome, 1971).

G. Benigni and others, *Saggi fenici I* (Rome, 1975).

Cambridge Ancient History, 3rd. edit., vol. II, pt. 2 (1975).

B. Couroyer, 'Origine des Phéniciens', *RB* 80 (1973), 264–76.

W. Culican, *The First Merchant Adventurers: the Ancient Levant in History and Commerce* (London, 1966).

J.C.L. Gibson, 'Inscriptions, Semitic' in *The Interpreter's Dictionary of the Bible,* Suppl. vol. (1976), 429–36 (on the value of the inscriptions for Biblical study).

Harden, *Phoenicians.*

G. Herm, *The Phoenicians: the Purple Empire of the Ancient World* (London, 1975) (popular) .

P.K. Hitti, *Lebanon in History* (London, 1957).

N. Jidejian, *Byblos through the Ages,* 2nd. edit. (Beirut, 1971).
———— *Tyre through the Ages* (Beirut, 1969).
———— *Sidon through the Ages* (Beirut, 1973).

H.J. Katzenstein, *The History of Tyre* (Jerusalem, 1973).

B. Mazar, 'The Philistines and the Rise of Israel and Tyre', *Isr. Ac. of Sciences and Humanities, Proceedings* 1, 7 (1964).

R. du Mesnil du Buisson, *Études sur les dieux phéniciens hérités par l'empire romain* (Leiden, 1970).

idem, *Nouvelles études sur les dieux et les mythes de Canaan* (Leiden, 1973).

Moscati, *Phoenicians.*

S. Moscati, *Problematica della civiltà fenicia* (Rome, 1974).

A. Parrot, M.H. Chebab, S. Moscati, *Les Phéniciens: l'expansion phénicienne: Carthage* (Paris, 1975).

H. Ringgren, *Religions of the Ancient Near East* (London, 1973).

J. Teixidor, *The Pagan God: Popular Religion in the Greco-Roman Near East* (Princeton, 1977).

W.A. Ward (ed.), *The Role of the Phoenicians in the Interaction of Mediterranean Civilizations* (Beirut, 1968).

B.H. Warmington, *Carthage* (London, 1960).

P. Xella, 'Studi sulla religione fenicia e punica', *RSF* 3 (1975), 227–44.

6. Bibliography. In addition to Teixidor's 'Bulletin' see the 'Bibliografia' by E. Acquaro printed annually in *RSF.*

INDEXES

NAMES OF DEITIES

PERSONAL NAMES

PLACE NAMES

SEMITIC TERMS

(Note: Only problematic or significant items are listed)

HEBREW BIBLE

OTHER REFERENCES

Map

| Lachish | B. | El-Kh. | | Azar. Cones | | Ahir. gr. | Yeh. Abi. Eli. Ship. Abda Nor. Cypr. | Kil. | Sev. Leb. Kar. pend. Prae. Ur Malta | Arsl. T. | |
| Bowl Ewer Shem. i | ii | iii | Gerb. Rap. Ruw. Al-B. Azar. Spat. i | ii | | | | i ii | | i | ii |

Old B.

7 cent. · 8 cent. · 9 cent. · late 10 cent. · 11–early 10 cents. · 12 cent. · 13 cent.

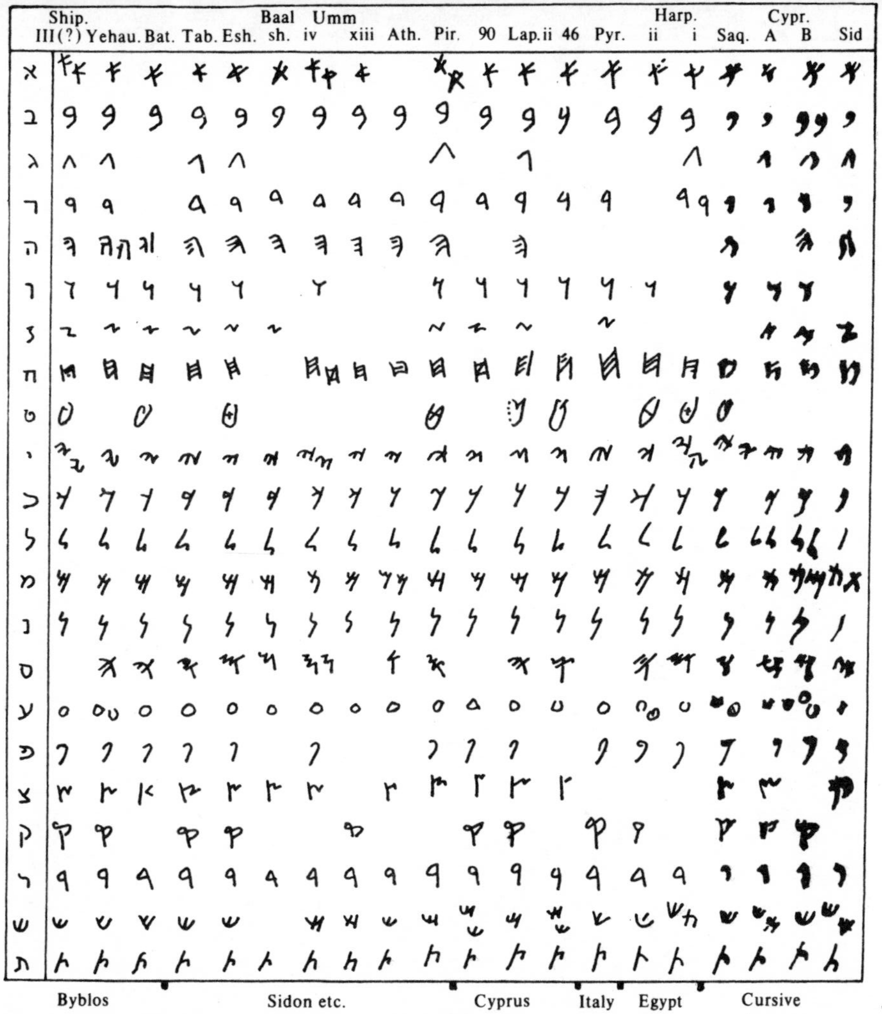
Ship. III(?)
Yehau.
Bat.
Tab.
Esh.
Baal sh.
Umm iv
xiii
Ath.
Pir.
90
Lap.ii
46
Pyr.
Harp. ii
i
Saq.
Cypr. A
B
Sid
א ב ג ד ה ו ז ח ט י כ ל מ נ ס ע פ צ ק ר ש ת
Byblos
Sidon etc.
Cyprus
Italy
Egypt
Cursive

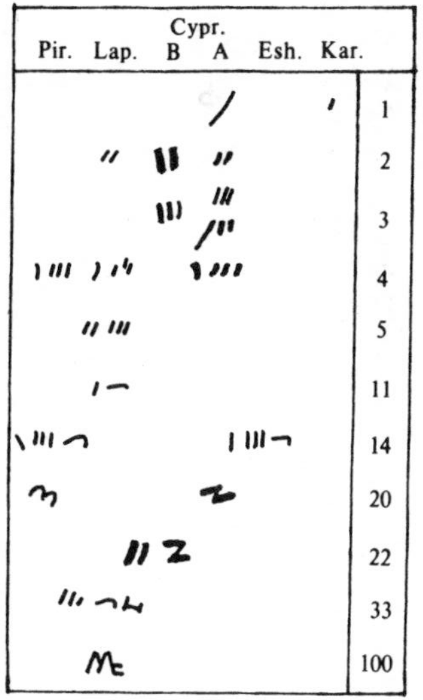
Pir.
Lap.
Cypr. B
A
Esh.
Kar.
1
2
3
4
5
11
14
20
22
33
100

Table of Scripts 6–2 centuries with numerical signs

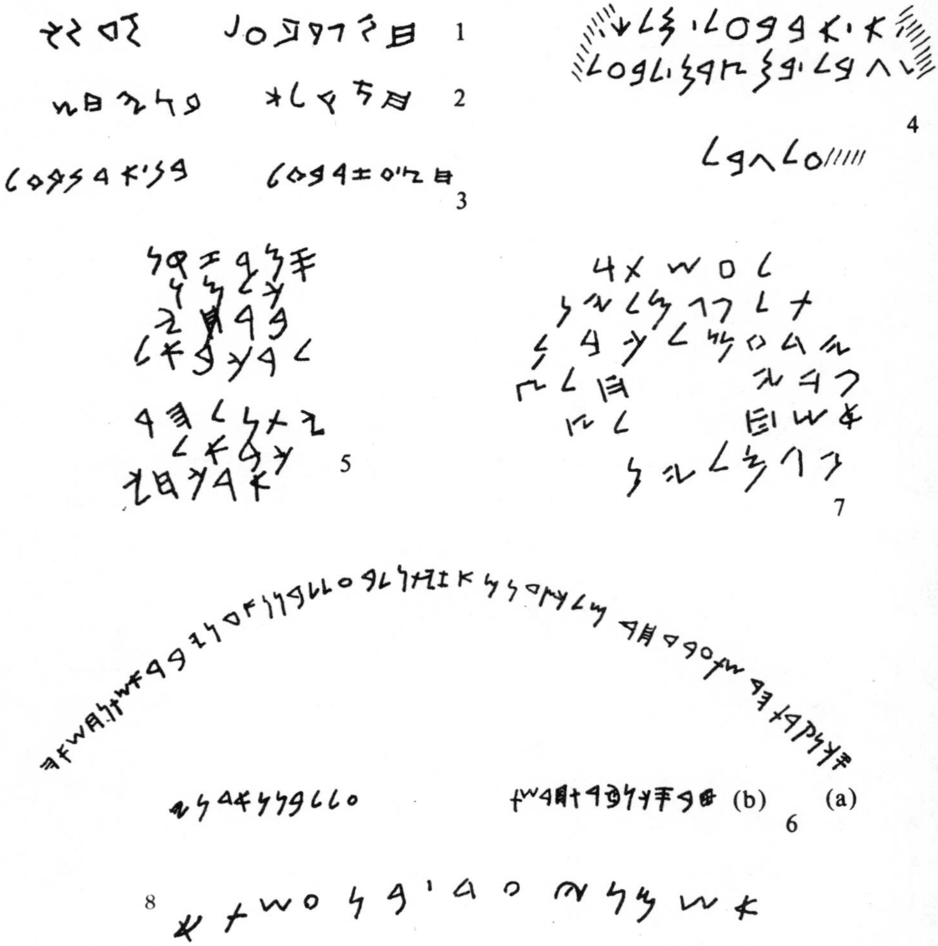

1

2

3

4

5

7

(b)   (a)
6

8

Figures 1–8

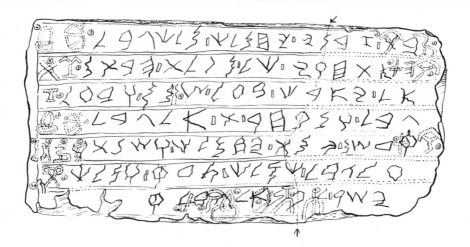

Figure 9

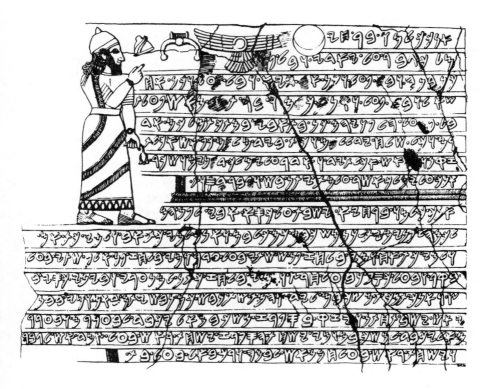

Figure 10

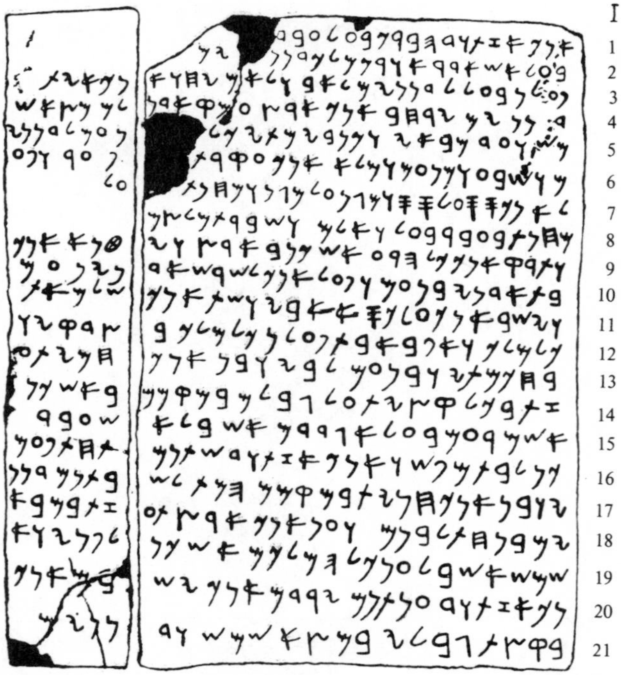

Figure 11

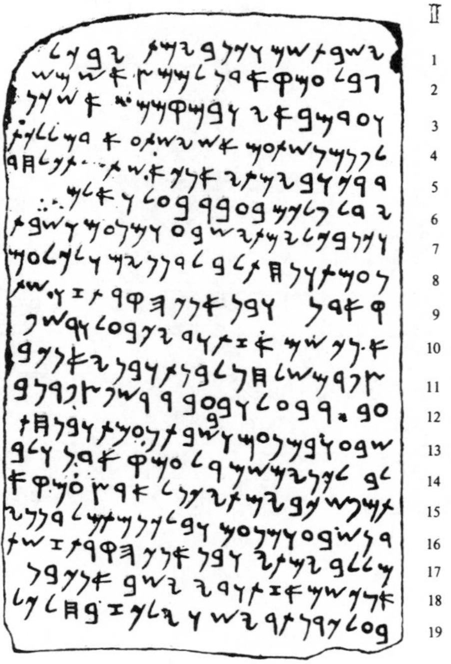

Figure 12

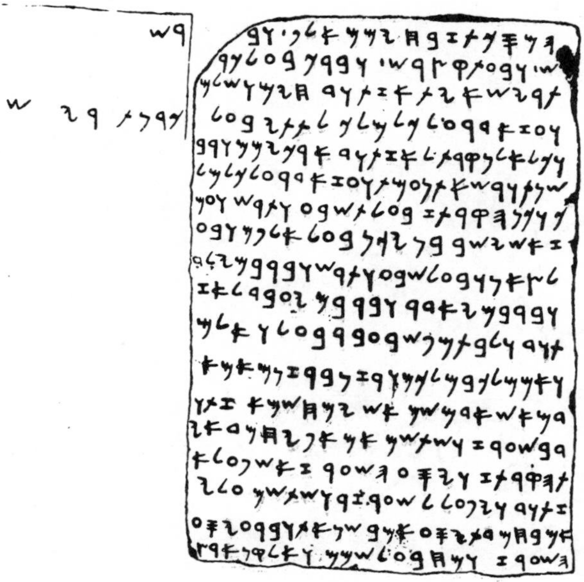

Figure 13

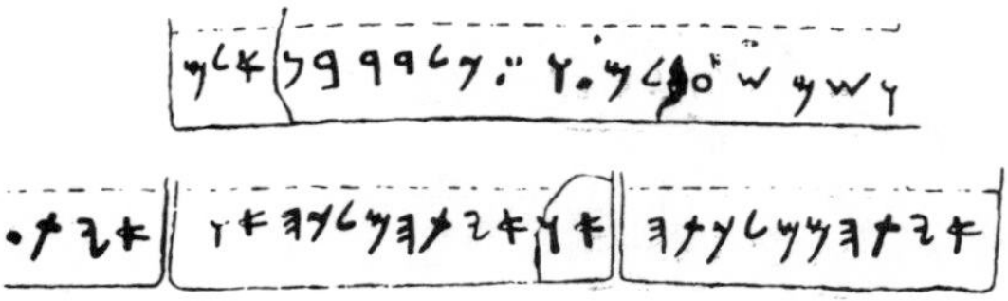

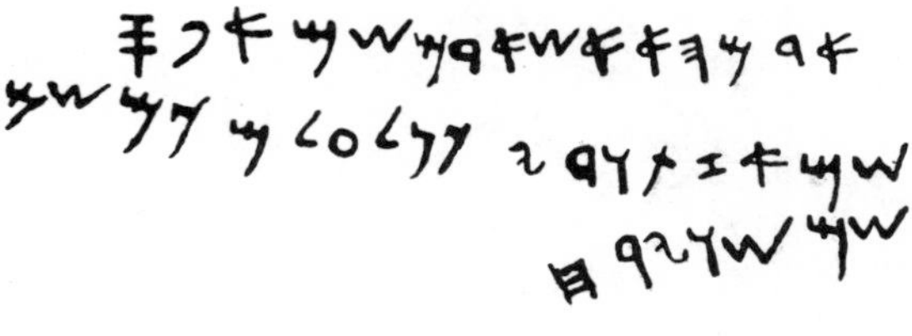

Figure 14

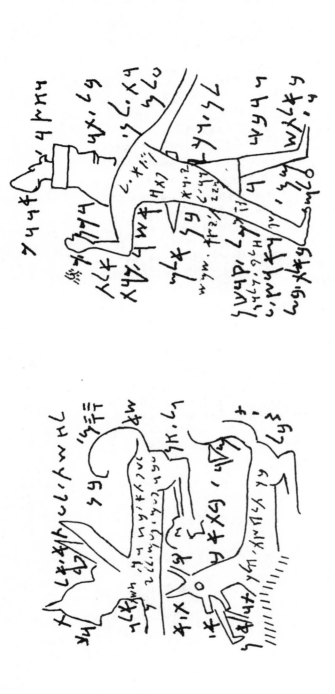

Figure 15

[186]

Figures 16–17

1

2

3

PLATE I

1

2

PLATE II

1

2

PLATE III

5

10

15

PLATE IV

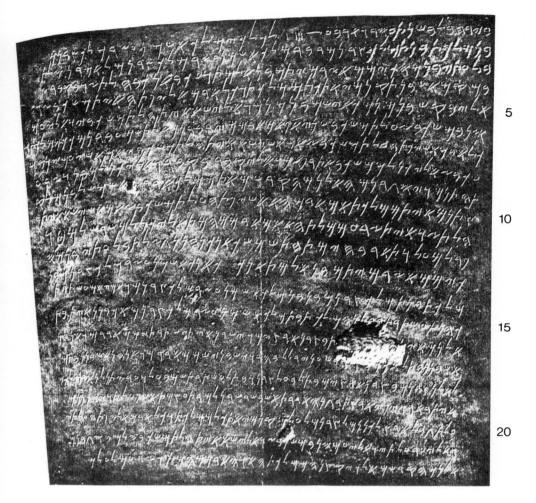

PLATE V

A

B

PLATE VI

PLATE VII

PLATE VIII